Literacy Classrooms That S.O.A.R.

Literacy Classrooms That S.O.A.R.

Strategic **O**bservation **A**nd **R**eflection in the Elementary Grades

Susan O'Hara
Robert Pritchard
Debi Pitta

Foreword by Douglas Fisher

TEACHERS COLLEGE PRESS
TEACHERS COLLEGE | COLUMBIA UNIVERSITY
NEW YORK AND LONDON

Published by Teachers College Press,® 1234 Amsterdam Avenue, New York, NY 10027

Front cover photo by Ridofranz / iStock by Getty Images.
Permissions lines for Figures 2.1 and 3.5 and Appendix A appear in the text below those figures.

Library of Congress Cataloging-in-Publication Data

Names: O'Hara, Susan (Susan Pauline), author. | Pritchard, Robert Henry, 1947– author. | Pitta, Debi, author.
Title: Literacy classrooms that S.O.A.R. : strategic observation and reflection in the elementary grades / Susan O'Hara, Robert Pritchard, Debi Pitta.
Description: New York : Teachers College Press, 2020. | Includes bibliographical references and index.
Identifiers: LCCN 2020030954 (print) | LCCN 2020030955 (ebook) | ISBN 9780807764787 (paperback) | ISBN 9780807764794 (hardcover) | ISBN 9780807779286 (ebook)
Subjects: LCSH: Language arts (Elementary)—United States. | Reflective teaching—United States. | Teachers—Professional relationships—United States. | Professional learning communities—United States.
Classification: LCC LB1576 .O38 2020 (print) | LCC LB1576 (ebook) | DDC 372.60973—dc23
LC record available at https://lccn.loc.gov/2020030954
LC ebook record available at https://lccn.loc.gov/2020030955

ISBN 978-0-8077-6478-7 (paper)
ISBN 978-0-8077-6479-4 (hardcover)
ISBN 978-0-8077-7928-6 (ebook)

Printed on acid-free paper
Manufactured in the United States of America

Contents

Foreword

Humans are social animals and much of our learning is communal, involving interactions with others. In fact, I would argue that much of what we each know developed as we interacted with others. And that process starts very young and continues throughout our lives.

When we interact with others, we have the potential for moving from the acquisition to the consolidation and deepening of our learning. Moving from acquisition to consolidation generally requires that we interact with others, sharing our thinking and listening to the ways in which it is received. As we interact with others, we come to understand what we think and why we think that.

This is why classroom conversations are so powerful. In fact, in John Hattie's massive review of educational research called Visible Learning (visible-learning.org), it was revealed that classroom discussions have an effect size of .82. In this database, which includes over 1800 meta-analyses and over 300 million students, the average impact on learning is .40. Effect sizes are descriptions of the impact that a specific influence has. It's an average, of sorts, across many studies. According to this research base, classroom conversations have double the average impact. That's pretty powerful.

Interestingly, classroom conversations are fairly rare. There are studies dating way back showing that teachers do a lot of talking, but when they talk less, students learn more. For example, Flanders (1970) reported that teachers of high-achieving students spent about 55% of class time talking, compared with 80% for teachers of low-achieving students. As Nystrand and Gamoran (1997) noted, the average length of whole-class discussion was 14–68 seconds per hour of instruction.

Perhaps these conversations are rare because teachers are not sure how to structure the interactions to ensure that consolidation occurs. We know that students will talk, but how can we ensure that they will talk about the learning at hand? We've all experienced lessons in which the student interactions were not productive and even off-task and off-topic.

The SOAR Teaching Frames provide a much-needed approach to help teachers elevate their literacy instruction and teach students how to have discussions, engage with complex text, identify and use evidence to support claims, and effectively communicate. All of the practices in the frames are mutually reinforcing. Teaching students how to engage in discussions is the starting place for learning that deepens and extends their understanding of complex content. These discussions provide an opening for students to explore complex texts and to mine those texts for evidence, which helps strengthen their oral and written communication skills. In other words, the discussions that we can facilitate in our classrooms are not the end point, but rather a vehicle for learning that allows students to become strong readers and thinkers who engage with ideas and one another as they learn and acquire the academic language needed to communicate these ideas. When the SOAR Teaching Frames are adopted as a framework by schools and districts where all teachers are using them and sharing their ideas, they become a powerful tool for elevating literacy instruction for all students and as a result for improving learning outcomes.

Imagine the changes that will be realized when students develop the habits necessary to interact with other humans in ways that include agreeing and disagreeing, using evidence to draw conclusions, and reaching consensus. Simply said, a better place to live and learn.

—Douglas Fisher

REFERENCES

Flanders, N. (1970). *Analyzing teacher behavior*. Addison-Wesley.

Nystrand, M., & Gamoran, A. (1997). The big picture: Language and learning in hundreds of English classrooms. In M. Nystrand, A. Gamoran, R. Karchur, & C. Prendergast (Eds.), *Opening dialogue: Understanding the dynamics of language and learning in the English classroom* (pp. 30–74). Teachers College Press.

Acknowledgments

We are deeply appreciative of all the teachers and administrators with whom we have worked, who strive every day to grow and help their students grow. We want to express special gratitude to:

- Isabel Aguirre, Maricela Sanchez Robles, and Michelle Staine of Los Angeles Unified School District, who recognized the potential of SOAR early in its development and facilitated its implementation across the district; and
- Ruben Reyes, Superintendent of Robla Elementary School District, for his unwavering commitment to student learning and the role SOAR can play in facilitating it.

We are extremely fortunate to have had many colleagues who contributed to the evolution of SOAR. We are particularly grateful to:

- Joanne Bookmyer, who was instrumental in forging the relationships that enabled us to introduce SOAR to so many teachers and school districts;
- Suzanne Abdelrahim, who took a leadership role in supporting schools implementing SOAR in the Los Angeles Unified School District; and
- Julie Webb, who early in the process contributed to the development of the classroom observation protocol and associated rubrics.

Literacy Classrooms That S.O.A.R.

CHAPTER 1

Introducing the SOAR Teaching Frames

New standards, including the Common Core State Standards (CCSS) and Next Generation Science Standards (NGSS), require that your students engage with complex informational texts, use evidence in writing and research, discuss sophisticated disciplinary content, and work collaboratively to present ideas and communicate multiple perspectives. The integration of English language arts (ELA) standards within each content area raises expectations for your students' use of language to explain concepts and relationships that become progressively more abstract throughout schooling. Consequently, the new standards require you to use your subject-specific knowledge to help all students learn the academic language and skills of their respective fields and understand how to draw on the cultural and linguistic backgrounds of all your students to facilitate this. The standards also require a shared responsibility for students' disciplinary language and literacy development among all teachers at your school.

As teachers across the country implement these new standards, they are looking for instructional approaches to help them meet the challenges these standards bring. We created the Strategic Observation and Reflection (SOAR) Teaching Frames to help elementary teachers navigate the language and literacy development of their students in all content areas. When developing the SOAR Teaching Frames, we used the definition of *academic language* in the California English Language Arts/English Language Development (ELA/ELD) Framework:

> Academic language broadly refers to the language used in school to help students develop content knowledge and the language students are expected to use to convey their understanding of this knowledge. It is a different way of using language than the type of English used in informal or everyday social interactions. (California Department of Education, 2014)

The SOAR Teaching Frames help teachers attend to the three features of academic language (vocabulary, syntax, and discourse) within sociocultural contexts for language use and do so in ways that respectfully encompass students' identities and social roles.

The frames offer teachers, instructional coaches, and administrators who are currently implementing new College- and Career-Readiness Standards a suite of tools that drives continuous improvement in teaching and learning. The tools can be useful for a variety of purposes: (a) informal or guided self-assessment of teaching practices, (b) peer-to-peer collaboration within learning communities to improve teaching, (c) site- and district-based professional-growth initiatives, and (d) formative and summative teacher assessment.

A RESEARCH-BASED APPROACH TO ELEVATING INSTRUCTION

Our work with schools and districts has shown us that instruction and student learning improve when an entire school is focused on a common set of high-impact instructional practices. This approach creates a common vision and language that promotes collaboration and engages all teachers, instructional coaches, and principals in a focused dialogue on achieving those goals. More specifically, principals and instructional coaches need to understand how teachers develop their professional practice and use this knowledge to facilitate dialogue about teaching and learning (O'Hara, Bookmyer, Martin, & Newton, 2018). Research suggests that there is a need to focus the process of instructional improvement on a set of targeted, high-impact instructional practices (Fogo, 2011; Grossman, 2018; O'Hara, Bookmyer, Martin, & Newton, 2018; O'Hara & Pritchard, 2016; Pritchard & O'Hara, 2016; Windschitl, Thompson, & Braaten, 2011). Teachers and instructional coaches benefit from opportunities to engage with one another using a common language and vision of effective instruction that explicitly articulates the instructional shifts needed for improvements in learning. Consequently, professional-learning initiatives should provide teachers and coaches with time for deliberate practice of new instructional moves that are aligned with this vision (Fogo, 2011; Grossman & Davis, 2012; O'Hara, Zwiers, & Pritchard, 2014; Thompson, Windschitl, & Braaten, 2013).

Supportive colleagues, engaged principals, and sufficient resources are key to fostering the professional growth of teachers and instructional coaches. In addition, tools that support reflective practice within a community of peers elevate instruction for everyone (Curtis, 2013; Gronn, 2002; Hunzicker, 2013). Learning to enact a new instructional practice requires the ability to see and understand the underlying instructional moves required to implement that practice in the classroom. As such, professionals need tools and experiences that help them unpack instructional practices and distinguish stronger and weaker versions of the practices (Grossman, 2018; McDonald, Kazemi, & Kavanagh, 2013; O'Hara et al., 2018; Pritchard & O'Hara, 2016).

Based on this research, we designed the Teaching Frames to help teachers elevate their instructional practice and to provide tools for instructional coaches and principals in supporting them to do so. This body of research also informed the content of the Teaching Frames, which emerged from the research and professional development we have been conducting for more than 10 years. This work, and the results of our research, have shown us that the SOAR Teaching Frames for Literacy provide a unique approach for planning, implementing, and elevating instruction that significantly affects student learning. Having identified the practices that are most predictive of student growth, our team also developed a corresponding set of classroom vignettes and instructional strategies and tools to illustrate how these practices can be enacted in your classroom. The Teaching Frames are designed to help teachers support the disciplinary language and literacy development of all students, including students at different stages of language development. In addition, the strategies and tools that we have developed to accompany the frames are intentionally designed to support differentiation of both content and language. The classroom vignettes we use in this book to illustrate implementation of the frames are a compilation of different SOAR lessons we have observed in diverse elementary classrooms with a wide range of language abilities, cultural backgrounds, academic levels, and reading levels. As such, we created teacher and student profiles that represent the classrooms where we have observed SOAR practices implemented.

ELEVATING TEACHING PRACTICE IN SUPPORT OF NEW STANDARDS

Consider the following scenario. Ms. Rahim and Ms. Aguirre are colleagues. They both teach 5th grade with many English learners, and they often plan and reflect on lessons together. They have both been reading *There's a Boy in the Girls' Bathroom*, by Louis Sachar, with their class. As part of a new professional-learning project at their school, they have been using the SOAR Teaching Frames as the lens through which they plan, teach, reflect on, and elevate their teaching practice. Their current focus is on designing instruction to support their students to engage in discussions so that students build new ideas and deepen their understanding of disciplinary content. Ms. Rahim observes the implementation of a lesson by Ms. Aguirre, which is described in the vignette below.

Step Inside Ms. Aguirre's Classroom

Ms. Aguirre introduces the prompt students are to discuss: "Was it fair that Carla was removed from Red Hill School as a counselor and placed at the other school as a kindergarten teacher, or was it not fair?" The students are familiar with this activity. Ms. Aguirre asks the class, "How many details do

I want?" "Three," the class responds. She surveys the class for how many believe it was fair and for how many believe it was unfair. Students raise their hands. More students believe that it was unfair. As more students raise their hands for the unfair position, she explains that they will begin by writing evidence for the unfair position. Ms. Aguirre gives them 2 minutes to write three pieces of evidence from the book. When the 2 minutes are up, she asks them to shift their brains and think about the opposite side. She gives them 2 minutes to find three pieces of evidence for the fair position.

Next, she asks the students to stand up with their journal and pick a partner from a different table. Once the students have chosen partners, they decide who partner A is and who partner B is. She explains that partner A will argue to partner B that it was fair that Carla had to leave, and partner B will argue to partner A that it was unfair that she had to leave. Ms. Aguirre states, "You have to take turns going back and forth, and you're building your case. You're not just saying the same thing over every time you speak. You have to add something else so that by the end your case—your point of view—is built. Use evidence from the book to support what you're saying." She asks partners B to begin, and the pairs engage in the discussion.

That afternoon Ms. Rahim and Ms. Aguirre meet to discuss the lesson. They use the SOAR Disciplinary Discussions Teaching Frame to help them reflect on the lesson, plan for ways to improve upon the lesson, and elevate their instruction. The teachers agree that the prompt was a good one; it was open-ended and allowed for rich discussions. However, what they heard from students was more back-and-forth comments without building on one another's ideas. They discuss several ways they can elevate this lesson to make it better for Ms. Rahim to teach to her students:

- The teachers decide that one thing that would have helped students do a better job in their discussions would be sharing their evidence with other students to strengthen their ideas before they have a discussion with their partner.
- Ms. Aguirre thinks she should have modeled what she expected the discussion to sound like when introducing and citing specific evidence from the text for the students.
- The teachers decide that giving students written sentence frames for citing evidence from text instead of sharing them orally would offer the students more support for their discussion.
- During the SOAR professional-learning project, Ms. Rahim and Ms. Aguirre learned about explicitly teaching students conversation skills to use during a discussion and how important that is. They have taught the conversation skills, but they realize that in this discussion students would be relying more on the skills of fortifying and negotiating ideas. Therefore, they should explicitly say that and review those skills with students.

- Ms. Rahim wonders what strategies they could use to help students monitor their own discussions and take action to move the discussion forward if they are off-topic or stuck.
- Ms. Aguirre states that she believes she needed to monitor the discussion more carefully and provide targeted feedback in a timely way. Doing so would have facilitated deeper conversations, a building-up of new ideas, and a greater understanding of the issue.

Near the end of the conversation, Ms. Aguirre expresses that she did not feel there was enough new learning by her students as a result of their conversations: "I want to design my instruction so that students develop new and deeper understanding as a result of participating in academic conversations. I don't want the academic conversations in my class to be busywork where students are simply stating what they already know." Ms. Rahim prepares the elevated lesson as they discussed, with plans for Ms. Aguirre to observe.

Step Inside Ms. Rahim's Classroom

Ms. Rahim introduces the prompt they are to discuss: "Today we are going to discuss: Was it fair that Carla was removed from Red Hill School as a counselor and placed at the other school as a kindergarten teacher, or was it not fair? Please prepare for this discussion by taking out your novel and the graphic organizer that you completed yesterday where you wrote three pieces of evidence for the agree position and three pieces of evidence for the disagree position. I'm going to give you some time to meet with your reading partner and share your evidence for each side of the argument. You can ask clarifying questions to help your partner be clearer with his or her ideas and evidence."

When students have finished sharing, she brings the class back together. "What is the conversation skill that we will use and develop for this activity and why?" Xiomara shares her thoughts: "The conversation skill we are focusing on is Fortify. We are working on how to get better at explaining how the evidence from the text supports our position." Ms. Rahim says, "You are correct, Xiomara. Now let's review the prompts and responses for Fortify. First, let's do the hand signal. (Place your hand palm down as if putting an idea on the table and use the fingertips of the other hand to support the palm.) What do the fingers under your palm represent? Yes, the evidence. Now let's read the prompt starters. 'Show me where. How do you know? Where do you notice that?' And the responses are . . . ? 'In the text . . . , I know because . . . , An example is . . . .' Good! Today, I am distributing more specific sentence frames for you to use to help us focus on explaining how the evidence supports your position. Let's read them together."

- I agree/think that it was fair that Carla was removed from Red Hill School and placed at another school because . . . .

- I agree/think that it was not fair that Carla was removed from Red Hill School and placed at another school because . . . .
- An example in the text is . . . .
- I agree with what you said about . . . , but/and I also think . . . .
- I understand that you think . . . , but I think . . . because . . . .

"I am going to model for you how you will state your opinion and cite the evidence from the text using the sentence frames. 'I think that it was not fair that Carla was removed from Red Hill School and placed at another school because she was an excellent counselor. She really helped Bradley be a better person. An example of that was when she tells Bradley that "friends handle their problems by talking about them. That's why we've become such good friends, because we've learned to talk to each other." This shows how she is helping him understand what friends are.' Now, if you were my partner, what would you say next? Talk to your partner and decide how you can add on or build off of my idea." Students share, and Ms. Rahim explains how their responses add to her ideas.

"Before we begin our discussions, I want to remind you about monitoring your discussions and using the conversation skills. What you should monitor during the discussion is your use of sentence frames and how you are explaining the ways in which the evidence connects to the position. I will monitor and provide feedback during the discussion on how effectively you explain the ways in which the evidence supports your position."

Ms. Rahim listens to students' discussions. She hears two students discussing how it was not fair for Carla to be removed from Red Hill. Maegan says, "I think when Carla told Bradley's mom that she had heard a lot of horror stories about Bradley, but couldn't wait to meet him, shows she was a good counselor." Justin responds, "I agree." Ms. Rahim asks Justin if he could add to Maegan's evidence besides just saying he agrees. Justin says, "I remember that Carla added that she thought Bradley sounded charming and delightful, which would show she was open-minded and didn't depend on what others thought." Ms. Rahim: "Much better, Justin! That adds to what Maegan said. I took notes and will use them to give you individual, written feedback on your discussions. Please return to your seats and take out your journals."

These vignettes illustrate how these two teachers used a SOAR Teaching Frame to reflect on their instruction and to elevate their practice. The first vignette in the scenario provides an example of a lesson in which many students were engaged, on-topic, and participating in a conversation. However, when the teachers reflected, they believed the lesson could have been stronger. Ms. Aguirre believed that not enough new learning for her students resulted from their conversations. She wanted the conversations students engaged in to lead to new learning and a deeper understanding of the disciplinary content. We can see how the new ideas that both teachers generated during their reflective discussion using the SOAR Teaching Frame led to an elevation of instruction seen in the Ms. Rahim vignette. For example, Ms. Rahim

- explicitly teaches the students about the conversation skills needed to engage in discussion and provides supports for students to use those skills,
- puts structures in place to ensure that all students participate in the discussions,
- reminds the students about monitoring their own discussions and provides supports for them to do so, and
- closely monitors the discussions and provides targeted feedback along the way.

We developed the SOAR Teaching Frames for Literacy to help teachers analyze their instruction and target the disciplinary language and literacy skills students need to successfully meet the expectations of new standards. The opening scenario is focused on the Disciplinary Discussions Teaching Frame, one of four Teaching Frames introduced in this chapter that form the basis for Chapters 2–5. Disciplinary Discussions is one of four High-Impact Practices that emerged from our extensive research as having significant potential to drive student learning as articulated in new standards like the CCSS and NGSS. In the sections below, we describe the SOAR practices and the associated SOAR Teaching Frames.

THE SOAR PRACTICES

We conducted an empirical study (O'Hara & Pritchard, 2016) using a Delphi panel technique (Steurer, 2011) to answer the question: Which instructional practices are most essential and provide the highest impact for promoting disciplinary language and literacy development for all students? The approach featured multiple rounds of survey analysis to develop group consensus around specific issues, in this case, taking instructional practices already identified in research literature and building consensus around those believed to have the most impact on student learning.

At the top of each of the four SOAR Teaching Frames is a High-Impact Practice that our research identified as driving student learning as articulated in the CCSS ELA and Anchor Literacy Standards. The four High-Impact Practices that we have identified appear in Figure 1.1. Below we describe these practices and the essential elements that comprise them.

- ***Disciplinary Discussions:*** This practice focuses on structuring, strengthening, and supporting *students' ability to engage in student-*

Figure 1.1. SOAR High-Impact Practices

to-student disciplinary discussions. Disciplinary discussions can consist of face-to-face interactions, online dialogues, and written conversations (Kazemi & Hintz, 2014; Zwiers & Crawford, 2011; Zwiers, O'Hara, & Pritchard, 2014b). When implementing this practice, effective teachers explicitly build students' conversation skills and support the application of these skills through extended opportunities to engage in discussions.

- ***Disciplinary Interactions With Complex Text:*** This practice focuses on structuring, strengthening, and supporting student interaction with complex text to develop academic language and disciplinary literacy (Cummins, 2013; Fisher & Frey, 2014; Fisher, Frey, & Lapp, 2012). When implementing this practice, effective teachers engage students in an analysis of text to examine how language, text features, and/or literary devices are used to convey meaning. Effective teachers also provide opportunities for students to interact with complex text to build academic language and disciplinary skills.
- ***Disciplinary Uses of Evidence:*** This practice focuses on structuring, strengthening, and supporting *uses of multiple forms of evidence in disciplinary writing and speaking* (Andrews, Torgerson, Low, & McGuinn, 2009; Kibler, Walqui, & Bunch, 2015). When implementing this practice, effective teachers foster students' ability to analyze textual and oral evidence for relevancy, and they provide opportunities for students to identify and use evidence to develop and support claims.

- ***Disciplinary Communication:*** This practice focuses on structuring, strengthening, and supporting the quantity and quality of *students' oral and written output using academic language* (Bernabei & Reimer, 2013; O'Hara, Pritchard, & Zwiers, 2014). When implementing this practice, effective teachers provide opportunities for students to produce and fortify both oral and written communication.

The qualitative findings from the Delphi panel suggest that these essential High-Impact Practices alone, although central to effective disciplinary language and literacy instruction, do not get to the core of teaching. Effective teachers enact a set of instructional moves in support of these essential High-Impact Practices. We labeled these moves Cross-Cutting Practices, and they include Facilitating Acquisition of Academic Language, Fostering Metacognition for Disciplinary Learning, and Monitoring and Guiding Disciplinary Learning.

- ***Facilitating Acquisition of Academic Language:*** This practice focuses on structuring, strengthening, and supporting the acquisition and use of the language needed to participate in knowledge construction and disciplinary tasks. Disciplinary language has three distinct features: vocabulary, syntax, and discourse (August, Branum-Martin, Cardenas-Hagan, Francis, Powell, Moore, & Haynes, 2014; Cook, Boals, & Lundberg, 2011; Nagy & Townsend, 2012). When implementing this practice, effective teachers introduce and refer to the academic language demands of texts and tasks, and they provide opportunities for students to acquire and use the features (vocabulary, syntax, and discourse) of academic language.
- ***Fostering Metacognition for Disciplinary Learning:*** This practice focuses on the degree to which a teacher visibly enacts and deconstructs metacognitive processes and strategies that *foster students' metacognitive knowledge*. Examples of metacognitive processes include self-monitoring, self-assessing, self-questioning, and selection of strategies (Marzano & Heflebower, 2011; Schoenbach, Greenleaf, & Murphy, 2012). When implementing this practice, effective teachers visibly enact metacognitive processes and strategies they want students to use, and they deconstruct those processes and strategies so that students understand how, why, and when to use them.
- ***Monitoring and Guiding Disciplinary Learning:*** This practice focuses on how effectively a teacher monitors and guides the disciplinary learning throughout each task and the lesson as a whole, as well as adjusts and supports disciplinary tasks to meet the current needs of all students in the classroom. This practice also includes providing

feedback and *gradually removing supports to foster students' ability to work flexibly and independently* (Marzano, Yanoski, Hoegh, & Simms, 2013; Wiggins, 2012). When implementing this practice, effective teachers monitor learning and adjust instruction to meet student needs, and they provide feedback during lessons to promote disciplinary learning.

Finally, in preparation for enactment of High-Impact and Cross-Cutting Practices, teachers employ a Foundational Practice.

- ***Designing Instruction for Disciplinary Thinking and Understanding:*** This practice focuses on the design of lessons and learning tasks *to promote academic language and literacy* and support the target High-Impact Practices. This practice also focuses on how clearly and directly the teacher aligns disciplinary learning targets with the lesson's texts and tasks and *enables students to meet the demands of the disciplinary content and academic language* (Marzano et al., 2013; Wilson, Sztajn, Edington, & Myers, 2015). When implementing this practice, effective teachers set learning targets that are aligned with content standards and the target High-Impact Practice, they structure and connect tasks that support these learning targets, and they establish high expectations and maintain the intellectual rigor of classroom activities.

SOAR TEACHING FRAMES

To illustrate the interconnectedness of the practices, we organized them into Teaching Frames. Each Teaching Frame consists of a different High-Impact Practice supported by the Cross-Cutting and Foundational Practices, which are common across all frames. Each of the High-Impact and Cross-Cutting Practices has two elements, whereas the Foundational Practice has three (Table 1.1).

Together, the SOAR Teaching Frames for Literacy and their associated implementation rubrics (which we present in Chapter 6) form a framework for improving these eight essential practices in the elementary grades. This framework allows teachers to understand, enact, and reflect on the practices to elevate their teaching. In addition, the framework provides a common language so that teachers and instructional coaches can provide constructive and strategic feedback to their peers.

When implemented in the field, the SOAR Teaching Frames are typically introduced and implemented one at a time, starting with Disciplinary Discussions and bringing in new frames in the order indicated in Figure 1.1. Teachers with whom we have worked, from preservice through induction to

Table 1.1. The SOAR Teaching Frame Structure

HIGH-IMPACT PRACTICE *One of the four High-Impact Practices sits on top of each teaching frame.*	• Element 1 of the practice • Element 2 of the practice		
CROSS-CUTTING PRACTICES *The same three Cross-Cutting Practices repeat across each teaching frame.*	Facilitating Acquisition of Academic Language (FAAL) • Element 1 of the practice • Element 2 of the practice	Fostering Metacognition for Disciplinary Learning (FM) • Element 1 of the practice • Element 2 of the practice	Monitoring and Guiding Disciplinary Learning (MG) • Element 1 of the practice • Element 2 of the practice
FOUNDATIONAL PRACTICE *The same Foundational Practice sits at the bottom of each teaching frame.*	Designing Instruction for Disciplinary Thinking and Understanding (DI) • Element 1 of the practice • Element 2 of the practice • Element 3 of the practice		

in-service, spend time understanding each Teaching Frame and engaging in cycles of inquiry where they use that Frame for planning, implementing, reflecting on, and elevating instruction. The common language of the Frames allows groups of teachers to collaborate on these cycles of inquiry together, which enhances teaching and learning.

The Cross-Cutting and Foundational Practices repeat across each of the four frames. Our work has shown us that although most teachers understand the need to build academic language, foster metacognition, and guide learning and language use, more explicit attention needs to be paid to a connected enactment of these practices in order to support the end goal for students. For example, if your aim as a teacher is to have your students engage in a rich disciplinary discussion, build up new ideas, and construct new understanding, then you should facilitate their acquisition of the academic language they need to achieve that goal. You also should help them realize when a discussion is stalled or not on track and provide them with strategies to use to get the discussion back on track. Finally, you should carefully monitor and guide their engagement in a discussion and their use of academic language during that discussion. And when you plan for a lesson where students will be engaged in disciplinary discussion, you should think through the moves you can make during instruction as well as the materials and support you need to help your students be successful. The structure of the Teaching Frames, therefore, provides support for making teaching more intentional and for facilitating tighter connections among teaching practices to help students be successful.

Having identified the practices that are most predictive of student growth, our team next developed a corresponding set of videos and materials to illustrate what these practices look like when enacted in the classroom. We developed a platform (soarpractices.org) designed around the SOAR Teaching Frames to

- help teachers and administrators deepen their understanding of the SOAR practices by engaging in a series of online modules and accessing additional instructional strategies;
- allow teachers and administrators to use SOAR for self-reflection and for formative and summative teacher assessment, by providing interactive activities to deepen understanding of the SOAR rubrics; and
- scaffold professional learning for teachers in different grade spans (pre-K–2, 3–8, and 9–12) and across content areas (ELA, social studies, science, and mathematics) by providing them with access to additional video examples of the practices implemented in a range of classrooms.

FINDINGS FROM OUR WORK IN THE FIELD

We conducted a series of studies based on our SOAR implementation work in the field. We worked with very large, mid-sized, and small districts in urban, rural, and suburban settings. The contexts for the studies varied with respect to student and teacher diversity. For example, we worked in

- a large urban district with a high English learner population and a very diverse teaching force,
- a small suburban district with a high percentage of English learners and a less diverse teaching force, and
- a mid-sized district with a low percentage of English learners, a high percentage of English-speaking students who struggled with disciplinary language and literacy, and a teaching force that was primarily white and female.

The work was conducted with teachers at various stages in their careers, from beginning teachers to veteran teachers. We designed studies to investigate the impact of teacher use of the SOAR Teaching Frames to plan, implement, reflect on, and elevate instruction. In each context, the work we facilitated aimed to build capacity for improved disciplinary language and literacy development of all groups of students.

The central research questions that cut across these studies were as follows:

1. How did training and engagement with the SOAR Teaching Frames affect teacher practices?
    a. To what extent did teachers begin to adopt the language of SOAR?
    b. Was participation in the intervention associated with improvements in teachers' confidence to effectively plan for and teach disciplinary language and literacy?
    c. How did teachers' instructional practices change, if at all, as a result of the intervention, and to what degree were changes in instructional practices aligned with SOAR elements?
2. How did training and engagement with the SOAR Teaching Frames affect student outcomes?
    a. To what degree did students incorporate academic language into classroom tasks and activities?
    b. To what extent were metacognitive strategies utilized by students during classroom tasks and activities?
    c. How did student performance on standardized tests change, if at all, as a result of teachers' participation in SOAR?

We developed several SOAR-aligned instruments to capture changes in instruction throughout implementation of the model. These instruments were field-tested to establish their reliability and validity.

Change in Instructional Practice

Across all studies, analyses of growth on SOAR rubric scores indicated significant positive differences between treatment and comparison groups. The observed large effect sizes for all practices (.47–.60) indicated significant main effects attributable to the intervention. The Cross-Cutting Practice with the largest observed effect was Fostering Metacognition for Disciplinary Learning, which focuses on the degree to which a teacher visibly enacts and deconstructs metacognitive processes and strategies that foster students' metacognitive knowledge. We also found large effects on teachers' intentional actions for Monitoring and Guiding Disciplinary Learning and Facilitating Acquisition of Academic Language.

The results we found from the analyses of SOAR rubric scores parallel teachers' self-reported increases in their knowledge about academic language and literacy and in their ability to integrate language and content during instruction. Analyses of scores from self-assessment surveys across studies show a statistically significant impact on teachers' knowledge and use of SOAR practices. Specifically, the most significant shifts were found on teachers' ability to integrate language and content through discussion, implement in-the-moment teaching moves, and engage in metacognitive teaching.

Change in Student Outcomes

The impact of these instructional changes was evident in student outcomes over the course of the SOAR interventions. Results across all studies show that students significantly improved their disciplinary discussion and communication skills as a result of the intervention. In one study, for example, we found very large effects ($d = 1.71$) on a measure of students' ability to engage in discussions. This analysis showed that students significantly improved their ability to build up an idea and to use academic language appropriately in a discussion. Finally, significant differences were found across all studies between treatment students' performance on the Smarter Balanced Assessment Consortium (SBAC) tests in math and ELA in comparison to their non-SOAR peers. The studies showed that these significant differences were also evident for subgroups, including students classified as English learners, students reclassified as English proficient within the prior 3 years, and students classified as English-only students.

CONCLUSION

This chapter describes essential instructional practices that drive student learning as articulated in the CCSS, NGSS, and state ELD standards as well as a framework for how these essential practices are interconnected in effective academic language and disciplinary literacy teaching. We designed this book to be a practical guide that will help you understand each of the SOAR Teaching Frames as well as to provide you with instructional strategies and tools for implementing the practices within each frame across content areas and grade levels. We also provide vignettes from actual elementary classrooms so that you can see what the SOAR Teaching Frames look like when implemented.

We are currently using the framework and corresponding support materials in professional-learning programs for teachers, instructional coaches, and instructional leaders in partner districts and schools across the United States. Consequently, the examples in the book come from a range of contexts. Findings from our work demonstrate that the SOAR Teaching Frames for Literacy provide a suite of powerful tools for supporting leaders', coaches', and teachers' adoption and enactment of these practices in their contexts, and ultimately for improving academic outcomes for all students.

CHAPTER 2

Disciplinary Discussions

The first part of this chapter will help you understand the practices in the Disciplinary Discussions Teaching Frame by illustrating how a teacher used this frame to enhance a lesson, elevate her instruction, and better develop her students' ability to engage in discussions of disciplinary content. The second part of the chapter provides you with classroom examples and instructional strategies and tools to help you implement the Disciplinary Discussions Teaching Frame in your classroom.

In Chapter 1 we described the SOAR practices and provided you with an overview of the SOAR Teaching Frames, which consist of five practices: one High-Impact Practice, three Cross-Cutting Practices, and one Foundational Practice. Each Teaching Frame focuses on a different High-Impact Practice. The Cross-Cutting Practices are the same for every Teaching Frame, although their implementation varies in the way they support the High-Impact Practice. For example, visibly enacting metacognitive strategies to help your students engage in discussion looks different than visibly enacting metacognitive strategies to help your students interact with complex text. The Cross-Cutting Practices—Facilitating Acquisition of Academic Language, Fostering Metacognition for Disciplinary Learning, and Monitoring and Guiding Disciplinary Learning—represent good pedagogy. These practices need to be present in every lesson to promote student learning. Without them, the lesson will be missing critical pieces that support the High-Impact Practice and student learning.

The Foundational Practice is called Designing Instruction for Disciplinary Thinking and Understanding. It too is the same for each Teaching Frame. This practice has teachers consider the alignment of the CCSS, the High-Impact Practice, and the learning target as well as how the tasks of the lesson connect

THINK BEFORE READING ACTIVITY

In what ways do you have your class engage in student-to-student discussions? How do your students' discussions inform your teaching? As you read the vignette below, think about how Ms. Vu would respond to these questions.

and support the learning target with a laser-like focus. Finally, it emphasizes maintaining high expectations and rigor throughout the lesson. We want teachers to create an environment that sets high expectations and that requires students to learn at high levels of rigor in meeting those expectations. As you review the three elements of the Foundational Practice, you will see that each of them needs to be addressed in every lesson, hence the name Foundational.

The goal of the Disciplinary Discussions High-Impact Practice is to have students engage in student-to-student discussions where they grapple with ideas to help them co-construct deeper understandings of a topic. In order for that to happen, you first need to explicitly teach and build your students' conversation skills (element 1; see Table 2.1).

The four conversation skills are Create Ideas, Clarify Ideas, Fortify Ideas, and Negotiate Ideas (see Table 2.2). These skills can be used in conversations across disciplines and grade levels as long as students learn how and when to use them as they talk.

Once your students understand and have practiced the skills, you need to provide students with time and support to dive into discussions, using the open-ended prompts you have provided, to reach deeper understandings of the content (element 2, see Table 2.1).

USING THE SOAR LENS TO PLAN AND REFLECT

SOAR is not a curriculum or an isolated set of strategies. SOAR is a lens you use to plan, teach, and reflect on your lessons and ultimately elevate your

Table 2.1. Disciplinary Discussions Teaching Frame

HIGH-IMPACT PRACTICE	Disciplinary Discussions (DD) **Element 1:** Build conversation skills (Create, Clarify, Fortify, Negotiate) **Element 2:** Provide extended and supported opportunities for students to engage in disciplinary discussions		
CROSS-CUTTING PRACTICES	Facilitating Acquisition of Academic Language (FAAL) **Element 1:** Introduce and/or refer to the academic language demands of texts and tasks **Element 2:** Provide extended and supported opportunities for students to acquire and use the features of academic language	Fostering Metacognition for Disciplinary Learning (FM) **Element 1:** Visibly enact metacognitive processes and/or strategies students are expected to use in support of disciplinary learning **Element 2:** Deconstruct metacognitive processes and/or strategies that support disciplinary learning	Monitoring and Guiding Disciplinary Learning (MG) **Element 1:** Monitor learning and adjust instruction, supports, and/or disciplinary tasks to meet student needs **Element 2:** Provide written and/or oral feedback during lessons to promote disciplinary learning
FOUNDATIONAL PRACTICE	Designing Instruction for Disciplinary Thinking and Understanding (DI) **Element 1:** Set disciplinary learning targets that are aligned with ELA/Literacy CCSS and the target high-impact practice **Element 2:** Structure and connect tasks that support the learning targets **Element 3:** Establish high expectations that support the learning targets and maintain the intellectual rigor of classroom activities and tasks		

Table 2.2. Conversation Prompts and Responses

Conversation Skill	The Skill Requires:	Prompt and Response Starters
Create Ideas	• Staying on topic • Building on others' ideas • Making claims • Considering multiple points of view	A: What is your idea? B: My idea is . . . A: What else can we say about that? B: I can add to that.
Clarify Ideas	• Elaborating on ideas • Paraphrasing what others say • Asking questions to deepen understanding	A: Can you elaborate on that idea? B: In other words, . . . A: Can you clarify that part? B: I think it is important because . . .
Fortify Ideas	• Supporting ideas with evidence (self, world, text, research) • Identifying multiple examples of evidence • Explaining how evidence supports an idea	A: Can you give me an example? B: An example from the text is . . . A: What other evidence can we use? B: I think this evidence supports that idea because . . .
Negotiate Ideas	• Agreeing and disagreeing • Combining ideas into a new idea • Adjusting your thinking in response to others' ideas • Coming to consensus	A: Where do we agree/disagree? B: I agree/disagree because . . . A: How can we combine these ideas? B: I think we can say . . .

instruction. The SOAR lens helps you think about how the five practices of a Teaching Frame are integrated during instruction to drive student learning. By keeping the SOAR Teaching Frame at the forefront of your planning and teaching, your lessons will more effectively reach all of your students and address their needs. Therefore, it is critical to understand how each practice works in conjunction with the others in the frame and to address each of them in your lesson design.

To get a deeper understanding of what is meant by using SOAR as a lens, let's first look at a non-model of a lesson created by a teacher who was unfamiliar with SOAR. When we have finished, we will consider why this is a non-model and how posing SOAR guiding questions as we plan helps us address all the practices of a Teaching Frame, strengthens our lesson, and ultimately affects student learning. After the non-model, we will examine a lesson created by a teacher who is familiar with SOAR and who has used SOAR as a lens in her planning. The annotated lesson shows the alignment with the five practices of the frame so that we can see how the teacher included each of the practices of the frame to plan her lesson. Finally, we will step inside a 3rd-grade classroom by reading a vignette that illustrates how the teacher uses the SOAR lens to implement the lesson.

3rd-Grade Non-Model Lesson

The teacher who created this non-model has been working with her students on opinion writing. They have been collecting research on the topic of whether there should be zoos. This lesson focuses on having the students discuss and develop their opinions in preparation for writing their essay.

Let's think about why this is a non-model. The box lists the standards the teacher will address in the lesson and the activities in which the students

Standards:

CCSS.ELA.SL.3.1 Engage effectively in a range of collaborative discussions (one-on-one, in groups, and teacher-led) with diverse partners on grade 3 topics and texts, building on others' ideas and expressing their own clearly.

CCSS.ELA.SL.3.3 Ask and answer questions about information from a speaker, offering appropriate elaboration and detail.

CCSS.ELA.RI.3.6 Distinguish their own point of view from that of the author of a text.

CCSS.ELA.W.3.1 Write opinion pieces on topics or texts, supporting a point of view with reasons.

- Recap the work we have been doing and how today's work supports the goal of writing an opinion essay.
- Read the standards to the class.
- Have students review the graphic organizer they created after reading several texts about zoos.
- Label four corners of the room: strongly agree, agree, disagree, strongly disagree. Have students go to corners, match up with students with different opinions, and discuss.
- Students return to their desks and use the Argument Evidence Scale (Figure 2.1 on p. 27) to sort their evidence into pro and con.
- Have students use the Argument Evidence Scale tomorrow to begin their essay.

will be engaged. Regarding the High-Impact Practice of Disciplinary Discussions, the students will be discussing their opinions. However, it is unclear as to what, if any, extent the teacher has prepared students for these discussions. For instance, how are the conversation skills (Create, Clarify, Fortify, Negotiate) being addressed, and what support is the teacher providing to help her students use them? The teacher could ask herself the following guiding questions as she plans her lesson to help her zero in on these critical elements:

- How will I refer to the conversation skills I want the students to use?
- What type of support can I provide to help them be successful?
- How can I structure the lesson so that students have extended opportunities to engage in the discussion successfully?

Now let's consider how the teacher addresses the three Cross Cutting Practices. For Facilitating the Acquisition of Academic Language, this lesson does not acknowledge any academic language or the language demands that are inherent in this type of activity. The teacher could ask the following questions as she plans the lesson:

- What academic language and structures do my students need to understand to be successful in their discussions?
- What supports do I need to provide so that my students use academic language in their discussions?

There is no evidence of metacognition. The lesson does not include any demonstration or think-aloud as a model for what is expected of students. The teacher could ask the following questions as she plans the lesson for this Cross-Cutting Practice:

- What process or strategy do I need to demonstrate so that my students understand what I am expecting them to do?
- In what way(s) can I enact, and explain how, when, or why to use, the process or strategy?

There is also no evidence of how the teacher will monitor the students or the type of feedback she will give them. The teacher could ask herself the following questions as she plans the lesson:

- In what ways will I monitor my students' learning during the lesson?
- What type of feedback will I provide to help my students improve?

There is evidence of the Foundational Practice. The standards are listed and include the speaking and listening CCSS. There does appear to be a connectedness among the activities and the end product, the essay. The lesson also seems rigorous. The teacher could ask the following questions as she plans the lesson to ensure a laser-like focus on those standards:

- How do the learning targets align with the CCSS and the High-Impact Practice, Disciplinary Discussions?
- How do the tasks support the learning targets?
- How will I establish high expectations and rigor and convey them to students?

By considering these guiding questions for each of the practices, the teacher could enhance the lesson to be more cohesive, which would help her students be more successful in engaging in disciplinary discussions.

3rd-Grade SOAR Model Lesson With Annotations

Now we are going to guide you through a process that will deepen your understanding of how SOAR can be used as a lens to plan. Let's look at this lesson again, only this time the teacher is aware of SOAR and has used guiding questions to reflect as she plans. We have identified where the teacher addresses each of the five practices in her planning.

As you read the annotated lesson below (see Table 2.3), note how much more intentional and thoughtful this lesson is and how each of the SOAR practices supports the High-Impact Practice of Disciplinary Discussions. It is evident that the teacher has been more thoughtful in her planning and is using the SOAR Teaching Frame as a lens. Our research in schools where teachers use the SOAR Teaching Frames as a lens shows that these teachers plan more thoroughly, which in turn positively affects student learning (O'Hara et al., 2018; Pritchard & O'Hara, 2016; Reyes, Bookmyer, O'Hara, Pitta, & Pritchard, 2020).

Now let's see how the teacher takes this lesson and enacts it with her students. As you read this vignette, reflect on how the five practices of the Disciplinary Discussions Teaching Frame are being implemented. Try to answer the following questions:

1. How do the Cross-Cutting Practices enhance and support Disciplinary Discussions?
2. How do the High-Impact, Cross-Cutting, and Foundational Practices work together to support student learning and the learning target?

Table 2.3. 3rd-Grade Annotated Model Lesson

Disciplinary Discussions (DD) Teaching Frame Elements	Teacher Actions
Designing Instruction E1–Teacher aligns the High–Impact Practice, Disciplinary Discussions, to the CCSS	DD-E1: Build conversation skills DD-E2: Provide extended and supported opportunities for students to engage in disciplinary discussions Standards: CCSS.ELA.SL.3.1 Engage effectively in a range of collaborative discussions (one-on-one, in groups, and teacher-led) with diverse partners on *grade 3 topics and texts*, building on others' ideas and expressing their own clearly. CCSS.ELA.SL.3.3 Ask and answer questions about information from a speaker, offering appropriate elaboration and detail. CCSS.ELA.RI.3.6 Distinguish their own point of view from that of the author of a text. CCSS.ELA.W.3.1 Write opinion pieces on topics or texts, supporting a point of view with reasons.
Designing Instruction E2–Teacher has students think about the tasks they have done and connects them to the larger task of opinion writing	Ask students to work with their partner and summarize the work we have been doing in ELA.
Designing Instruction E2–Teacher connects tasks	Call on some students to share out. Listen to clarify any misconceptions.
Designing Instruction E1 & 2–Teacher aligns High–Impact Practice to CCSS and connects all the tasks to the end product	Read the standards in student-friendly language and explain that today they are going to be having discussions with partners to deepen their understanding of the issue.
Disciplinary Discussions E1–Teacher builds conversation skills	Review the norms of interaction, emphasizing *speak and act respectfully* since they will be discussing different points of view.
Designing Instruction E2–Teacher connects tasks	Review each skill (Create, Clarify, Fortify, Negotiate) on the Conversation Prompts and Responses.

Table continues on next page

Table 2.3. 3rd-Grade Annotated Model Lesson (continued)

Disciplinary Discussions (DD) Teaching Frame Elements	Teacher Actions
Disciplinary Discussions E1–Teacher builds conversation skills through diverse partners and use of sentence frames Disciplinary Discussions E2–Teacher provides extended opportunities by having students use the conversation skills	Working with another partner, have students review the graphic organizer they created after reading several texts about zoos. Then discuss the authors' points of view, as well as the evidence or reasoning the authors used to support their viewpoints.
Fostering Metacognition E1–Teacher enacts metacognitive process by demonstrating a model and non-model so that students know what is expected	Distribute sentence frames and demonstrate a model and non-model of how to use the skills to discuss different points of view.
Monitoring & Guiding E1–Teacher monitors students' discussion	Circulate and monitor students' use of the conversation skills.
Monitoring & Guiding E2–Teacher provides feedback	Provide specific feedback on how the students can improve.
Facilitating Acquisition of Academic Language E2–Teacher provides opportunities to acquire and use academic language of agreeing and disagreeing Designing Instruction E1–Teacher establishes high expectations and intellectual rigor	Label four corners of the room: strongly agree, agree, disagree, strongly disagree. Have students go to corners, match up with students with different opinions, and discuss. Explain this discussion is a bit different since they are discussing their points of view. Provide sentence frames: • What is your point of view? My point of view is . . . because . . . . • I hear you saying . . . ; however, I disagree because . . . . • I understand that you believe . . . , but have you considered . . . because . . . ? • I see evidence to support a different point of view . . . . • I agree with the statement . . . , but I could be persuaded that . . . . • I would like to add to your point of view . . . .
Disciplinary Discussions E2–Teacher provides extended opportunities by having students use the conversation skills	After one minute, have students switch partners. Do that three times.

Table 2.3. 3rd-Grade Annotated Model Lesson (continued)

Disciplinary Discussions (DD) Teaching Frame Elements	Teacher Actions
Monitoring & Guiding 1 & 2–Teacher monitors and provides feedback	Use a checklist to track students' use of conversation skills and provide feedback.
Fostering Metacognition E1–Teacher enacts the metacognitive process by modeling how to weigh the evidence Facilitating Acquisition of Academic Language E2–Teacher provides opportunities to acquire and use academic language with their partner by discussing pros and cons Designing Instruction E3–Activity is intellectually rigorous by having students think deeply about the evidence	Return to their desks and meet up with their partner. Use a think-aloud to demonstrate how to use the *Argument Evidence Scale* to sort the evidence into pro and con with their partner.
Fostering Metacognition E1–Teacher enacts the metacognitive process by modeling how to weigh the evidence Disciplinary Discussions E1 & 2–Teacher refers to conversation skills and provides opportunities to use them	Once that is done, model how to weigh the evidence from most important to least and how to discuss it using Clarify, Fortify, and Negotiate conversation skills.
Monitoring & Guiding E1 & 2–Teacher monitors and provides feedback to students	Monitor students and provide support as needed.
Designing Instruction E2–Teacher connects tasks by reviewing what was done today and how it connects to the essay	Review today's outcomes in preparation for writing their opinion essay tomorrow.
Fostering Metacognition E2–Teacher draws attention to metacognitive process by having students stop and reflect	Have students reflect on what worked today and how it helped them decide their position.
Fostering Metacognition E1–Teacher has students be metacognitive by rating themselves in the use of the norms and skills	Have students do *Fist to Four* on how well they adhered to norms of interaction and their conversation skills.

Step Inside Ms. Vu's Classroom

Ms. Vu has an expectation that her 3rd-graders have student-to-student discussions every day in every subject. One of her protocols is to have students identify different partners to talk to instead of always turning to their elbow partner. For this unit she uses names of different zoo animals (e.g., walrus, zebra, rhino) for their learning partners. In ELA, they are learning about opinion writing and how authors use evidence and reasoning to support their point of view. Her class is preparing to answer the focal question: Should there be zoos? Students have read a number of articles in favor of and against animals being kept in zoos. They recorded the pros and cons presented by each author on a graphic organizer.

> Having students think about and discuss what they have been working on confirms for the teacher that students understand how the tasks are connected.

Ms. Vu begins the day by asking students to take a moment to reflect on what they have been working on and to discuss it with their walrus learning partners. After students have had a few minutes to think and discuss, she calls on a few students to share. Felipe says, "We have been reading about should there be zoos. We have read four different articles that have different points of view. We have taken notes about them on our graphic organizer."

"Great job summarizing, Felipe," said Ms. Vu. "Does anyone want to add to what Filipe has said?"

Penelope says, "I would like to add to what Felipe said. We wrote on a graphic organizer if the article was in favor of animals being in zoos or if they were against animals being in zoos."

Quincy says, "Oh, I would like to add to Penelope. We also wrote why they were in favor of or against zoos."

"Okay, Felipe, I would like to come back to you to see if you want to add anything else."

"Umm, maybe that I think we called it pro when they were in favor and con when they were against. And we are going to write our own essay," Felipe replied.

> Ms. Vu provides feedback to students to reinforce how they are listening and adding on.

"Wow, I am so impressed with all of your great summarizing of what we have been studying. I'm especially impressed by how well you listened to one another, so you were able to add to what others said! So, today we are going to continue our work by thinking about our own opinion of whether there should be zoos. Today we are going to review our graphic organizer to see what other authors thought about zoos and discuss them with our zebra partner to try to formulate our own opinion. Then we are going to work with another partner using the Argument Evidence Scale to firm up our opinion before we start our opinion essay."

Ms. Vu points to the standards she has written in *I Can* statements and reads them to the students, explaining that these are the standards they will be addressing today.

- I can state my opinion and support it with evidence.
- I can keep an open mind and listen to someone else's opinion.
- I can ask and answer questions to negotiate meaning.
- I can keep the conversation going when it stalls.

Since a lot of today will be discussing what they have learned, Ms. Vu references the Conversation Prompts and Responses (Create, Clarify, Fortify, Negotiate; Table 2.2) students have at their desks and reviews each skill, highlighting the language students need to use for each of the skills (e.g., Can you elaborate? Can you paraphrase? Can you add to my idea?). She also reviews the norms of interaction, emphasizing the need to speak respectfully even if they do not agree with their partner.

> Ms. Vu supports all students by having them review the graphic organizer and discuss it with their partner. This allows students an opportunity to formulate their opinion.

Ms. Vu then asks students to take the graphic organizer they have been working on and meet with their rhino partner. Once they are with their partner, she explains, "I want you to review your graphic organizer and discuss the authors' points of view and the evidence or reasoning the authors used to support their viewpoints. If you need to go back and look at the articles to confirm your notes or thinking, please do that. Good researchers go back to the text to confirm their thinking. And we are good researchers!

"Before you start, I want to use our puppets to model how to use the sentence prompts and responses in your conversations." She points to the anchor chart on the board.

> She supports students in their discussion by having them hear and see the conversation with the sentence prompts and responses.

Puppet 1: In the article *An Argument for Zoos: Extinction and Endangered Animals,* the author claimed that animals like the passenger pigeon became extinct because of humans. What did you write about this article?

Puppet 2: I agree with your evidence. I also wrote down that Atlas bears became extinct because they lost their habitat. So, what do you think was the author's reasoning for why there should be zoos?

Puppet 1: He said in the last sentence that a good zoo can provide food, shelter, and preservation of wildlife.

Puppet 2: I agree with you.

"I want you to answer these questions with a thumbs-up if they did or down if they didn't: Did they stay on topic?. . . Did they take turns?. . . Did they add to one another's ideas? Good, so now with your partner discuss the other articles."

While the students are working, Ms. Vu circulates around the classroom. She has a clipboard with all the students' names and columns labeled *stays on topic*, *elaborates*, *paraphrases*, and *adds on*. She puts check marks under columns when students show evidence of performing them during the conversation.

This checklist helps Ms. Vu track what skills all students are using and not using. This allows her to be explicit with her feedback and any necessary reteaching.

Once students complete their discussion, she asks students to think about what they researched and to decide which way they were leaning in regard to whether or not there should be zoos. She explains, "You are going to talk to other classmates who have a different opinion than you. This will help you think more deeply about your opinion and whether or not you want to change it. However, when we talk about our point of view, the conversation sounds a bit different. I want to give you these prompts and responses to use when sharing your point of view. Let's read these together."

- What is your point of view? My point of view is . . . because . . .
- I hear you saying . . . ; however, I disagree because . . .
- I understand that you believe . . . , but have you considered . . . because . . . ?
- I see evidence to support a different point of view . . .
- I agree with the statement . . . , but I could be persuaded that . . .
- I would like to add to your point of view . . .

Sentence frames support students' use of academic language.

She then has students go to one of the four corners of the room labeled strongly agree, agree, disagree, and strongly disagree. She has students meet up with students from opposite corners to discuss their position. Using their conversation prompts and graphic organizer, students discuss their points of view and the reasoning that supports them. After a few minutes, she has the students move to a new partner and discuss again. She repeats this process three times, giving students multiple opportunities to hear other points of view and to think more deeply about their own. During this time, Ms. Vu continues to walk around with a clipboard, tracking students' use of the conversation skills. She also uses this opportunity to provide feedback to her students.

Ms. Vu asks students to return to their seats and meet with a different learning partner. She distributes the Argument Evidence Scale (see Figure 2.1). She demonstrates how to use this by modeling the process. "I am going to look at my graphic organizer and think about what I learned from the four corners discussion to come up with the reasons and evidence for having zoos and not having zoos. I will write each piece of evidence I find on a different

Figure 2.1. Argument Evidence Scale

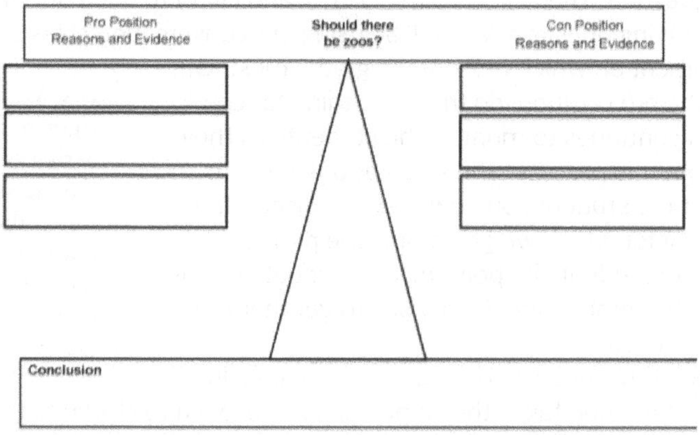

Source: Adapted from *Common Core Standards in Diverse Classrooms: Essential Practices for Developing Academic Language and Disciplinary Literacy* by Zwiers, O'Hara, & Pritchard. 2014a. Copyright 2014 by Stenhouse. Adapted with permission.

card. If the evidence or reasoning is for zoos, I am going to write it on one of the green cards and place it under the pro position of the argument scale. If the evidence or reasoning is con, I am going to write it on an orange card and place it under the con position. This will help me determine which position is stronger. You are going to be working with your hippo partner to list all of these, so you need to use your conversation skills as you discuss them. Remember to use our academic vocabulary that is listed on our word wall, for example, extinct, endangered, habitat."

Ms. Vu sees two students struggling and asks them, "What was one of the reasons the author used in the 'Zoochosis' article?" One student responds that the animals are separated from their families. Ms. Vu then asks the students where they would write it and where it would be placed on the Argument Evidence Scale.

When the students finish, Ms. Vu then models the next process. "As I walked around, I noticed that all of you have a number of reasons and evidence under each pro and con position. So now we need to think about which reason or evidence weighs the most. That means we need to think about the reasoning in a different way—which reasoning is stronger or more important. I want you and your partner to negotiate and put them in order from most to least important. Let me give you an example. If I look at the evidence I have under the pro position, I think the reasoning for keeping animals from being extinct is more important or weighs more than the reasoning that zoos are educational. I am going to explain my idea to my

> Teacher thinks aloud to demonstrate how to use the conversation skill "negotiate" to come to agreement on what evidence weighs the most.

partner and then ask him if he can build on my idea, elaborate on it, or ask a clarifying question. Then I'll ask him his idea, and I'll try to build on, elaborate, or ask a clarifying question. We will be using our conversation skills to come to an agreement on which reasons weigh the most. Once you finish the pro position, do the same thing for con."

Ms. Vu adds rigor to the activity by having students think about their reasoning, which will strengthen their opinion essay.

Ms. Vu continues to monitor the students as they work through this process. She stops at one table to compliment the students on how they are discussing the reasoning for which weighs more. She prompts another set of students by pointing to Negotiate on the Conversation Prompts and Responses to get them to come to consensus.

She calls time when most students have concluded this section. She then takes this opportunity to explain to students that today was about discussing the evidence for and against having zoos. "We began the day by reviewing our graphic organizers with our walrus partner. Then we went into the four corners to talk to our classmates about each of our points of view. After that, we collected the evidence and placed them under the pro or con position and then placed them in order of most to least important. All of this work is to prepare you to write your opinion essay tomorrow. Weighing the evidence should have helped confirm for you what your opinion is. So I want you to take a minute and think about what your position was before class today and what your position is now. Write down on a piece of paper what helped you reach a position today." Finally, Ms. Vu asks students to use *Fist to Four* to rank how well they used the norms of interaction. She points to the anchor chart on the wall (four being an expert, three being a practitioner, two being an apprentice, and one being a novice) to remind them of the strategy. She repeats the process for their use of conversation skills.

She has them think metacognitively about their own position and how it might have changed.

Think After Reading Activity

In the preceding vignette, you read about ways in which Ms. Vu used the SOAR Teaching Frame as a lens to plan, teach, and reflect on instruction designed to engage students in disciplinary discussions. Her activities were tied directly to the learning target. She supported her students by having them discuss the evidence that supported their opinions so that they would be successful in writing their essays. Before reading the next section of this chapter, think about how you could use the Disciplinary Discussions Teaching Frame to enhance a lesson you have previously taught and, as a result, engage your students more deeply in co-constructing knowledge.

IMPLEMENTING THE DISCIPLINARY DISCUSSIONS TEACHING FRAME

In the following section, we provide you with instructional strategies and example lessons to support the implementation of the Disciplinary Discussions Teaching Frame in your classroom. These resources will deepen your understanding of the SOAR practices, demonstrate the purposeful planning required to implement the practices, and explain why, when, and how to use these strategies and tools in different content areas.

Instructional Strategy: Introducing Disciplinary Conversation Skills

This strategy supports element 1, *Build conversation skills*. Students need conversation skills to engage in productive disciplinary discussions. We define these skills as students' ability to Create, Clarify, Fortify, and Negotiate ideas (Table 2.2) during student-to-student interactions. You should use this strategy to explicitly introduce each skill to your students.

Why Use This Strategy: Disciplinary conversation skills are essential for disciplinary learning and for student success in CCSS and NGSS classrooms. An understanding of these skills and the ability to use them effectively helps students hold purposeful discussions in which they deepen their thinking and co-construct meaning through multiple exchanges with peers. These skills are necessary across contexts and disciplines and will be used by students for the rest of their lives.

When to Use This Strategy: Use this strategy when you want to introduce students to a new conversation skill or when you want to remind students of conversation skills you have previously taught. This strategy can also be useful when you want to provide prompt and response starters (see Appendix A) associated with each skill or highlight its purpose in a discussion. The visuals and hand signals included with this instructional strategy are helpful reminders for students before they engage in disciplinary discussions.

How to Use This Strategy: Begin by introducing conversation norms and rules for discussion. With your students, create an anchor chart that illustrates your expectations. These norms could include sit knee to knee, use a quiet voice, and one person talks at a time. Rules for discussion could include taking turns, using academic language, and building on others' ideas. Have students practice these norms and rules. Once they are established, introduce each of the conversation skills using prompt and response starters to help students develop these skills.

Example Lesson

1. In small groups, have students discuss norms that are effective for a discussion. Ask groups to share what they have discussed and then create an anchor chart for the classroom.
2. Groups discuss what a disciplinary discussion would look like. Create a T-chart on the whiteboard and label one column *looks like* and the other column *sounds like*. Then students share their ideas while you record responses on the T-chart. Be very explicit and intentional about the outcome: for students to understand that disciplinary discussions are different than the way they typically talk to their friends.
3. Process the T-chart by asking students to answer and discuss these questions: Why are disciplinary discussions important? How do disciplinary discussions help us learn? What makes a disciplinary discussion a good disciplinary discussion?
4. Now introduce each of the four conversation skills one at a time. Provide a model and a non-model conversation for the conversation skill Create and have students discuss the qualities and effectiveness of each one. Repeat the same steps with different partners for the skills of Clarify, Fortify, and Negotiate. Introducing the skills and giving students the opportunity to use them happens over a number of days.
5. Once students have an understanding of the conversation skills, have them apply them one at a time. Project a visual text and provide a model and non-model of how you could create an idea with this visual text. Then have students work with a partner and create an idea using the sentence stem "I noticed . . ." Students should practice this skill for a few days until you feel they have grasped it. Follow the same process for the other three conversation skills.

Instructional Strategy: Building Disciplinary Conversation Skills

This strategy supports element 1, *Build conversation skills*. In the previous instructional strategy, we introduced the four disciplinary conversation skills: Create, Clarify, Fortify, and Negotiate. This instructional strategy provides students with a chance to build these skills through structured and supported practice. The Conversation Prompts and Responses (Table 2.2) provide support for students.

Why Use This Strategy: Introducing disciplinary conversation skills is not enough for students to be able to use them effectively to engage in extended, productive discussions. To take ownership of these skills, students need extended opportunities to practice applying them in structured and supported ways. Building disciplinary conversation skills is a strategy that integrates all four skills and maintains the intellectual rigor necessary for CCSS and NGSS instruction. You need to carefully consider the prompts you use to engage students in disciplinary conversations. Prompts that are at the literal level or that require little thinking will produce limited responses. Rich prompts engage and excite students while encouraging them to think more deeply about the content.

When to Use This Strategy: Students, especially English learners, need many opportunities to practice disciplinary conversation skills in structured and supported ways. These opportunities should occur as often as possible in all content areas so that students understand that discussion is a tool to deepen their learning across the curriculum.

How to Use This Strategy: Explain to students that they are going to have an opportunity to practice the conversation skills. Students are given a text (written, visual, audio, or multimedia) and asked to create an idea with their partner. Model what this sounds and looks like using the prompt and response starters. Repeat the process for Clarify, Fortify, and Negotiate. The amount of scaffolding that you provide should decrease as students become more proficient in using the skills.

Example Lesson

1. It is important for students to meet with different learning partners. Distribute matching pairs of cards to students to find their partners (e.g., peanut butter and jelly, or SpongeBob and Patrick), or have students select different learning partners themselves.
2. Tell students they will have an opportunity to practice using conversation skills with a partner. Students have been studying American symbols. Project a number of American symbols on the board (e.g., Statue of Liberty, American flag, Capitol Building, American eagle). Ask students to "Think about the symbols we have been studying. Which American symbol do you think best represents America?"
3. Ask students to turn to their discussion partners and discuss their ideas. The following sentence stems can help students discuss the ideas they have created and clarify their thinking:

Disciplinary Conversation Skill: Create

Prompts	Responses
What is your idea?	One idea could be . . .
What do you notice about the other symbols?	I noticed . . .

Disciplinary Conversation Skill: Clarify

Prompts	Responses
Why do you think that?	I think it because . . .
Tell me more about . . .	In other words . . .

4. Supply students with an informational text about American symbols. An example of a primary one is in Appendix B. Choose an approach to reading the passage that best matches the needs of the students in your classroom. For example, you may ask students to read the text on their own, with a partner, or in a guided reading group. Prompt students to consider what they originally thought about the symbols. Ask them to share with their partners how their thinking has changed based on the informational text they just read. Tell them to start with "Now I think . . ."

Disciplinary Conversation Skill: Fortify

Prompts	Responses
Show me where . . .	An example is . . .
How do you know that?	I know that because . . .

5. Have students negotiate and see whether they can agree with one another about which American symbol best represents America.

Disciplinary Conversation Skill: Negotiate

Prompts	Responses
What is your opinion?	My opinion is . . .
Do you agree/disagree? Why?	I agree/disagree because . . .

Strategies for Engaging Reluctant Speakers

Students may be reluctant to talk for a variety of reasons, including language proficiency, academic language development, lack of experience with using the conversation skills, and cultural norms. However, all students need to talk to express themselves, and this is critical when students are first practicing the conversation skills.

One idea is to provide language supports such as prompt and response starters for each of the conversation skills so that students have something to use as a model. Another idea is to give students the opportunity to draw or write a response to a discussion prompt before asking them to use the conversation skills with a partner.

Yet another approach is to provide more scaffolding for students who need it by making available sentence frames, monitoring student use of the sentence frames and conversation skills, and asking guiding questions as needed. Talking Chips is a strategy in which each student is given two to three manipulatives. After a student speaks, the students place a chip in the middle of the table and cannot speak again until all the others in the group have shared their ideas. Finally, do not forget the importance of wait time. Giving students the time to construct a response while letting them know they cannot outwait you reinforces the message that everyone must participate.

Instructional Strategy: Layering Texts

This strategy supports element 2, *Provide extended and supported opportunities for engaging in disciplinary discussions.* This strategy uses text sets to engage students in disciplinary discussions that lead to the synthesis of information. Text sets are collections of resources from different genres, media, and levels of reading difficulty that support readers with a range of abilities, experiences, and interests.

Why Use This Strategy: Synthesizing across multiple texts is a necessary skill for 21st-century learning, and layering texts in a text set raises the intellectual rigor of this task. Synthesis includes summarizing key information, uncovering patterns within texts, and integrating ideas. In order to synthesize information across texts, students must first analyze each text to determine important information conveyed by the authors. Then students compare that information across texts to form new ideas and understandings. Layering Texts offers students multiple entry points into the texts, which enable all students to participate more fully in discussions.

When to Use This Strategy: Layering Texts is particularly effective when the reading and language abilities of your students vary significantly because the texts in a text set are linked by their topic or content, which provides different pathways to the concepts you are studying. Layering Texts also increases student engagement, since the different formats featured in the text set can heighten student interest and motivate students to read. This is also an effective way to address the information gap.

How to Use This Strategy: Strategically decide the order in which the texts will be presented to students based on students' prior knowledge and proficiency levels as well as the learning targets. These texts help students construct knowledge as they engage in discussions and deepen their understanding of content.

Example Lesson

1. The layers of this text set include photographs, an informational text, and song lyrics to support student discussions about the Buffalo Soldiers who served in the American Civil War. Students can use the Conversation Prompts and Responses (Appendix A) to support them in their disciplinary discussions.
2. Display three photos of Buffalo Soldiers. A good resource for photos and information can be found here: https://nmaahc.si.edu/explore/manylenses/buffalosoldiers. Distribute the graphic organizer in Table 2.4 and ask students to think about what they see in the images. At this point, do not supply them with any information; rather, allow them to tap into their background knowledge or begin to make inferences based on what they see. Direct them to turn to a partner to discuss what each of them noticed using the conversation skills they have learned. Ask them what they can conclude about the people in the pictures and have them fill in the Picture column in the graphic organizer using the prompts provided as needed. After they have discussed the pictures, have them complete the prompt in the last row of that column: "We think . . ."
3. Provide students with copies of the informational text entitled *Buffalo Soldiers* found in Appendix C. Set the purpose for the reading by

Table 2.4. Layering Texts Graphic Organizer: Buffalo Soldiers

Picture	Article	Lyrics
Prompts: • I think . . . because . . . • I also noticed . . . which supports my idea. • I can see what you mean, but it could also be . . . • What else do you notice?	*Prompts:* • What did we learn from the text? • What part of the passage supports our ideas from the photo? • How has our thinking changed based on our reading?	*Prompts:* • How do the lyrics inform our thinking? • We can say that . . . • How can we bring these ideas together? • Even though some might think that . . . we could conclude that . . .
We think . . .	Our thinking has changed . . .	This adds . . .
We can conclude from the three texts that . . .		

explaining to students that they are going to be reading about the people in the photos. While reading, they should think about what information in the text supports what they discussed when viewing the pictures and what new information they are learning. Choose an approach to reading the passage that best matches the needs of the students in your classroom. For example, you may ask students to read the text on their own, with a partner, or in a guided reading group. When students have completed the reading, direct them to talk with their partners and fill in their graphic organizers under the Article column.

4. Play the song "Buffalo Soldier," by Bob Marley, and ask students to follow along with the lyrics found here: https://www.azlyrics.com/lyrics/bobmarley/buffalosoldier.html. Then tell students to engage in another discussion with their partners regarding what they learned from the lyrics and write that in the Lyrics column. Now have students discuss and, when they come to a consensus, respond to the prompt "We can conclude from the three texts that . . ."
5. Facilitate a class discussion by asking students to share with the entire class the evidence they recorded on their organizers. Document their responses on a corresponding anchor chart.
6. Process the use of conversation skills with your students by citing different students' use of the conversation skills that you witness during their discussion. Ask students to rate their use of each of the conversation skills and set goals for the next opportunity.
7. Layered text in a primary classroom can be a video, poem, and text where students find, compare, and discuss the facts from each source.

Instructional Strategy: Silent Discussions

This strategy supports element 2, *Provide extended and supported opportunities for engaging in disciplinary discussions*. Silent Discussions is an effective tool that can be used in any subject to engage all students in reading, writing, and thinking. Working in complete silence, a pair or triad of students respond to each other about a prompt that you provide. They write responses to the prompt just as if they were talking out loud. Beginning readers or early language learners could draw pictures to represent their ideas. The students pass the paper back and forth until each one has written three or four responses. The result is a visual record of their thoughts about the topic as well as their ability to stay on topic and build on each other's ideas.

Why Use This Strategy: In addition to the valuable record of student thinking and conversation skills it provides for future planning, this strategy informs your next instructional steps in regard to the students' content understanding and use of the conversation skills. Silent Discussions slow down student thinking and provide an opportunity for students to focus on the perspectives of their partner(s) in ways that are difficult in an oral conversation. When this strategy is followed by a whole-class discussion, students are far more prepared and inclined to speak because they have had a chance to process the information and formulate their thoughts.

When to Use This Strategy: Silent Discussions are useful when students are not as likely to engage in a verbal conversation. This might be due to a lack of background knowledge related to the topic, a sense of insecurity about their language ability, or some other factor. This strategy also helps students who might be too eager to talk, requiring them to carefully consider the ideas of others.

How to Use This Strategy: Explain to students that they will be engaging in a different type of discussion. They will be working in pairs or triads to respond to a prompt you will provide, but instead of talking to each other, they will respond to each other in writing. They must not talk at any time during the activity, even when they exchange the paper. You can provide additional prompts or sentence frames to help if the discussion stalls.

Example Lesson

1. Explain to the students how and why they are doing this strategy: "You are going to have a silent, written discussion with your partner. Partner A will respond to the prompt first. Once A has finished writing to the prompt, A will pass their paper to B, and B will read the response and add to it. The paper will pass back and forth between the two partners. When you read your partner's response, you are 'listening' carefully to it so that you can be more thoughtful when responding."
2. Provide a model for students to deconstruct and read it to your students. Ask them to discuss what they noticed about the conversation with their neighbor and to find areas where the partners built on each other's ideas using the conversation skills of Clarify, Fortify, and Negotiate.
3. Provide a non-model for students to deconstruct and rewrite. Read the non-model to students, asking them to talk to their partners about the differences between the two silent conversations and emphasizing areas you want students to use. Working in pairs, have students rewrite the non-model.
4. Provide a well-constructed, open-ended prompt that aligns with your learning target. Consider possible student responses to the prompt to ensure that it will generate the requisite number of exchanges. Rewrite the prompt if necessary.

5. Have students participate in their silent discussion. At times it may be appropriate to set the minimum number of turns you want them to take.
6. When they have finished, process the activity by asking students what they learned about their use of conversation skills and about their co-construction of knowledge.

Strategies for Engaging All Students in Discussions

Think about why some of your students are not engaged. Is it because they have nothing to say? If that is the case, you should reflect on how you are setting up the room and the discussion. First, when you are asking two, three, or four students to engage in a discussion, their seats need to be arranged so that the students are facing one another. Next, ensure that students have the opportunity to think about their responses through graphic organizers, visuals, or text before the discussion. Having students read content or listen to a brief video before a discussion can also be a great way to make sure they have something to say. Another approach is to have your students interview one another about the topic in advance of any discussion; that way, they have the opportunity to listen to the opinions of others or adapt other ideas and use them as their own. Another reason your students might not engage is because they are not sure what the discussion should sound like and therefore are unsure about how to participate. One way to help these students is to provide a model of what you want the discussion to sound like. Models and non-models are a great way for students to understand the structure of a discussion.

Cross-Cutting Practice: Facilitating Acquisition of Academic Language

Proficiency in the three features of academic language—vocabulary, syntax, and discourse—strengthens students' ability to comprehend and analyze texts, speak and write effectively, and acquire disciplinary content in all subject areas. All students, regardless of their first language, are developing academic language as they progress through school. Academic language development is also associated with student achievement, as demonstrated by the correlation between measures of academic language proficiency and content-assessment scores. Academic language development is especially challenging for English learners. Studies show that academic language that is weak or missing is a major contributor to gaps in achievement between English learners and native speakers of English (Anstrom, DiCerbo, Butler, Katz, Millet, & Rivera, 2010; Pritchard & O'Hara, 2016).

The practice of Facilitating Acquisition of Academic Language consists of two important elements:

- Element 1: Introduce or refer to the academic language demands of texts and tasks
- Element 2: Provide extended and supported opportunities for students to acquire and use the features of academic language

The instructional strategies and tools that follow will help you understand what these elements would look like when implemented in your classroom.

Instructional Tool: Sentence Starters and Frames (SSFs)

This strategy supports element 1, *Introduce or refer to the academic language demands of texts and tasks*. Using sentence starters and frames (SSFs) throughout a lesson helps students use academic language. Often, we associate the use of SSFs with English learners. However, the appropriate use of SSFs can facilitate academic language development of all students. Referencing their Conversation Prompts and Responses (Table 2.2) and highlighting the language of those skills make the academic language clear to students. Inserting SSFs on a graphic organizer to support students in their discussion is also a way to explicitly reference the conversation skills.

Why Use This Tool: SSFs enable students to use academic language to formulate responses by providing words and syntactical structures for their discussions. They also help students build understanding of academic vocabulary through context. Even students who are conversationally proficient need exposure to and practice with academic language in order to function successfully in school.

When to Use This Tool: SSFs can be used in any subject when students need scaffolding and support in acquiring a conversation skill or language structure. SSFs can be differentiated by the number of words used in the frame and should be designed to provide a model of language just beyond students' current abilities. Research has shown that teachers get more on-topic talk and more clearly articulated answers from students when using SSFs (O'Hara, Pritchard, & Zwiers, 2016).

How to Use This Tool: Give students SSFs, model how to use them, and explain why they are helpful tools.

1. Identify which conversation skill, language structure, or vocabulary your students need.
2. Use the appropriate SSFs from the Conversation Prompts and Responses, or create them based on your students' needs and the language demands of the task or text.

3. Provide students with a copy of the SSFs as an individual resource and model how to use them.
4. Provide a meaningful context for students to use SSFs, prompt for them as needed, and monitor student use.
5. Revise the SSFs periodically as students become more independent in their use of academic language and need less scaffolding.
6. Have students practice using the SSFs until they become internalized and a natural way of speaking.

Instructional Strategy: What's the Gist?

This strategy supports element 2, *Provide extended and supported opportunities for students to acquire and use the features of academic language.* Finding the main idea of a passage requires students to individually select the most important words in a passage, work with partners to develop a group list of words, and write a gist statement using the group's list. Although students may be expected to accomplish this task on their own, their language and literacy development may be facilitated when they work collaboratively with other students on the strategy What's the Gist? For younger students, a teacher can read the passage aloud and have students discuss the most important words with partners. Students share their words and the teacher writes them on the whiteboard. Then, as a class, students can eliminate unimportant words and write a gist statement.

Why Use This Strategy: What's the Gist? is a strategy that incorporates all three features of academic language—vocabulary, syntax, and discourse—in an engaging process that requires students to listen, speak, read, and write. As a result, students are able to see how each of the three features is essential to oral and written communication.

When to Use This Strategy: This strategy is used most effectively in conjunction with a lesson that requires students to read an informational text and determine its main idea. Academic language instruction too often focuses on vocabulary development at the expense of syntax and discourse. What's the Gist? establishes clear expectations for each feature by asking students to identify important words (vocabulary), write a sentence (syntax), and capture the main idea (discourse).

How to Use This Strategy: Give students a nonfiction passage to read, have them choose important vocabulary words, and then use those words to create a sentence that captures the main idea, or gist, of the passage.

1. Distribute a nonfiction passage for students to read. You may also project the text and read it to students.

2. After students read the text, they individually go back through the text, highlight 20 words they believe are essential to the main idea of the article, and write them on a piece of paper.
3. Have students meet with their partner and discuss each of their 20 words (a total of 40 words between them). The goal is to eliminate less important words until they have only 10 words between them. Students write those 10 words on their paper.
4. Now have two pairs of students work together and discuss their lists. During the discussion, they should come to a consensus about the five most important words and write them on their papers.
5. Individually or with a partner, students use their five words to write a sentence that captures the main idea of the article. Students may add linking and connecting words to complete their sentence.
6. Have some students share their sentences and write them on the whiteboard.
7. You can adapt this strategy for younger or less proficient readers by providing a shorter text, reducing the number of words they initially select, or doing it as a whole-class activity.

Cross-Cutting Practice: Fostering Metacognition

The use of metacognitive processes and strategies helps students become aware of their own understanding, strengths, and weaknesses. These insights enable students to identify what constitutes good work on a given task and what they need to do to complete it successfully. This self-knowledge allows students to select, vary, and modify strategies for solving problems and develop independence in directing their own learning, which in turn improves student achievement.

The practice of Fostering Metacognition for Disciplinary Learning consists of two important elements:

- Element 1: Visibly enact metacognitive processes and/or strategies that students are expected to use in support of disciplinary learning
- Element 2: Deconstruct metacognitive processes and/or strategies that support disciplinary learning

The instructional strategies that follow will help you understand what these elements would look like in practice in your classroom.

Instructional Strategy: Talk Detectives

This strategy supports element 1, *Visibly enact metacognitive processes and/or strategies students are expected to use in support of disciplinary learning*. Talk Detectives (Minero, 2016) requires a small number of students (usually two or three) to circulate and observe other students engaging in discussions. The students who are assigned this role have a sheet of paper with discussion-related behaviors and skills written at the top (e.g., following norms of discussion, staying on topic, building on previous turns) and space underneath them where the Talk Detectives can write students' names and what the students said that did or did not address the focus items.

Why Use This Strategy: Talk detectives' observations provide students with feedback that will help them understand which discussion skills and behaviors they did and did not use appropriately. The opportunities to think metacognitively about their discussions help students understand the importance of monitoring their discussion skills and being a reflective learner. An ancillary benefit is that the talk detectives get to practice their listening and speaking skills in a fun and engaging way.

When to Use This Strategy: The Talk Detectives strategy can be used across disciplines and in all grade-level classrooms to help students become more reflective participants in disciplinary discussions. The only caveat is that the skills and behaviors the talk detectives are observing should be ones that your students have already had the opportunity to practice.

How to Use This Strategy: Identify a number of discussion-related behaviors and skills that you have previously introduced to your students. Assign two or three students the role of talk detectives and explain to the class that they will be circulating to observe these behaviors and skills during discussion time. When the discussions are done, talk detectives report and reflect on their observations while you provide scaffolded support as needed.

Example Lesson

1. After teaching the conversation skills and using models and non-models of discussions, ask students to discuss with a partner the skills we need to use to have a good discussion (e.g., build on each other's ideas, paraphrase your thinking or your partner's, ask a clarifying question). Chart these or reference your anchor chart.
2. Explain the Talk Detectives strategy and its purpose.
3. With your students, create an observation sheet that will be used by the talk detectives and discuss the types of evidence for each category so that students have a clear understanding of what the talk detectives will be looking for.
4. Model how the talk detectives will walk around and look for evidence. For example: "I notice Juan is asking his partner for his idea. I will write Juan's name here and write what he said."

5. Once the observation sheet is completed, select two or three students to be the talk detectives and have students begin their discussion.
6. After the discussion, ask the talk detectives to report out on what they heard and saw. Debrief the activity with students, summarizing what they did well and what they need to continue to improve on.

Instructional Strategy: Metacognition in Discussions

This strategy supports element 2, *Deconstruct metacognitive processes and/or strategies that support disciplinary learning*. When some student pairs are off-topic in their discussions, you can refer them to the Metacognition in Discussions Anchor Chart (see Figure 2.2). The anchor chart is organized around three issues students may become aware of when engaged in a conversation: they have a problem that is interfering with the conversation, their partner has a problem, or they both have a problem. Each of these issues has three strategies students can learn to use when the need arises.

For younger students, the anchor chart would be adapted to meet their language needs and the level at which they can engage in discussion (see Figure 2.3).

Why Use This Strategy: Research investigating metacognition has identified a wide range of strategies students can use when they encounter problems while reading or writing. In contrast, relatively little research has investigated what students should do when they encounter problems in a discussion. Our

Figure 2.2. Metacognition in Discussions Anchor Chart

What I can do when I don't understand

- I can reread the prompt to refocus my thinking.
- I can summarize my ideas to clarify my thinking.
- I can ask my partner for help to get back on track.

What I can do when my partner doesn't understand

- I can paraphrase my partner's ideas to help my partner refocus their thinking.
- I can ask a question to prompt my partner to reconsider their thinking.
- I can explain my thinking to move my partner beyond their misunderstanding.

What we can do when we both need help to move the conversation forward

- We can clarify why the discussion has stalled to figure out how to move forward.
- We can retrace the discussion to identify where the breakdown occurred.
- We can explain why we are stuck and ask for help to enable us to move forward.

Figure 2.3. Primary Metacognition in Discussions Anchor Chart

What I can do to have a successful discussion with my partner

- I can stay on topic.
- I can take turns.
- I can express my ideas clearly.

What I can do to help my partner

- I can ask my partner a question.
- I can add to what my partner said.
- I can paraphrase my partner's ideas.

What we can do to help each other

- We can restate the prompt.
- We can use examples to support our ideas.
- We can summarize our discussion.

Metacognition in Discussions framework provides you with a research-based approach you can teach students to use when a conversation breaks down.

When to Use This Strategy: Students often do not know what to say when a conversation begins to break down. In addition, teachers often do not know what type of scaffolding to provide to enable students to persevere when this happens. This framework, which has been used successfully with students in kindergarten through high school, is a resource for students and teachers to use in these situations.

How to Use This Strategy: Determine which of the nine strategies from the Metacognition in Discussions Anchor Chart you want to model for your students. Then select or write a short conversation that contains a point at which that strategy could be utilized. Explain to your students that you want to show them how they could react when they are engaged in a discussion and a problem arises.

Example Lesson

1. Decide which of the three issues has been the most common challenge for your students. Then choose which of the three strategies in that category you want to highlight. (For the sake of this example, we will use "I can reread the prompt to refocus my thinking" from "What I can do when I don't understand.")
2. Begin by explaining to students that, just as we need to monitor our reading comprehension, we must monitor our discussions. Ask students to talk to their partner about what it means to monitor our learning and what that might look like when we are having a discussion.

3. Say you have been noticing that some students have not always stayed on topic or built on their partner's comments when engaging in discussions. When that happens, one partner usually ends up carrying the discussion. Ask students to discuss with a partner a time when that has happened to them.
4. Explain that we need to work together and help one another so that both partners are contributing to the discussion: "Today you are going learn the first of a number of strategies that you will be able to use to make that happen."
5. Distribute this model student discussion scenario for students to read.

Example: Essential Question—How do we respond to nature?

Prompt: Generate questions to guide your inquiry about observing nature.

Partner A: "My first question to guide our inquiry is 'What can we observe in nature?' What is your idea?"
Partner B: "My first question is 'What do owls eat?' What is another question you want to use?"
Partner A: "Another question for us is 'How does nature affect each of us?' What is another question you want to use?"
Partner B: "Another question I have is 'How do owls survive the winter?' (Pause) Umm. My questions are different from yours. My questions are very specific. Too specific, I think."
Partner A: "Are we supposed to be specific or not? I'm going to reread the prompt. 'Generate questions to guide your inquiry about observing nature.'"
Partner B: "That doesn't make it clear, but the essential question is 'How do we respond to nature?' The essential question makes me think that our questions should not be too specific."
Partner A: "I agree with you. Can you ask a question that is not very specific?"
Partner B: "My question is 'What can we learn from observing nature?'"

6. Ask students the following guiding questions:
   - Where does the discussion break down?
   - What makes the student aware that the conversation has broken down? (Their questions are different than their partner's.)
   - What does the student do? (Reread the prompt.)
7. Provide another script for students to work through as guided practice.
8. Explain that the Metacognition in Discussions Anchor Chart is a resource that will remain in the classroom as a reminder of the strategy and that they will be learning the other strategies soon.
9. Prompt students during conversations to use the strategy.

Cross-Cutting Practice: Monitoring and Guiding

Monitoring students' discussions helps teachers determine what instructional moves need to be taken. Guiding disciplinary learning helps students know exactly what they need to do to meet learning targets. Specific and timely feedback is fundamental to helping students understand their work and the steps they need to take to improve it.

The practice of Monitoring and Guiding Disciplinary Learning consists of two important elements:

- Element 1: Monitor learning and adjust instruction, supports, and/or disciplinary tasks to meet student needs
- Element 2: Provide written and/or oral feedback during lessons to promote disciplinary learning

The instructional tools that follow will help you understand what these elements will look like when you implement them in your classroom.

Instructional Tool: Student-to-Student Discussion Checklist

This tool supports element 1, *Monitor learning and adjust instruction, supports, and/or disciplinary tasks to meet student needs.* You can create a checklist to monitor student discussions and use it to capture the conversation skills students are using. Based on this formative information, you can adjust instruction to meet the needs of your students.

Why Use This Tool: Effectively monitoring and guiding student learning is a major factor in improved learning outcomes for students. The purpose of the Student-to-Student Discussion Checklist (see Table 2.5) is to keep track of student use of conversation skills and provide feedback to students. These data also inform the next instructional step or any adjustments needed. At the surface level, you might think students are having deep conversations because you see them talking and they appear on task. However, you need to more closely monitor what specifically is being said in the discussion.

Table 2.5. Student-to-Student Discussion Checklist

Student	Creates clear ideas	Stays on topic	Adds to others' ideas	Elaborates	Paraphrases	Supports ideas with evidence	Synthesizes

When to Use This Tool: You need to monitor students' acquisition and use of the conversation skills as often as possible. This informs instruction about which students are and are not fully understanding their use. This information allows you to make the necessary instructional moves (e.g., more modeling of specific conversation skills, providing more prompts and responses) to get students to the next level of discussion. It also provides you with the data and opportunity to give targeted feedback as necessary.

How to Use This Tool: Creating a Student-to-Student Discussion Checklist when designing your lesson requires the following steps.

1. Create a Student-to-Student Discussion Checklist based on the skills you have taught and are expecting students to use.
2. Share the checklist with your students and explain that you will be monitoring their use of the skills while they are having their student-to-student discussions.
3. Explain that the purpose of monitoring their discussions is to have concrete data regarding which skills they are using, which skills need to be reviewed or retaught, and which skills need to be introduced.
4. Use the Student-to-Student Discussion Checklist when students are engaged in a discussion to provide them with feedback or to model prompts and responses they could be using.
5. Review the data from the checklist to look for patterns and decide on the next instructional step. This data could also be shared with students to make them aware of what they need to do to improve their discussions.

Instructional Tool: Formative Assessments of Student Talk–DD

This tool supports element 2, *Provide written and/or oral feedback during lessons to promote disciplinary learning.* Checklists can be quick, useful tools for monitoring student-to-student discussions to determine which elements of a discussion students are or are not demonstrating. At times, however, a more thorough analysis is necessary to provide students with the type of in-depth, constructive feedback that will enhance their use of conversation skills, academic language, and metacognitive strategies. The Formative Assessments of Student Talk–Disciplinary Discussions, or FAST-DD (see Appendix D), is a tool that teachers can use to monitor disciplinary discussions, analyze student participation, and provide constructive feedback.

Why Use This Tool: FAST-DD contains three dimensions, each of which can be scored individually using a four-point rubric. The first dimension, Building Up an Idea, focuses on the clarity of the discussion, the extent to which it addresses the prompt or task, and whether or not it leads to co-construction of new ideas. The second dimension, Using Academic Language, focuses on which academic language features are used in a discussion, and whether or not the discourse feature is used appropriately to convey ideas. The third dimension, Applying Metacognitive Strategies, focuses on whether or not students are monitoring their own discussions and, when needed, applying strategies appropriately and independently to keep the discussion on topic and moving forward.

When to Use This Tool: As noted above, FAST-DD is a tool that you can use when you want to monitor disciplinary discussions, analyze student participation, and provide constructive feedback or prompts to help move the discussion forward. You can use it effectively to assess all three dimensions or to focus on one dimension at a time, depending on the grade level, your specific learning targets, and your students' needs.

How to Use This Tool: You can use FAST-DD to monitor discussions in one of two ways. During a lesson in which students are engaged in discussion, you can listen to one or two student pairs for evidence of one or more dimensions and use that to provide in-the-moment guidance. You can also use FAST-DD to analyze a written transcript or videotape of student discussions after a lesson and provide students with targeted feedback to help strengthen their next discussion. Like other one-on-one assessment tools, the more you use FAST-DD, the better you will be at analyzing student discussions and providing effective feedback to your students.

Foundational Practice: Designing Instruction

Explicit expectations for student learning establish clear goals and enable students to monitor their progress. Cohesively designed and logically sequenced instruction, in which lessons work together to support student learning, improves the likelihood that students will achieve the learning targets. When teachers have high expectations for students and provide tasks that are engaging and of high interest, students build self-esteem, increase confidence and motivation, and improve academic performance.

The practice of Designing Instruction for Disciplinary Thinking and Understanding consists of three important elements:

- Element 1: Set disciplinary learning targets that are aligned with ELA/Anchor Literacy CCSS and the target High-Impact Practice
- Element 2: Structure and connect tasks that support the learning target
- Element 3: Establish high expectations that support the learning targets and maintain the intellectual rigor of classroom activities and tasks

The instructional tool that follows will help you understand what element 1 would look like in practice in your classroom. Examples for elements 2 and 3 are described in Chapters 3, 4, and 5.

Instructional Tool: Language Demands Flowchart

This instructional tool supports element 1, *Set disciplinary learning targets that are aligned with ELA/Anchor Literacy CCSS and the target High-Impact Practice*. When designing a lesson at any grade level, it is essential to identify the language demands inherent in texts, support materials, and instructional tasks. The Language Demands Flowchart is a tool that provides teachers with a consistent, systematic process for identifying, sorting, and prioritizing the academic language demands students need to understand.

Why Use This Tool: The CCSS and NGSS clearly establish high expectations for students in regard to academic language usage. Yet, in too many classrooms academic language development is reduced to teaching vocabulary. So you must be aware of the full range of academic language features (discourse and syntax as well as vocabulary) and systematically analyze the language demands of all three features that are inherent in the texts and tasks students use in your lessons.

When to Use This Tool: You need to identify the academic language demands students will encounter in virtually every lesson you design. This is true across all grade levels and content areas. In addition, you usually identify many more demands (e.g., words, language functions, text structures) than you have time to teach. So a tool that helps you think through how to prioritize those demands can be used on a daily basis.

How to Use This Tool: Using the Language Demands Flowchart when designing your lesson requires five steps:

1. Reflect on the learning target(s) of your lesson and the academic language needs of your students. What language knowledge and skills do they most need to develop?
2. Analyze the texts you plan to use, remembering that texts include any written, visual, audio, or multimedia message that conveys information or ideas. Identify the most challenging discourse, syntax, and vocabulary demands in those texts.
3. Analyze tasks that will be used, including activities, handouts, and assessments. Identify the most challenging discourse, syntax, and vocabulary demands in those tasks.
4. Choose the most useful and important language demands that are needed to support the learning target(s).

5. Use the language identified in step 4 to create a language objective for your lesson. Figure 2.4 is an example of how one teacher used the Language Demands Flowchart and the Layering Texts Strategy as she planned a unit on bullying.

ADDITIONAL IMPLEMENTATION CONSIDERATIONS

Teaching Disciplinary Discussions is complex, and those complexities can often get in the way of students successfully co-constructing learning. In addition to understanding the practices, strategies, and tools described above, you need to be mindful of a number of other considerations as you implement the practices in the Disciplinary Discussions Teaching Frame.

Figure 2.4. Example of the Language Demands Flowchart

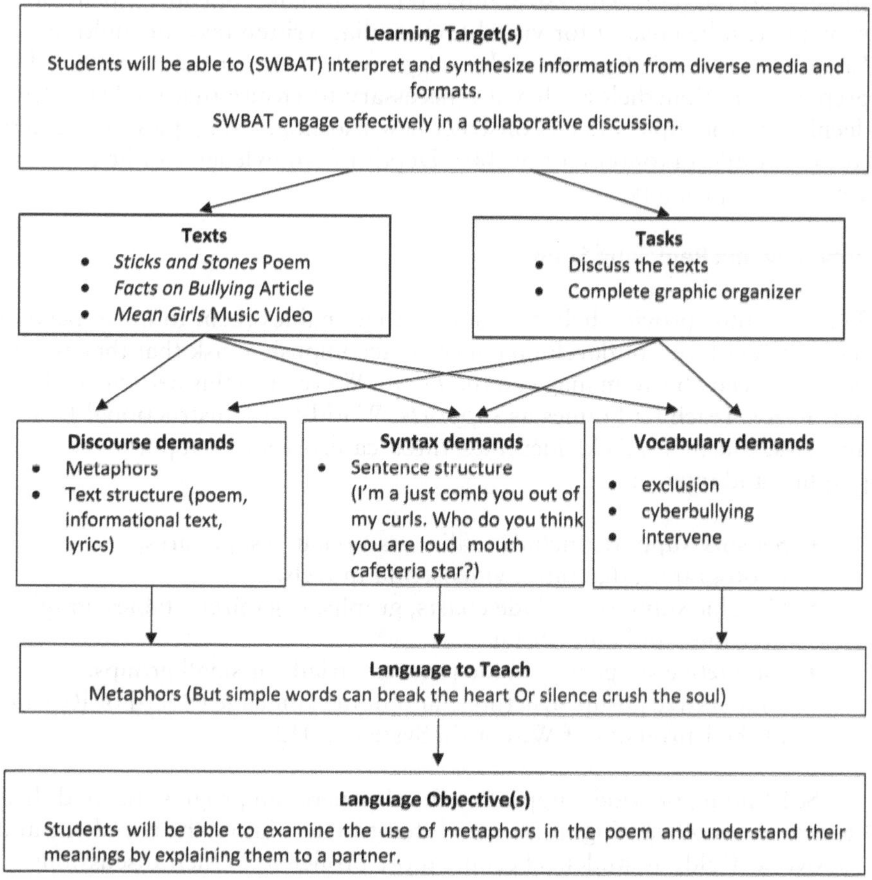

Using Discussion Routines

Establishing routines for classroom discussions is just as important as any other classroom routine. It saves instructional time and helps students understand what is expected and how to perform the routines. Discussion routines are taught by modeling your expectations, providing opportunity for guided practice, and giving feedback about how well students follow the routine. The routines we have found to be crucial for successful student-to-student discussions are (a) getting students to find their partner quickly and efficiently, (b) asking students to hold up the number of fingers for the number of minutes they need to complete the task, and (c) getting students' attention after a discussion.

Developing Open-Ended Prompts

Open-ended prompts stimulate and challenge students' thinking by asking students to analyze, synthesize, interpret, and think critically. Open-ended prompts can be created for visual text, realia, written text, or multimedia. Creating open-ended prompts that align with your learning targets takes preparation. Nonetheless, they are necessary to ensure that students delve deeply into the topic and co-construct new learning. Using question starters from Bloom's Taxonomy or Webb's Depth of Knowledge can help you in creating the prompts.

Providing and Removing Supports

Teachers must provide help to students that enables them to move beyond their current levels of development or to accomplish a task that they would not have been able to manage on their own. We refer to this help throughout our SOAR Teaching Frames as *supports*. World-Class Instructional Design and Assessment (WIDA) identifies three categories of supports—sensory, graphic, and interactive:

- Sensory supports include realia, manipulatives, pictures, photographs, diagrams, videos, and models.
- Graphic supports include charts, graphic organizers, tables, graphs, timelines, and number lines.
- Interactive supports include partners, triads or small groups, cooperative group structures, and home language (Board of Regents of the University of Wisconsin System, 2012).

Scaffolding provides support so that learners can progress beyond their current levels of learning. It is crucial that teachers know their students and remove scaffolds as students become more proficient in their discussions.

CONCLUSION

The purpose of this chapter has been to deepen your understanding of the Disciplinary Discussions Teaching Frame by unpacking the language of and rationale for the instructional practices that comprise it. The model lesson and associated classroom vignette provide additional insight into these practices by illustrating the dynamic and interdependent ways in which they work together in the context of a Teaching Frame to drive both teacher and student growth. You have seen that when teachers develop the language needed for use of conversation skills, explicitly teach metacognitive strategies, and guide their students during discussions, lessons are richer and learning is enhanced for all students. Finally, the instructional strategies and tools are designed to deepen your understanding of the Disciplinary Discussions Teaching Frame and to provide you with concrete examples of approaches teachers are currently using in their classrooms to implement it. These strategies will equip you to utilize Disciplinary Discussions as a powerful learning tool for your students.

CHAPTER 3

Disciplinary Interactions With Complex Text

This chapter focuses on the Disciplinary Interactions with Complex Text Teaching Frame. Element 1 of the High-Impact Practice engages students in examining the complexity of text by having them analyze how the author uses language, text features, and literary devices to convey meaning. Element 2 of this practice emphasizes the importance of providing support and opportunities for students to grapple with complex text as they build academic language and disciplinary skills. Please take a few minutes to review the Disciplinary Interactions with Complex Text Teaching Frame in Table 3.1.

USING THE SOAR LENS TO PLAN AND REFLECT

As we did in Chapter 2, we will first look at a non-model lesson created by a teacher who is not familiar with SOAR. Our goal is to use the SOAR lens to enhance it. After reviewing this lesson, we will examine the same lesson created by a teacher using the SOAR Teaching Frame as a lens to plan. This annotated lesson will demonstrate how each element of the five practices of the frame has been integrated into the lesson during the planning process. Finally, we will present a vignette of the lesson to deepen your understanding of how the practices can be implemented in an elementary classroom.

THINK BEFORE READING ACTIVITY

What percentage of your students are able to read complex, grade-level texts? Think of two things that need to happen for that percentage to increase. As you read the first part of this chapter, consider how you could use the strategies that Mr. Ortiz implements to bridge the gap between the reading levels of your struggling students and the difficulty level of your reading materials.

Table 3.1. Disciplinary Interactions With Complex Text Teaching Frame

<table>
<tr><td>HIGH-IMPACT PRACTICE</td><td colspan="3">Disciplinary Interactions with Complex Text (DICT)
Element 1: Engage students in an analysis of text to examine how its language, text features, and/or literary devices work together to convey meaning and/or purpose
Element 2: Provide and support extended opportunities for students to interact with complex text to build academic language and disciplinary skills</td></tr>
<tr><td>CROSS-CUTTING PRACTICES</td><td>Facilitating Acquisition of Academic Language (FAAL)
Element 1: Introduce and/or refer to the academic language demands of texts and tasks
Element 2: Provide extended and supported opportunities for students to acquire and use the features of academic language</td><td>Fostering Metacognition for Disciplinary Learning (FM)
Element 1: Visibly enact metacognitive processes and/ or strategies students are expected to use in support of disciplinary learning
Element 2: Deconstruct metacognitive processes and/ or strategies that support disciplinary learning</td><td>Monitoring and Guiding Disciplinary Learning (MG)
Element 1: Monitor learning and adjust instruction, supports, and/ or disciplinary tasks to meet student needs
Element 2: Provide written and/or oral feedback during lessons to promote disciplinary learning</td></tr>
<tr><td>FOUNDATIONAL PRACTICE</td><td colspan="3">Designing Instruction for Disciplinary Thinking and Understanding (DI)
Element 1: Set disciplinary learning targets that are aligned with ELA/Literacy CCSS and the target high-impact practice
Element 2: Structure and connect tasks that support the learning targets
Element 3: Establish high expectations that support the learning targets and maintain the intellectual rigor of classroom activities and tasks</td></tr>
</table>

5th-Grade Non-Model Lesson

The teacher who created the non-model below has been working with his students on interacting with a variety of texts to gather key information. They have been studying the American Revolution. This lesson focuses on having students compare and contrast the overall structure of information in two texts.

Let's think about why this is a non-model. The lesson lists the standards that will be addressed and the activities in which the students will be engaged. Regarding the High-Impact Practice of Disciplinary Interactions with Complex Text, the students do have multiple opportunities to engage with different texts. However, it is unclear to what extent the teacher is supporting students in analyzing how the language and text features are used to convey meaning. It is also unclear to what extent the teacher is providing students with extended and fully supported opportunities to build their academic language skills at the vocabulary, syntax, and discourse levels. The teacher could ask himself the following guiding questions as he plans his lesson to help him zero in on these critical elements:

- How can I have my students examine the author's use of language, text features, or literacy devices to understand the author's purpose?
- What supports or structures can I provide to help my students engage with and comprehend the complex text?
- Have I built in supported opportunities to allow students time to build academic language as they interact with the text?

Standards:

CCSS.RI.5.1 Quote accurately from a text when explaining what the text says explicitly and when drawing inferences from the text.
CCSS.RI.5.2 Determine two or more main ideas of a text and explain how they are supported by key details; summarize the text.
CCSS.RI.5.5 Compare and contrast the overall structure (e.g., chronology, comparison, cause and effect, problem solution) of information in two or more texts.

- Explain that students are going to read two texts about the allies of the American colonists during the Revolutionary War. Explain what an ally is.
- Text 1: "Non-colonists in the American Revolution." Read the first paragraph together. Give a quick explanation of these terms from the text: enlightenment, republicanism, and democracy.
- Have students number their paragraphs. Ask students to read text independently.
- Explain to students about transition words and signal words. Point to the anchor chart.
- Have students read the paragraphs looking for signal words.
- Explain that they are going to read text 2: "American Revolution for Kids: Allies." Have students read independently.
- Have students work with their partner and compare and contrast the information in the two texts.
- Have students compare and contrast the overall structure of the two texts.
- Have students write a paragraph explaining why groups became allies of the colonists in the Revolutionary War.

Now let's consider how he addresses the three Cross-Cutting Practices. For Facilitating the Acquisition of Academic Language, this lesson does address academic language by having students identify transition words, but the teacher could offer more modeling and support for students to allow them to acquire and use academic language. The teacher could ask the following questions as he plans the lesson:

- What are the academic language demands of this task at the word, sentence, and discourse levels that I need to identify and address with my students?
- How can I embed multiple opportunities for students to acquire and use academic language in an authentic and meaningful way?

In this lesson we see no evidence of metacognition. The lesson does not include a demonstration or think-aloud as a model for what is expected of the students. The teacher could ask the following questions as he plans how to incorporate this Cross-Cutting Practice:

- What process or strategy do I need to demonstrate so that my students understand how to access the complex text?
- How can I deconstruct the reading process in a way to help my students utilize these strategies?

In this lesson there is no explanation of how students will be monitored and no reference to the type of feedback the teacher might provide. At the planning stage, it is always important to think through the structures or tools that will be used to monitor students during classroom activities. The teacher could ask the following questions as he plans the lesson:

- What approaches or tools could I use to monitor my students' learning during the lesson to inform my instruction?
- What questions can I ask to elicit student thinking, assess their understanding, and provide them with feedback?

We do see evidence of the Foundational Practice. The standards are listed and appear to connect to the High-Impact Practice, although the connection is not articulated. The activities do appear to be connected and rigorous. The teacher could ask the following questions as he plans the lesson to ensure a laser-like focus on those standards:

- How can I make the ways the tasks are connected transparent to my students?
- How can I ensure that students see how the tasks build up and support student understanding of the text?
- How will I establish and maintain high expectations and rigor for all my students?

5th-Grade SOAR Model Lesson With Annotations

As we did in Chapter 2, we are now going to guide you through a process that will deepen your understanding of how the Disciplinary Interactions with Complex Text Teaching Frame can be used as a lens to plan. Let's look at this lesson again, only this time the teacher is aware of SOAR and has used guiding questions to reflect as he plans. We have identified where the teacher addresses each of the five practices in his planning. The Juicy Sentences strategy referenced in the lesson will be explained more fully on pages 65–67 of this chapter.

As you read the annotated lesson (see Table 3.2), note how much more intentional and thoughtful this lesson is and how each of the SOAR practices supports the High-Impact Practice of Disciplinary Interactions with Complex Text. It is evident that the teacher has been more strategic in his planning and has used the SOAR Teaching Frame as a lens to enhance the lesson.

When you have finished reviewing Table 3.2, read the vignette that follows to see how the teacher enacts this lesson with his students and implements the five practices of the Disciplinary Interactions with Complex Text Teaching Frame. Try to answer the following questions:

- How do you facilitate acquisition of academic language, foster metacognition, and guide learning to support students' interactions with complex text?
- How do all the practices in the Teaching Frame work together to support student learning and the learning targets?

Table 3.2. 5th-Grade Annotated Model Lesson

Disciplinary Interactions with Complex Text (DICT) Teaching Frame Elements	Teacher Actions
Designing Instruction E1–Teacher aligns the High–Impact Practice to CCSS	DICT–E1: Analysis of text to examine how its language, text features, and/or literary devices are used to convey meaning and purpose DICT–E2: Provide and support extended opportunities to interact with complex text to build academic language and disciplinary literacy Standards: CCSS.RI.5.1 Quote accurately from a text when explaining what the text says explicitly and when drawing inferences from the text. CCSS.RI.5.2 Determine two or more main ideas of a text and explain how they are supported by key details; summarize the text. CCSS.RI.5.5 Compare and contrast the overall structure (e.g., chronology, comparison, cause/effect, problem/solution) of information in two or more texts.

Table 3.2. 5th-Grade Annotated Model Lesson (continued)

Disciplinary Interactions with Complex Text (DICT) Teaching Frame Elements	Teacher Actions
Designing Instruction E1–Teacher explicitly states standards to the students	Introduce the standards for today. Explain that students are going to read two texts about the allies of the American colonists during the Revolutionary War.
Facilitating Acquisition of Academic Language E2–Students are given opportunity to acquire and use academic language in a meaningful way	Ask students to turn to their partners and discuss the term "ally" and give an example. Discuss as a class, provide student-friendly definition, and have students write in their vocabulary book, adding a picture to represent the term.
Disciplinary Interactions with Complex Text E1–Teacher is providing opportunity to examine the author's use of language to convey meaning	Text 1: "Non-colonists in the American Revolution." Have students predict what the article will be about. Read the first paragraph together. Give a quick explanation of these terms from the article: enlightenment, republicanism, and democracy. Ask students to discuss the last sentence: "Some countries found that watching wasn't enough—they joined the fight."
Fostering Metacognition E1–Teacher is enacting a metacognitive process by conducting a think-aloud	Do a think-aloud helping students see what message the author is conveying in this sentence and how it informs what they can expect in the rest of the article. Have students think about reasons. Have students number their paragraphs. Ask students to read text independently.
Disciplinary Interactions with Complex Text E1–Teacher explains how text features work to convey meaning	Explain to students that it is important to understand how transition words and signal words alert readers to what is coming next in the text. Use examples: but, and, at first. Point to the Transitions anchor chart.
Fostering Acquisition of Academic Language E1–The teacher has identified the language demands for students	Explain that the text structure varies in the text.

Table continues on next page

Table 3.2. 5th-Grade Annotated Model Lesson (continued)

Disciplinary Interactions with Complex Text (DICT) Teaching Frame Elements	Teacher Actions
Disciplinary Interactions with Complex Text E1–Teacher is leading students through an examination of how language works to convey meaning Disciplinary Interactions with Complex Text E2–There are structured opportunities for students to interact with complex text to build academic language and disciplinary literacy	Have students look at paragraph 2. Look for signal words. "One of these countries . . ." tells us what as readers? This is signaling an addition. "For a number of reasons . . ." Have students underline the reasons the French supported the Americans. "This resulted . . ." Have students identify the cause.
Disciplinary Interactions with Complex Text E1–Students examine how language works to convey meaning	Look at paragraph 3. Look for the signal words "At first," which is time order. Discuss what we expect would follow.
Disciplinary Interactions with Complex Text E1–The teacher is providing a structured opportunity for students to examine how language works to convey meaning Disciplinary Interactions with Complex Text E2–The students are provided with an opportunity to build academic language and disciplinary literacy	Project the fourth paragraph and deconstruct the first sentence: "In February 1778, France officially recognized the United States (following the Battle of Saratoga, in which the Continental Army decisively defeated the British army and gave a resurgence of hope to the colonists' fight for independence), and the countries signed an alliance." Remove the parenthetical phrase, explaining how and why you do it. Be sure students understand what "decisively" and "resurgence" mean. Look at the rest of the paragraph. Why did France provide more assistance to the Americans? Use evidence from the text.
Disciplinary Interactions with Complex Text E2 & Fostering Acquisition of Academic Language E2–Students are provided opportunities to build academic language at the discourse level	Look at paragraph 5. Find signal words for compare and contrast structure (also, but, like). Summarize this paragraph with a partner.
Facilitating Acquisition of Academic Language E2–Students are provided opportunities to acquire academic language at the vocabulary level	Look at paragraph 6. Where did the Hessians get their name?

Table 3.2. 5th-Grade Annotated Model Lesson (continued)

Disciplinary Interactions with Complex Text (DICT) Teaching Frame Elements	Teacher Actions
Disciplinary Interactions with Complex Text E2–Students are provided opportunities to build academic language and disciplinary literacy	Look at remaining paragraphs for signal words: 7—(also, so, in total, for instance), 8—(not only, but), 9—(other). Summarize each paragraph with a partner.
Disciplinary Interactions with Complex Text E2–Students interact with text to build academic language and literacy	Explain that they are going to read text 2: "American Revolution for Kids: Allies." Explain that the purpose for reading this text is to compare its information and structure to the first text. Have students read independently.
Disciplinary Interactions with Complex Text E2–Students interact with text to build academic language and literacy	Have students work with a partner and compare and contrast the information in the two texts using the graphic organizer.
Fostering Metacognition E1–Teacher models the expectations for students	Model expectations.
Monitoring & Guiding E1–Teacher monitors student work	Monitor students' work.
Disciplinary Interactions with Complex Text E1–Students examine how text features and language convey meaning	Have students compare and contrast the overall structure of the two texts. What do they notice is different? Have them talk to a partner.
Monitoring & Guiding E1–Teacher monitors student work	Walk around and monitor students working. Students should note that this text has bold headings and the first part is in question-and-answer format. Discuss how that affects the reader and why an author would choose to have headings and Q-and-A format.
Disciplinary Interactions with Complex Text E2–Teacher provides students with opportunities to interact with text to build academic language and disciplinary literacy Designing Instruction E3–Using evidence from the two texts provides rigor through complexity	Have students write a paragraph explaining why other groups became allies of the colonists in the Revolutionary War. Use evidence from the texts to support their thinking.
Fostering Metacognition E1–Teacher visibly enacts metacognitive strategies students are meant to use during activities	Review the reading strategies they used while reading the two texts and add to the reading strategy anchor chart.

Step Inside Mr. Ortiz's Classroom

Mr. Ortiz has the following learning targets, which align to the CCSS and the High-Impact Practice, written on the whiteboard.

- I can compare and contrast the overall organizational structure of two informational texts.
- I can examine informational text to see how its language, text features, and literacy devices are used to convey meaning and purpose.
- I can interact with complex text to build academic language and disciplinary literacy.

Mr. Ortiz begins the lesson by introducing the day's standards to his 5th-grade students. He explains to the students that they are going to read two texts about the allies of the American colonists during the Revolutionary War. He asks students to turn to their partners and discuss the term "ally" and give an example of what an ally is. They discuss the term as a class, and he provides the students with a kid-friendly definition. He asks them to take a moment to write their own definition of ally in their vocabulary notebook, give an example, and draw a picture to represent the term.

> Mr. Ortiz introduces the concept of "ally," not only as a vocabulary word, but as the theme of these two articles.

Mr. Ortiz introduces the first text, "Non-colonists in the American Revolution," and has students number the paragraphs. He asks his students to turn to their partners and talk about what the prefix "non-" means and to predict what they think this article will be about. He reads the first paragraph to the students and gives a quick explanation of the Enlightenment, republicanism, and democracy.

> Through his think-aloud, Mr. Ortiz demonstrates how to pose questions as you read. He also sets the purpose of the reading.

Mr. Ortiz then asks students to think about the last sentence in the first paragraph: "Some countries found that watching was not enough—they joined the fight." He does a think-aloud to demonstrate how to think more deeply about the text. He poses the question, "I wonder why other countries thought they needed to do more by joining the fight? Did they want to help the colonists, or did they want to hurt the British? I think this sentence is the main idea of the entire article. The author is going to explain why some countries felt they needed to join in the revolution."

> He builds students' knowledge before reading to enhance their engagement with the text. He also explains strategies good readers use.

Mr. Ortiz then says, "Talk with your partner and come up with two reasons other countries would want to help the colonists and two reasons they would want to hurt the British. You can use the sentence stems on the whiteboard in your discussion." After students discuss the reasons, Mr. Ortiz writes their ideas on the whiteboard and explains that they just made predictions about the reasons some countries would have joined the revolution. He adds, "Good readers monitor their reading and stay engaged with the text by posing questions, making predictions, and summarizing what they have read. Let's see if our reasons become the reasons the author lists."

Next, Mr. Ortiz has students read the text independently. When they have finished, he explains to students that it is important to understand how signal words and transition words guide the reader to understand how the author organized the text. They connect ideas and introduce shifts. He uses the word "but" as an example of a transition word and states, "If I said, 'I would love to go over to your house but . . . ,' what are you expecting to hear once I say but? . . . Yes, that is right, a reason why I can't come over. As a reader you do the same thing. You hear the word 'but' and you expect a contrast or reason. The same thing is true with 'and.' If I said 'I would love to come to your house and,' what are you expecting to hear? . . . Yes, you would expect an addition to my statement, something more."

> Mr. Ortiz methodically has students look at signal words as a strategy to anticipate the author's message.

"Remember the anchor chart we made on informational text structure and the type of signal words that goes with each type of structure (see Figure 3.1)? You are going to look at the text again and identify

> He explains that text structure is a language demand of this article.

Figure 3.1. Informational Text Structures and Signal Words

Informational Text Structures				
Description	Problem and Solution	Compare and Contrast	Cause and Effect	Sequence
Text provides details or characteristics of something	Text gives information about a problem and gives one or more solutions	Texts discusses similar and differences between people, places, things, etc.	Text describes how or why something happened (cause) and the results (effects) that follow	Text outlines chronological events or a list in a procedure
	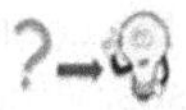			
Signal words	Signal words	Signal words	Signal words	Signal words
for example, specifically, for instance, in addition, another	problem, solve, because of, so, therefore due to, leads to, as a result	similar, alike, both, different, unlike, just like, on the other hand, in contrast, but, however	since, because, due to, if, so, as a result of, then, consequently, therefore	first, next, then, last, finally. before, after, prior to, later

signal words. We are doing this so that we pay attention to how the author is using text structure to convey meaning. However, what we know is that texts typically do not stick to one type of text structure. For instance, one section of a chapter may include a compare-and-contrast paragraph as well as a cause-and-effect paragraph. So, you need to be an alert reader to figure out what the author is doing. For this text in particular, this can be a language demand on you, the reader."

Mr. Ortiz has the students look at paragraph 2 and identify signal words with their partner. He points out the first one is "One of these countries . . . ." He asks students to think about what they would expect to follow this phrase. A student shares that there are more countries. Mr. Ortiz affirms the response by saying, "Yes, as a reader you are waiting to read about the others. So, this is signaling to us as readers that we need to expect there will be more countries." The students point out the second one, "For a number of reasons . . . ," which means there is more than one reason. He asks students to underline the reasons the French supported America.

When students have done that, he asks them to check the whiteboard to see if their predictions regarding the reasons some countries would join were accurate. He explains there is one more signal phrase and asks if anyone found it. A student says, "This resulted . . . ." Mr. Ortiz asks what that signal phrase indicates and the student responds, "Cause and effect." Mr. Ortiz states that since the effect was the loss of the North American territories, he wants them to talk to their neighbor to identify the cause (France lost the Seven Years' War to Britain). He reminds students to use the skills Clarify and Fortify in their discussion. He continues to do this with paragraph 3.

> Mr. Ortiz deconstructs a juicy sentence explaining how, when, and why to use this strategy.

Then Mr. Ortiz projects paragraph 4. He explains, "Many times informational text will have long, complex sentences. It is important not to just glaze right over the sentence, but to stop and deconstruct it to figure out what the author is really saying. Juicy Sentences is a strategy that readers use to do that. The first sentence in this paragraph is a great example of that. As a reader you could get confused by all the words and not comprehend what the author means. 'In February 1778, France officially recognized the United States (following the Battle of Saratoga, in which the Continental Army decisively defeated the British army and gave a resurgence of hope to the colonists' fight for independence), and the countries signed an alliance.' Let's first take out the phrase in parentheses. What does the sentence say with the parenthetical phrase removed? Who is the subject? . . . Yes, France. What did they do? . . . Yes, they recognized and . . . signed. . . . So, let's restate that. France recognized and signed an alliance. Now let's look at the parenthetical phrase. So, what happened in the Battle of Saratoga? There is an 'and' in the phrase, so I will be expecting two things. Talk to your neighbor and find the two things that happened."

Mr. Ortiz walks around the room to listen to students discussing the two things. "Who can tell me the two things? . . . Yes, that is correct. Who knows what decisively means? The author uses this word purposely to explain the defeat." Mr. Ortiz defines the term: acting quickly and effectively. "What tone does this convey? We have talked about the importance of word choice when we write. What does resurgence mean? That is a big word. Can we figure it out by breaking it apart? What does the prefix 're-' mean? What does 'surge' mean? So, because of the victory in the Battle of Saratoga, what did France do? Talk with your neighbor. . . . Excellent. We just broke apart a very long sentence. Turn to your partner and each of you paraphrase that sentence. Now let's look at the rest of the paragraph. What assistance did France give to the Americans? Discuss this with your neighbor using evidence from the text."

He explains how the author's word choice conveys meaning.

Having students paraphrase the sentence helps Mr. Ortiz monitor whether they understood it.

Mr. Ortiz continues to have students identify signal words in the rest of the paragraphs and summarize each paragraph with their partners. He first asks them to turn to their partner and explain to each other what it means to summarize. He points to the anchor chart they created and explains that summarization is when you create a short statement in which you identify the main idea and key details. The signal words help you identify the main idea and key details. He walks around and listens to students as they work through each paragraph.

The next day, Mr. Ortiz summarizes the standards they are working on and asks students to turn to their partner and explain to each other what they did yesterday. He explains that they are now going to address the CCSS RI 5.5 by comparing and contrasting the overall structure of two texts. He tells them they are going to read a second text, "American Revolution for Kids: Allies," and compare its structure to the article they just read. He has students read this article independently.

He explains and connects the tasks to the standards.

After they have read the second article, Mr. Ortiz explains that they are going to begin by comparing and contrasting the information in the two texts. He models how he wants the students to approach the texts and use the graphic organizer (see Figure 3.2). He walks around and monitors the students' work. For some of his students, he has filled in one similarity and one difference for them on their graphic organizer to help them get started.

He differentiates the graphic organizer for those who need more support.

He stops at one table and asks the students, "What information have you found so far that is the same?" Students respond, "They both say France and Spain were

Mr. Ortiz provides feedback through his questioning and comments.

Figure 3.2. Compare and Contrast Graphic Organizer

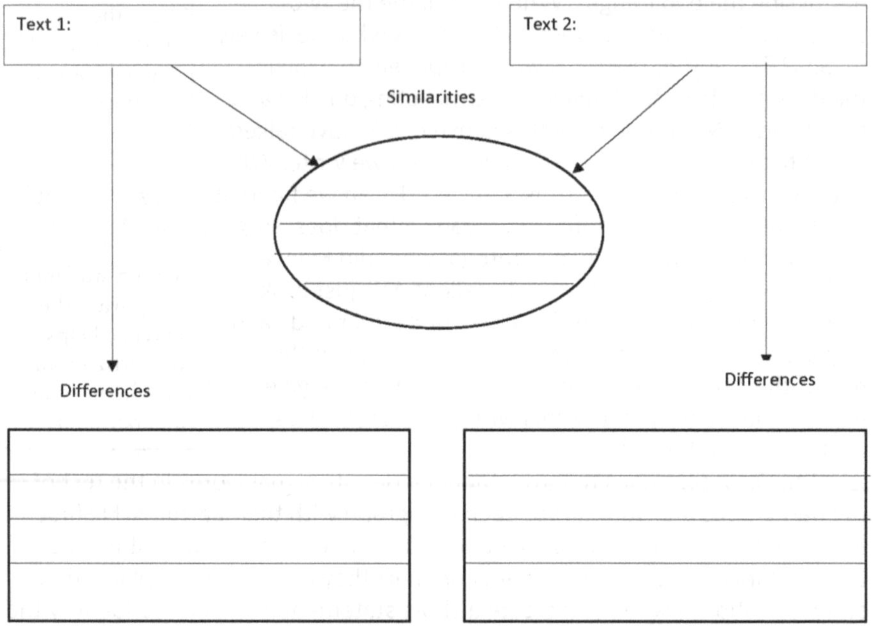

allies, but this one also says the Netherlands. But the first one doesn't say anything about the Netherlands." Mr. Ortiz asks them where they are going to put that information on the graphic organizer. The students look at him quizzically. He responds, "What does this bubble say? . . . Yes, similarities. So, what would you put in there? . . . . Yes, France and Spain. Where would the Netherlands go? . . . Yes, differences, but under which text? . . . Very good. I liked how you went back to the text to decide which information went where in your graphic organizer."

> He pushes the students' thinking about why the two authors chose the structures they did.

When students complete that task, Mr. Ortiz then has them look at the overall structure of the two texts. He asks, "What do you notice is visually different about these two texts? Talk with your partner about what you notice." He again walks around to listen to students' discussions and prompts them when necessary. He calls on a few students to share what they noticed. One student says, "The second article has bold headings." Mr. Ortiz asks students to discuss with their partner how that affects the reader and why an author would choose to have headings. Students share their ideas. He asks what else they noticed. A student says, "Some of the headings are questions." Mr. Ortiz asks them why an author would choose to use that format. Another student says, "The second article numbered the reasons." Again, Mr. Ortiz asks students to think about the author's purpose in doing that.

Mr. Ortiz compliments the students on how hard they worked today. He asks them to talk to their partner and discuss what they learned about the Revolutionary War from these two articles. Students share. He then reviews the strategies they learned and applied to these articles, and he adds them to the reading strategy anchor chart. He then asks students to get out their graphic organizer and write a paragraph comparing and contrasting the information in the two articles.

> He discusses reading strategies the students utilized in the two-day lesson. He keeps a chart in the class as a reference for students.

Think After Reading Activity

Through the vignette of Mr. Ortiz's classroom, you have explored the Disciplinary Interactions With Complex Text Teaching Frame. Mr. Ortiz carefully guided his students through the analysis of complex text. He supported them through the structures he put in place (e.g., chunking the text, giving explicit instructions, summarizing each paragraph). Before moving on to the next section, examine a lesson of your own in which students are expected to read complex text. What are some ways you can enrich your lesson by what you have learned from Mr. Ortiz and the Disciplinary Interactions With Complex Text Teaching Frame? What are some supports you can include in your lesson to ensure that students are gaining information from the text?

IMPLEMENTING THE DISCIPLINARY INTERACTIONS WITH COMPLEX TEXT TEACHING FRAME

Now that we have introduced you to the Disciplinary Interactions With Complex Text Teaching Frame, we will explore instructional strategies and tools you can use to engage students in analyses of text and to facilitate their interactions with complex text. As in Chapter 2, these strategies and tools are designed to deepen your understanding of the SOAR practices, demonstrate the purposeful planning required to implement the practices, and explain why, when, and how to use these strategies and tools in different content areas and in different grade levels.

Instructional Strategy: Juicy Sentences

This strategy supports element 1, *Engage students in an analysis of text to examine how its language, text features, and/or literary devices work together to convey meaning and/or purpose.* The Juicy Sentences strategy (Wong Fillmore & Fillmore, 2012) engages students in instructional conversations about linguistically rich and complex sentences—in other words, about the academic language they will encounter in complex texts. It draws students' attention to parts of a sentence and how each part contributes to the meaning of the sentence as a whole. These conversations provide both the focus on language and the language support students need for disciplinary learning.

Why Use This Strategy: Reading lengthier and more complex sentences is essential for student success in Common Core classrooms. Unfortunately, too many students do not know what to do when they come to these types of sentences. Unpacking juicy sentences provides students with a strategy that will help them navigate a complex text by understanding the ways in which meaning relates to words, phrases, and clauses in the text. This approach helps students gain access to meaning as well as to the language itself.

When to Use This Strategy: Teachers can use this strategy whenever students will be encountering linguistically rich and complex sentences in their reading materials and need instructional support to gain access to ideas and information. It is particularly useful when students are attempting to access a text at a complexity level beyond their independent reading level. Juicy Sentences is also a valuable modeling tool when students are learning to add details to their writing.

How to Use This Strategy: Begin by choosing a compelling and complex text that supports your learning target. Build background knowledge and establish a purpose for listening or reading. When choosing a juicy sentence, consider these factors:

1. Is the sentence complex and important enough to deserve attention and discussion?
2. Does it contain Tier 2 vocabulary (Marzano & Simms, 2013)?
    a. Does it contain figurative language whose meaning needs to be explained?
    b. Does it contain specific language functions (e.g., cause and effect, compare and contrast, sequencing) that are essential to understanding the text?

Choose a juicy sentence to deconstruct with your students and decide in advance how to break up the sentence phrase by phrase to identify the information conveyed in each part. Post the sentence using sentence strips. Have your students break the sentence apart to deepen their analysis. Older students can use the author's structure as a model when writing a new sentence. Be transparent about why you are doing this activity with your students—to help them understand how the language in a sentence works together to convey meaning.

Example Lesson

To support your 1st-graders' study of planets (ESS1.A Universe and Its Stars), read the book *What Makes Day and Night* by Franklyn M. Branley.

1. Choose as your juicy sentence: "The earth also turns, or rotates, like a top as it goes around the sun."
2. Post the sentence on a long sentence strip, read it to your students, and have the students chorally read it as a whole class.
3. Ask students what the sentence is about. Students respond, "The earth." Have a student tear "The earth" off the sentence strip.
4. Ask, "What does the earth do?" Some students respond, "turns" and others say "rotates." Use this opportunity to explain context clues (appositives) that authors use to help define vocabulary words. Explain that the author says "turns, or rotates," which means they are synonyms. A student tears "turns" and "rotates" off the sentence strip.
5. Ask students to read the words they have torn off: "The earth turns" and "The earth rotates." Ask students if these sentences make sense. Ask them to turn and talk to their partner about why the author added all the other parts to the sentence if these three words make sense. Explain that "The earth turns" and "The earth rotates" are complete sentences, but the author added more details to make the sentence more interesting and to give us more information.
6. Ask students what the author is comparing the earth to. Students respond, "A top." If your students are not familiar with a top, have one ready to demonstrate. Ask students what type of figure of speech it is when we use "like." Reinforce that the author added this detail to help us visualize the earth. A student tears this off the strip.
7. Ask students where the earth rotates. Students respond that it rotates as it goes around the sun.
8. The teacher helps students put the parts together to create new sentences: "The earth also turns around the sun. The earth also rotates around the sun. The earth also turns, or rotates, around the sun."
9. Give the torn pieces to students to reconstruct the original sentence or reconstruct it through an interactive writing activity.
10. Ask students to turn to their partner and explain what they know about the earth.

Instructional Strategy: Cross-Text Analysis

This strategy supports element 1, *Engage students in an analysis of text to examine how its language, text features, and/or literary devices work together to convey meaning and/or purpose.* Cross-Text Analysis guides readers through the analysis of comparing and contrasting multiple texts to see how the author uses language, text features, or literary devices to convey meaning or purpose.

Why Use This Strategy: Analyzing two or more texts provides students with the opportunity to make inferences and draw conclusions based on how the author used language, text features, and literary devices to convey meaning or purpose. Students gain more information, think more critically, and learn to synthesize when they analyze multiple texts. Asking students to identify similarities and differences through comparative analysis leads to large gains in student achievement.

When to Use This Strategy: This strategy can be used in any content area with either literary or informational texts when students will be encountering challenging language, text features, or literary devices. It is particularly useful when students need instructional support to construct meaning from these reading materials.

How to Use This Strategy: Begin by deciding what text comparison aligns with the CCSS and your learning target. Look for texts that lend themselves to being analyzed. The text can be visual, audio, or written. Once you have decided on the text, analyze the text yourself to be sure it is effective in helping students see how the author used language, text features, or literary devices to convey meaning or purpose.

Example Lesson

Students are going to be reading two books on octopuses: *Octopus (A Day in the Life: Sea Animals)* by Louise Spilsbury, and *Gentle Giant Octopus* by Karen Wallace.

1. Explain that the first purpose is to identify the facts they learn from each text. As a class, they are going to create a large graphic organizer to analyze the facts from each book.
2. Read *Octopus (A Day in the Life: Sea Animals)*. After the first read-through, reread each page and have students talk to their partner about any facts they heard. Have students share and record their comments on the whiteboard.
3. The next day, read *Gentle Giant Octopus*. After the first read-through, reread each page and have students talk to their partner about any facts they heard. Record the facts on the whiteboard.
4. Have students help you identify the facts that appear in both books and write them on the large Compare and Contrast Graphic Organizer (Figure 3.2). Do the same with the differences.
5. Have students discuss the facts and decide which one was most intriguing.

6. On the next day, explain to students that they will be analyzing the two books, focusing on how the authors wrote them (structure and style), and why the authors chose to do it that way.
7. Show students the table of contents in *Octopus* and the first page of *Gentle Giant Octopus* so that students can compare them. Ask students what they notice about each one (chapters are questions, each chapter is two pages, there is a glossary, body map, find out more, and an index). Write the responses on the class compare and contrast analysis chart.
8. Project or show students the first page of text in each book. Ask them what is the same and what is different about each book. As students identify similarities and differences, add them to the class chart.
9. Ask students what the author's purpose was in writing *Octopus* using this style.
10. Ask students to think about *Gentle Giant Octopus* and the way the author used poetic language to present the information using this style.
11. Explain that they as authors also have choices about how they present information. Have students write a fact sentence about octopuses using either of the two ways demonstrated in the books.

Strategies for Engaging All Students in Analysis of Text

Analyzing a text may seem too daunting a task to some students, making them hesitant to engage. One approach is to chunk the text into smaller parts for those students. After each part is completed, they can share their analyses with a partner or small group. Another approach is to gradually release responsibility from teacher to student in the analysis of text. You would begin by modeling the analysis and then providing an example for students to analyze with guided support. Next, you would have students do the analysis with a partner and, finally, by themselves. To challenge your more advanced students, you can pair them with small groups of less proficient readers and have them think aloud as they analyze a piece of text to determine how an author uses descriptive language to convey meaning. The modeling process benefits your more advanced learners by helping them take more responsibility for their own self-regulated learning. It helps your less proficient readers understand how to complete the analysis and meet the learning target.

Instructional Strategy: Chunking the Text

This strategy supports element 2, *Provide and support extended opportunities for students to interact with complex text to build academic language and disciplinary skills*. This strategy gives students the opportunity to break down difficult passages into more comprehensible pieces or smaller parts. By doing this, students are able to identify key ideas and words, increase their ability to paraphrase, organize their thinking, and synthesize information.

Why Use This Strategy: Teaching readers to break difficult passages into more manageable segments allows for more efficient use of short-term memory. As a result, students who struggle with reading comprehension improve significantly when reading material is chunked into smaller units.

When to Use This Strategy: This strategy can be used with any complex text in any content area. However, its greatest impact is with complex texts in which meaning relates to and is affected by the language, text features, or literary devices of the material.

How to Use This Strategy: Choose an appropriate text. Determine how and where to chunk it. Model the strategy, and then guide students through the process using your identified chunk. Evaluate the students' levels of understanding before allowing them to chunk the text on their own. Give students the opportunity to work with a partner to evaluate decisions they made while utilizing this strategy.

Example Lesson

1. Begin by teaching the Paraphrasing strategy as referenced in a later section in this chapter.
2. Then explain to students that Chunking the Text is a reading strategy that will help them better comprehend text. Breaking a text into chunks and paraphrasing each chunk makes a complex text more manageable. After you have paraphrased each chunk, you go back and read what you paraphrased and put it into one big idea.
3. Read a chapter of a grade-level text such as *Because of Winn-Dixie* (by Kate DiCamillo) for students to enjoy and discuss their text-to-self connections. Return to the chapter and read one chunk at a time, stopping to ask students to paraphrase to their partner what was in the chunk.
4. Now practice with an informational text that you have chunked. Have students read the chunk, write a paraphrased version, and share it with a partner. If you notice students are writing more of the text word for word, take an example and have students highlight words that are in both the text and the paraphrase. Use this to help students recognize that this is not a paraphrase. Then have them rewrite it.

Instructional Strategy: Anticipation Guide

This strategy supports element 2, *Provide and support extended opportunities for students to interact with complex text to build academic language and disciplinary skills.* An anticipation guide (McKenna, 2002) is a series of teacher-generated prompts about a topic that students respond to before interacting with a text. A pre-reading discussion of student responses to the prompts elicits preconceived ideas that students have about the topic and encourages students to consider those ideas in relation to the information presented in the text. Prompts are revisited during or after interacting with the text so that students can check their predictions and understanding.

Why Use This Strategy: This strategy promotes active, in-depth engagement with and processing of the text by activating background knowledge, establishing purposes for reading, and arousing student interest. It also enables you to assess class knowledge before your students begin a lesson or unit by revealing student inaccuracies and misconceptions.

When to Use This Strategy: Use an anticipation guide to structure meaningful discussions that review what students already know and encourage them to think critically about the concepts presented in the text. Students can respond to an anticipation guide before reading an entire text or passage, or you can divide a difficult text into more comprehensible, smaller chunks for students to process.

How to Use This Strategy: Begin by considering the major concepts that you want students to focus on in the text and identify those that are likely to support or challenge students' preconceived ideas. Develop statements that will grab students' attention or arouse their curiosity. The statements do not have to be factually accurate and can be a combination of statements that can and cannot be confirmed by the text. Arrange the statements in a format that requires students to respond positively or negatively to each one—for example, true or false, yes or no, or agree or disagree. As an alternative, you could include columns labeled yes or no at the end of each statement, with an additional column for revisiting the statement after students have interacted with the text. Direct the students to complete the guide individually and discuss their responses with a partner. Then have students read or interact with the text in some other way to determine whether their initial responses to the prompts are supported and whether their beliefs about the topic have changed. You can extend this strategy by asking students to write a brief explanation of their post-interaction reasoning using relevant information from the text.

Example Lesson

1. Construct the anticipation guide (Figure 3.3). It should be simple, with four or five statements about the key ideas in the text, some true and some false. For the book *Enemy Pie* by Derek Munson, the main theme is about friendship, so the statements represent that theme.

Figure 3.3. Anticipation Guide: Enemy Pie

Name________________________________ Date______________

Anticipation Guide: *Enemy Pie*

Mark whether or not you agree or disagree with each statement under Before Reading. At the end of the lesson, go back and mark whether you still agree or disagree under the After Reading column.

Before Reading			After Reading	
Agree	Disagree	Statement	Agree	Disagree
		A good friend understands you.		
		Making friends takes time.		
		An enemy can't ever be a friend.		
		A good friend listens and shares.		
		Don't judge a person if you don't know them.		

2. Explain to the students that they are going to be reading (or listening to you read) the book *Enemy Pie*. But before they do, they are going to read (or listen to) some statements and indicate whether they agree or disagree.
3. Model the first statement: "A good friend understands you. I think I agree with that statement because my best friend always knows if I am happy or sad and asks me how I am doing. I am going to mark this with a happy face."
4. Students then respond to each statement and, when they are done, share their reasoning.
5. Read the text aloud or have students read it themselves, and then have students respond in the After Reading column.
6. Then ask students if they changed their minds about their positions. Ask them to explain any changes using examples or evidence from the text.

Strategies for Making Complex Texts Accessible to English Learners

One approach that can be effective is having beginning English learners pair up with more advanced English speakers to engage in a structured conversation about the text with which they are interacting. You can also have students work in pairs or groups to conduct a close reading of the text, rather than asking students to do this activity independently. Another approach to consider is providing multimedia options (e.g., pictures, songs, videos) as a way to introduce the content to your students before reading the text. In addition, you can differentiate the language supports you provide to your students based on their language proficiency levels. Beginning English learners might need additional supports such as key vocabulary in both English and their first language, visual supports, or realia that provide more scaffolding. Remember to monitor the language needs of your students over time so that you can reduce the supports as their language proficiency increases.

Cross-Cutting Practice: Facilitating Acquisition of Academic Language

Students' ability to comprehend and interpret the kinds of texts they encounter in school and beyond depends to a great extent on their increasing proficiency and sophistication in academic language. As we acknowledge the role of academic language in literacy development, we must also recognize that meeting the College- and Career-Readiness Standards requires students to be able to construct different kinds of meaning from images and digital resources. The requirement that students make sense of complex text beyond the printed page—that is, multiliteracy development—reinforces academic language's role as the medium of literacy and learning. We now provide instructional strategies designed to help you implement these elements in the context of helping students interact with complex texts.

Instructional Strategy: Introducing Discourse Patterns

This strategy supports element 1, *Introduce and/or refer to the academic language demands of texts and tasks.* This strategy focuses on the discourse feature of academic language—that is, how authors use language, text structure, and images to convey information, influence their readers, and evoke responses. This is one of the most significant academic language demands of complex texts. Introducing Discourse Patterns is a way you can introduce this demand to your students and explain how it is connected to the disciplinary text or task you expect them to complete. These patterns can be introduced to younger students through whole-class read-alouds and in guided reading groups with leveled readers.

Why Use This Strategy: College- and Career-Readiness Standards like the CCSS and the NGSS place great emphasis on grade-level, informational text. As a result, the linguistic complexity in textbooks students are expected to read has increased. Introducing Discourse Patterns is a strategy you can use to help your students identify and understand how ideas in an informational text are organized, which improves both reading comprehension and expository writing.

When to Use This Strategy: Introducing Discourse Patterns should be used with informational text in which one or more of the five most common patterns are evident. These patterns—description, sequence, compare and contrast, cause and effect, and problem solution—rarely appear consistently throughout an entire piece of text; in fact, they may differ from paragraph to paragraph. Nonetheless, identifying and understanding the patterns will help your students process the information they are reading and organize the information they are writing.

How to Use This Strategy: Begin by deciding which discourse pattern you want to teach. Our recommendation is to use the one you believe will be easiest for your students to understand. In our experience, compare and contrast is a good starting point. Identify a short text that you can use to introduce the pattern you have chosen as well as words from the text that signal the structure—for example, on one hand, on the other hand. Then ask students to read the text and, working with a partner, identify the signal words and label the pattern. This instructional sequence requires different degrees of modeling and scaffolding depending on your students. For instance, you and your students can construct an anchor chart listing each pattern and its signal words. In addition, a graphic organizer can be used to help students organize the information. Once students have learned the patterns, they will be able to survey a text, identify signal words, and determine the discourse pattern(s) on their own.

Example Lesson

1. Have students tell their partner the structure of a narrative text (e.g., setting, characters, plot, resolution).
2. Explain to students that informational text also has a structure and that recognizing the structure helps us be better readers because we can anticipate what the author is telling us.
3. Begin by creating an anchor chart listing the five types of informational text structures.
4. Distribute a short informational text with the compare and contrast structure or use a mentor text like *Cats vs. Dogs* by Elizabeth Carney. Ask students to read the text and work with a partner to decide which of the five structures this text represents.
5. Then ask students to explain how they recognize that structure. Students should point out the signal words that were the clues. Add those signal words to your anchor chart.

6. Ask students what they would be looking for if they were reading a compare and contrast text. (What is the author comparing? How are they the same? How are they different?)
7. Add the responses to the anchor chart.
8. Continue this process with the other four text structures.

Instructional Strategy: Possible Sentences

This strategy supports element 2, *Provide extended and supported opportunities for students to acquire and use the features of academic language.* Possible Sentences (Stahl & Kapinus, 1991) is a pre-reading strategy that focuses on the vocabulary feature of academic language. Students are given a list of words that they will encounter in the text they will be reading. Based on their prediction of the text's content, students create a sentence for each word. After students finish reading, they check to see if their possible sentences were accurate. If not, students revise them.

Why Use This Strategy: This strategy activates background knowledge about the topic of the text and encourages students to make predictions about what they will be reading, both of which research has shown facilitate reading comprehension (Duke & Pearson, 2009). Possible Sentences also focuses student attention on the most important concepts in the text and provides students with multiple exposures to those concepts before, during, and after reading.

When to Use This Strategy: Possible Sentences is most effectively used when students have at least some familiarity with the topic of the text. If this is not the case, then the sentences students create are based entirely on guesswork. Consequently, this strategy is not typically used at the beginning of a unit or with a topic that students know nothing about. For lower-level or struggling readers, you can discuss each word with your students and then choose two words for pairs of students to create a possible sentence. Have some students share their sentences with the class and write them on the whiteboard. You can continue this process until all the words have been used.

How to Use This Strategy: Identify key vocabulary from the selection to be read. Share the words with students and ask them to pair together words they believe are related. Working individually, students then create sentences they predict could appear in the reading using the paired words. Next, students work with a partner to compare their sentences and discuss why they paired their words. Have students read the text and compare their sentences with actual sentences in the text. Sentences that are not accurate should be revised.

Example Lesson

1. Read the text and choose vocabulary words that represent the key concepts of the text. You can use an informational or narrative text. Choose both words that students know and words they do not know.
2. Explain to students that they are going to be reading the book *And Then What Happened, Paul Revere?* by Margot Tomes. Distribute the worksheet for Possible Sentences (Figure 3.4) and explain that all of these words are in the text they are about to read. They are going to predict the possible sentences that are in the text.
3. Have students read the words and define them. If students do not know a word, give them a brief definition.
4. Have students work with a partner to group like words and create possible sentences using two of the words in each sentence.
5. Have students share their sentences, explain why they thought those words went together, and write them on the whiteboard.
6. Have students read the text looking for the words from possible sentences. Review their sentences and modify them as necessary.
7. Have a class discussion about the accuracy of the possible sentences and write new ones based on the information in the text.

Figure 3.4. Possible Sentences: *And Then What Happened, Paul Revere?*

Name____Date________________

Key Vocabulary:

Boston	bells	silver	English	Sons of Liberty
rider	prisoners	pistol	galloped	Lexington

Make a prediction: Before reading this selection, write three sentences using the words from above that you think could be in the text. Use at least two words from above in each sentence.

1.

2.

3.

Modifying Predictions: After reading the selection, review the sentences you wrote. Correct any information that is inaccurate.

1.

2.

3.

8. Have students reflect on how this strategy helped them in their reading and improved their academic language.

Cross-Cutting Practice: Fostering Metacognition

Modeling and verbalizing reading strategies can shift responsibility from teachers to students by enabling students to be independent learners. To accomplish this, you must think about how your instruction will activate and develop your students' metacognition. More specifically, you must help students understand what strategies are, how to use them, and when and why to apply them. This approach will empower students and enable them to persevere when they interact with complex texts. The instructional strategies that follow are designed to help you understand what these elements look like in practice in your classroom in the context of helping students interact with complex text.

Instructional Strategy: Comprehension Rating

This strategy supports element 1, *Visibly enact metacognitive processes and/or strategies students are expected to use in support of disciplinary learning.* Comprehension Rating is a strategy you can use to help students understand the importance of monitoring their reading comprehension as well as applying a process for doing so. It incorporates carefully designed guided practice, with a gradual release of responsibility built into the instructional sequence, to enable students to develop the knowledge and confidence they need before applying it in independent practice.

Why Use This Strategy: Modeling the thought processes of a proficient reader and consistently engaging students in reflective processes are at the heart of effective reading instruction. Students ask themselves questions such as: Does this word, sentence, or paragraph make sense? Can I explain or retell it in my own words? What could I do differently to increase my understanding of it? This fosters reflective thinking and helps build self-awareness. When you consistently and systematically integrate reflection into your teaching, it permeates the curriculum and gets built into your daily teaching activities.

When to Use This Strategy: Students can and should start learning about comprehension monitoring at an early age. The earlier you introduce your students to the concept and guide them to become self-reflective, self-directed readers who understand when they do and do not comprehend what they are reading, the better equipped they will be to handle the reading challenges inherent in complex texts. Providing opportunities to apply this learning across the curriculum will enable your students to improve their academic performance in all subjects.

How to Use This Strategy: Comprehension Rating has two components. The first is to *focus your students' attention on comprehension* by giving them sentences to read and rate for comprehension: a + if they understand and a – if they do not. Next, you *establish criteria for understanding* by giving students a paragraph and having them rate their comprehension in terms of how well they can explain it to a partner: 1 means *I understood it well and can explain it to my partner*, 2 means *I understood it somewhat and can explain some of it*, and 3 means *I did not understand it and cannot explain it*. Then give students the opportunity to repeat the process with a three-to-five-paragraph passage. Students rate their understanding of each paragraph individually and then rate the passage as a whole.

Example Lesson

1. Explain to students that the purpose of reading is to make meaning from the text, not just to read words. Meaning-making requires you to monitor your comprehension by thinking and reflecting as you read. Being metacognitive while you read enables you to be aware of when you do not understand so that you can fix what caused the breakdown.
2. Choose a short text like an article from the magazine *TIME for Kids* and either project it or provide a copy so that students can follow along. Read it aloud to your students, stopping to demonstrate questions you ask yourself to self-monitor your reading.
3. Have students explain to a partner what you just demonstrated.
4. Next, display a sentence that you know students will understand and ask them to put their thumbs up if they understand it and put their thumbs down if they do not. Then display a nonsense sentence and have students do the same thing. Debrief with students the difference between the two sentences and how it felt as readers.
5. Now provide students with new paragraphs and have them rate them + (it makes sense) or – (it does not make sense). When they have finished, have them discuss the paragraphs and their ratings with their partners.
6. Now that students have had these experiences, introduce the three-point rating task. Create an anchor chart with your students explaining the three points.
7. Provide sentences, paragraphs, and longer passages for students to rate. Debrief with the class and have students identify why comprehension broke down. Restate the purpose of this activity.
8. Now that students understand how to monitor their comprehension, you can teach them fix-up strategies.

Extension. Stop and Check is a way to have your students continue to think about their comprehension.

1. Select stopping points in a short text and have students pair up to read it.
2. Partner A explains two facts or ideas at the first stopping point to Partner B. Partner B either agrees with or modifies Partner A's facts or ideas and provides two other facts or ideas. Students continue to read and process the text, switching roles at each stopping point.
3. Students then rate their understanding of the text using the three-point rating scale and, if appropriate, explain where their comprehension broke down.

Instructional Strategy: Stop, Think, Tag

This strategy supports element 2, *Deconstruct metacognitive processes and/or strategies that support disciplinary learning*. Stop, Think, Tag is a way to help students stay metacognitively aware and actively engaged in their reading. As they read, students identify the specific strategies they use to recognize and address comprehension breakdowns that occur. These strategies are ones you have previously taught and posted in columns on a wall chart, bulletin board, or display surface. After using a strategy, students put a sticky note with their name on it in the appropriate column. This provides you and your students with a visible record of which strategies your class has used.

Why Use This Strategy: A great deal of research indicates that the explicit teaching of strategies to students will improve their learning and help them become more independent readers (Kolic-Vehovec & Bajsanski, 2006; Ness, 2011). Our work with the SOAR Disciplinary Interactions With Complex Text Teaching Frame has also demonstrated that the key to the successful teaching of strategies is explicitly demonstrating what the strategy is, how to use it, and when and why to use it. Stop, Think, Tag provides students with the scaffolded support they need to develop their metacognitive abilities while providing you with important information to guide your strategy instruction.

When to Use This Strategy: Students often do not know what is causing their reading problems or what to do when they occur. Stop, Think, Tag is an interactive resource for students to use in these situations. It is also a teaching tool that you can use to help students understand their reading strengths and weaknesses as well as what strategies are effective and available.

How to Use This Strategy: You and your students work together to determine which strategies should be displayed. You will start, of course, with those you have recently taught, but as time goes on some will need to be removed while new ones will be added. You need to balance ones that students use most often as they read with those that you think are being ignored. You should also use the strategy display to identify and discuss patterns that emerge (i.e., which strategies are used the most and which need to be used more) and to provide students with opportunities to share why they chose particular strategies.

Example Lesson

1. Create a reading strategy anchor chart with different reading strategies listed and, as you introduce and model different strategies, add them to the chart. Once you have three strategies listed, introduce Stop, Think, Tag.
2. Begin by asking your students to share with a partner why it is important to self-monitor your comprehension. Explain that the first step in becoming a metacognitive reader is being aware of when you are comprehending and when you are not. The second step is being able to take action. So when comprehension breaks down, you need to be able to do something about it. You should have some strategies you can use to get back on track with your reading.
3. Explain that the Stop, Think, Tag strategy is a way to publicly acknowledge and celebrate the reading strategies that you use.
4. Model the Stop, Think, Tag strategy by pairing up with a student and reading a paragraph. Now Stop and Think about what strategy you used. Discuss it with your partner. Take a sticky note and write your name or initials on it and Tag it on the chart under the strategy. Explain to students that they will do this for the entire article.
5. When students have finished reading and placing their sticky notes on the strategy chart, debrief with them.
6. Once students have practiced this strategy, have them implement it independently when they read.

Cross-Cutting Practice: Monitoring and Guiding

A strong positive connection exists between your monitoring of students' reading comprehension and your students' academic performance. Formative assessment is an essential component of monitoring, and its development can raise student achievement. Adjusting instruction based on formative assessment results and translating formative assessment results into frequent descriptive feedback for students provides them with specific insights into how to improve their interactions with complex texts. The instructional strategies we describe below will help you monitor and guide your students' learning as they interact with complex texts.

Instructional Strategy: Paraphrasing

This strategy supports element 1, *Monitor learning and adjust instruction, supports, and/or disciplinary tasks to meet student needs*. Paraphrasing requires readers to restate what they have heard or read in their own words. It can be both a reading comprehension strategy for students and an assessment strategy for teachers. In the SOAR context, we use Paraphrasing as a monitoring tool for you to determine and track how well your students are comprehending what they read. Students read an excerpt of text (or, in the case of young students, listen to you read), ask themselves what it was mainly about, and try to put it into their own words.

Why Use This Strategy: The ability to identify and restate key information from written material is fundamental to learning. Paraphrasing actively engages students in the reading process and allows you to monitor how well they can recall text and understand main ideas.

When to Use This Strategy: You need to monitor students' reading comprehension as often as possible. Paraphrasing informs your instruction regarding which students are comprehending the text and which are not. This also provides you with the data and opportunity to provide targeted feedback as necessary.

How to Use This Strategy: Begin by thinking about the skills you want students to exhibit in their paraphrase. Here are some questions you can ask: Was the paraphrase in the student's own words? Were key points or details identified and understood? Was the message of the author maintained? Were synonyms of vocabulary words used? After teaching students the paraphrasing process, you can circulate around the class and ask individual students to paraphrase a section of text that you have identified and copied. When a student has finished reading the passage, you remove it and ask the student to tell you everything they can remember about what they have just read. Answers need to be tied directly to the information in the passage and not be derived from previously learned information. Over time you can track individual student progress in terms of the amount of information recalled.

Example Lesson

1. Begin by explaining that paraphrasing is putting what you read into your own words, whereas summarizing is restating just the main points. A summary is substantially shorter than the original text, whereas a paraphrase can be as long as the original text. Show students an example of a paraphrase and a summary from the same text and have them work with a partner to identify the differences.
2. Teach the four R's of paraphrasing: Reword (replace words and phrases), Rearrange (rearrange ideas), Realize (some words and phrases cannot be replaced, e.g., names, dates, titles), and Recheck (make sure it conveys the same meaning as the original text).

3. Model a chunk of text as a think-aloud using the four R method.
4. Distribute a short text and have students practice with a partner, taking turns paraphrasing.
5. Ask some students to model for the rest of the class and then debrief by pointing out what was done well and what needs improvement.
6. Provide opportunities for independent practice. Keep anecdotal notes on how well students understood the text and were able to paraphrase it. Use your notes to provide feedback to your students on the steps they need to improve.

Instructional Strategy: Academic Feedback

This strategy supports element 2, *Provide written and/or oral feedback during lessons to promote disciplinary learning*. Academic Feedback, a strategy you can use to help students meet learning targets, is one of the most powerful tools you have to influence your students' achievement. It begins with you and your students having a clear idea of what the learning target is and what good work looks like. This enables you to identify, and students to understand, what they have done well and what needs to improve.

Why Use This Strategy: Research is very clear that when feedback is done correctly, it is ranked among the highest of hundreds of educational practices (Hattie, 2012). However, research also demonstrates that effective feedback's value is not just its impact on student performance and achievement. It also impacts student confidence, self-awareness, and enthusiasm for learning.

When to Use This Strategy: Academic Feedback, which can be written or oral, is an integral part of formative assessment. Your students not only receive the feedback prior to any summative assessment, but in time to have an opportunity to learn from and use it. Thus, the more timely your feedback is, the better your students' performance will be.

How to Use This Strategy: Effective Academic Feedback has four primary characteristics. First, it needs to be clearly and specifically linked to the learning target(s). Next, it needs to be descriptive rather than evaluative; for example, "When you paraphrased this paragraph, you included all the details and restated it in your words" rather than "You did a very good job of paraphrasing the paragraph." It is also important to explain how the student can improve the next time they engage in the task. "I noticed you used some great synonyms in your paraphrase. Your next step will be to reread the original paragraph and your paraphrase and then underline any details you left out." The third characteristic is timeliness. The sooner you provide feedback, the better the chance the student can and will use it. Finally, limit your feedback to the amount the student can realistically process and act upon. Concise, prioritized feedback is more digestible for students and therefore more likely to be implemented.

Example of Academic Feedback

1. You circulate and monitor your students as they generate questions while reading. All of the responses that follow should be timely.
2. You say, "The questions you generated from your reading tell me you really understood what you read (descriptive). This question in particular shows me you were interacting with the text (specific). To improve your questions, you need to ask questions that move beyond the text and think about what the author's message is (actionable)."
3. You say, "I can see from your questions that you were trying to understand what the text was about. However, your questions can be answered with a yes or no. I would like you to use these sentence stems to create your questions (actionable)."
4. You say, "It looks like you are stuck. Can you tell me what you have read so far? Based on what you just said, can you think of a question you might have about the character? You could use how, why, or where as a beginning."

Foundational Practice: Designing Instruction

If you use the Anchor Literacy Standards as a guide for creating appropriate literacy experiences for your students, you will build activities and select instructional strategies that focus on what your students should be able to learn and do in regard to their literacy development. For instance, to provide the scaffolding that students need to be successful, you should design and connect activities that maintain high expectations and that are keyed to a variety of texts and content. Interacting with and working their way through a variety of complex texts is essential if students are to grow as readers and learners, so the regular use of rigorous texts and content at all grade levels is essential. Below we provide an instructional tool that addresses element 3 to help you establish high expectations that support your learning targets and maintain intellectual rigor in a lesson focused on interactions with complex text. You will find an example for element 2 in Chapter 4.

Instructional Tool: Measuring Rigor Scale

This tool supports element 3, *Establish high expectations that support the learning targets and maintain the intellectual rigor of classroom activities and tasks.* Maintaining the intellectual rigor of instructional activities and tasks is essential to helping students meet the high expectations of the College- and Career-Readiness Standards. The Measuring Rigor Scale (Figure 3.5), adapted from Strong, Silver, and Perini (2001), is a tool that provides teachers with a research-based, comprehensive process for determining what kinds of rigor are addressed or lacking in a given set of instructional activities and tasks.

Why Use This Tool: Rigor as it relates to curriculum and instruction is too often thought of as the quantity or difficulty of the content to be covered. The Measuring Rigor Scale is based on a broader conceptualization of the term—"the goal of helping students develop the capacity to understand content that is *complex*, *ambiguous*, *provocative*, and *personally or emotionally challenging*" (Strong, Silver, & Perini, 2001, p. 11). Embracing this definition and tool enables you to develop rigorous activities and tasks that will establish high expectations and help students understand complex ideas and difficult concepts.

When to Use This Tool: Considering the extent to which you have established the rigor of your instructional activities and tasks is something you

Figure 3.5. Measuring Rigor Scale

Complexity	Emotion
To what extent are the activities and tasks organized around complex, interrelated concepts?	To what extent do the activities and tasks elicit strong feelings?
1 — 2 — 3 — 4	1 — 2 — 3 — 4
Provocativeness	**Ambiguity**
To what extent are the activities and tasks concerned with critical issues that challenge students' previous understandings?	To what extent do the activities and tasks focus on symbols and images that contain multiple meanings?
1 — 2 — 3 — 4	1 — 2 — 3 — 4

Source: Measuring Rigor in Instructional Activities and Tasks. Adapted from "Teaching What Matters Most: Standards and Strategies for Raising Student Achievement" by R. Strong, H. Silver, & J. Matthew. 2001. Copyright 2001 by ASCD. Adapted with permission.

must do for virtually every lesson you design. This is true across all grade levels and content areas. At the same time, the extent to which you address each dimension of rigor may vary from lesson to lesson. So a tool that helps you think through how to prioritize those dimensions can be used on a daily basis.

How to Use This Tool:

1. Take your Measuring Rigor Scale and your lesson activities and tasks. Look at the first quadrant: Complexity. Consider these questions as you rate your lesson.
   a. To what degree does your lesson
      i. ask students to synthesize information across multiple texts?
      ii. have students transfer knowledge to new and unfamiliar situations?
      iii. move students beyond the surface level to deeper layers of meaning?
   b. Decide where your activities and tasks rate on the four-point scale. If appropriate, consider ways to increase the rigor.
2. Then move to the next quadrant: Emotion. Consider these questions as you rate your lesson.
   a. To what degree does your lesson
      i. challenge students' feelings?
      ii. trigger empathy for characters or causes?
      iii. elicit sympathy for characters or causes?
   b. Decide where your activities and tasks rate on the four-point scale. If appropriate, consider ways to increase the rigor.
3. Move to the next quadrant: Ambiguity. Consider these questions as you rate your lesson.
   a. To what degree does your lesson contain symbols or images that
      i. leave students in a state of suspension?
      ii. engage students in divergent thinking?
      iii. require cognitive stamina?
   b. Decide where your activities and tasks rate on the four-point scale. If appropriate, consider ways to increase the rigor.
4. Now move to the last quadrant: Provocativeness. Consider these questions as you rate your lesson.
   a. To what degree does your lesson engage students in
      i. identifying problems?
      ii. dealing with dilemmas?
      iii. analyzing multiple perspectives to create a new position or perspective?
   b. Decide where your activities and tasks rate on the four-point scale. If appropriate, consider ways to increase the rigor.

This tool is meant to help teachers find ways to make their activities and tasks more rigorous. Nonetheless, it is important to note that your activities and tasks do not have to be equally rigorous in all quadrants. Some activities and tasks might lean more heavily to one quadrant than the other three because of the nature of the materials or the learning target.

We believe that this tool is as relevant for primary teachers as it is for intermediate teachers. An example of Complexity for primary might be comparing different versions of the gingerbread man story. For Emotion, you could consider a book like *Ira Sleeps Over* by Bernard Waber and identify the emotions both Ira and Reggie felt and why they felt that way. Ambiguity can be experienced when trying to understand the Princess's reaction to the Prince in *The Paper Bag Princess* by Robert Munsch. For the Provocative dimension, students can take a position about whether Goldilocks was right or wrong in entering the Three Bears' house.

ADDITIONAL IMPLEMENTATION CONSIDERATIONS

The best, and for some students the only, place they will encounter the structures and language necessary to interact successfully with complex texts is in the materials they will read in school. So creating classroom environments where students have consistent, scaffolded access to these materials is essential. In addition to understanding the practices, strategies, and tools described above, you must be mindful of two other considerations as you implement the practices in the Disciplinary Interactions with Complex Text Teaching Frame: defining complex text and understanding the reading process.

Defining Complex Text

A complex text can be any written, visual, audio, or multimedia message that conveys information or ideas. This expanded notion of what a text can be is particularly important when we embrace the fact that using complex texts is not just the responsibility of ELA or ELD teachers. All teachers across all disciplines are being asked to help students comprehend complex literary or informational texts independently and proficiently. This shift within the CCSS also emphasizes less pre-reading instruction, more close reading, and a greater focus on evidence from text in student answers. So, whether the complex text is a novel, lab report, sheet of music, or work of art, you must be able to create the kind of environment that students need to develop complex academic language and disciplinary literacy. Creating these environments requires you to understand the three factors affecting text complexity, identified in the CCSS as follows:

- Quantitative factors such as word length and frequency, and sentence length and structure;
- Qualitative factors such as levels of meaning, purpose and clarity of text, and difficulty of language; and
- Reader and Task factors such as motivation and background knowledge as well as the purpose and complexity of the task assigned.

Understanding the Reading Process

Supporting students' language and literacy development is dependent on you understanding the reading process. Although the ultimate goal of reading is comprehension, the process is likely to break down unless the reader controls the skills involved in individual word recognition. However, simply reading words with fluency and accuracy will not enable students to handle the conceptual demands of complex texts. Thus, your students' reading abilities depends on the strategic integration of word recognition, vocabulary development, and comprehension strategies.

As your students move through the grades, they will be asked to apply the reading process to a variety of tasks that have different purposes, require different processing, and result in different consequences. As a result, it is possible to adjust the difficulty of a text and a student's ability to comprehend it by altering the task. How well students comprehend the text and perform the task also depends on their proficiency in the language of the text, prior knowledge of the topic, level of motivation for and interest in the task, and their perceptions of themselves as readers. Thus, the reader, text, and task interact to determine the quality of comprehension experienced by the reader.

Finally, as Figure 3.6 illustrates, the reading process occurs in dynamic sociocultural contexts that shape and are shaped by the reader. This means that language and literacy development are closely linked to the culture and society in which they are used. Consequently, a reader's comprehension can be influenced by variables such as race, ethnicity, gender, social class, and sexual orientation, all of which you must consider when supporting your students.

CONCLUSION

The purpose of this chapter has been to deepen your understanding of the Disciplinary Interactions with Complex Text Teaching Frame by unpacking the language of and rationale for the instructional practices that comprise it. The model lesson and associated classroom vignette provide additional insight into these practices by illustrating the dynamic and interdependent ways in which they work together in the context of a Teaching Frame to

Figure 3.6. The Reading Process

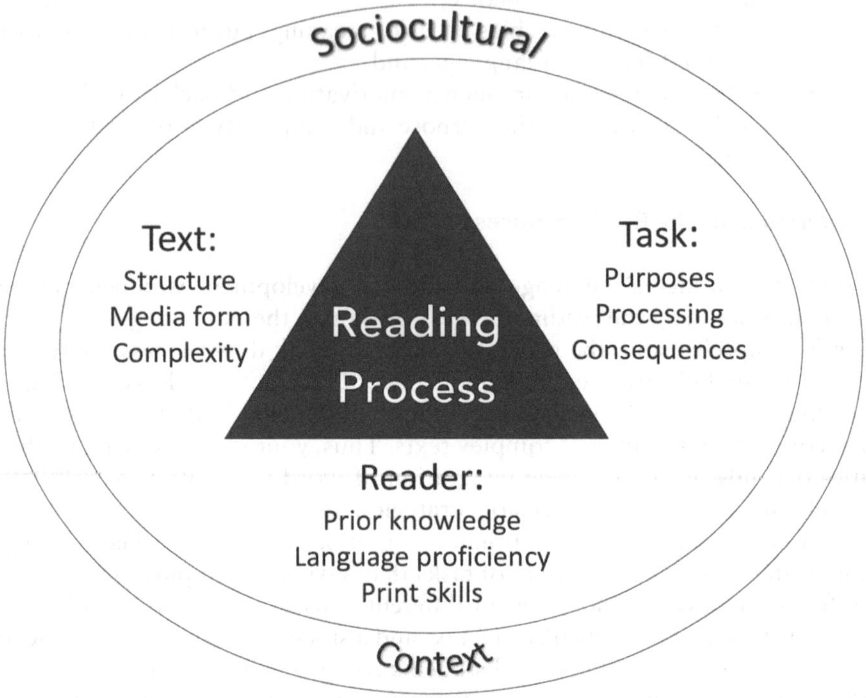

drive both teacher and student growth. Teachers need to develop students' academic language, help them become independent readers, and monitor and guide their text interactions to facilitate access to a range of complex texts. This all requires intentional planning with the goal of supporting students' ability to interact with appropriate texts in mind. Finally, the instructional strategies and tools are designed to deepen your understanding of the Disciplinary Interactions with Complex Text Teaching Frame and to provide you with concrete examples of approaches teachers are currently using in their classrooms to implement it. These strategies will help you to support your students with text interactions, which is an essential 21st-century skill.

CHAPTER 4

Disciplinary Uses of Evidence

Supporting claims with logical reasoning and relevant evidence is heavily emphasized in the CCSS and NGSS and is the focus of the next SOAR Teaching Frame for Literacy: Disciplinary Uses of Evidence. The High-Impact Practice focuses on structuring, strengthening, and supporting uses of multiple forms of evidence in disciplinary writing and speaking. Two essential elements make up this practice: effective teachers engage students in identifying and analyzing textual and oral evidence for relevancy (element 1), and they provide opportunities for students to identify and use sufficient evidence to develop and support claims (element 2). Please take a few minutes to review the Disciplinary Uses of Evidence Teaching Frame in Table 4.1.

USING THE SOAR LENS TO PLAN AND REFLECT

The SOAR Teaching Frames provide a systematic way for you to plan and reflect on your teaching. In the non-model and model lessons that follow,

Table 4.1. Disciplinary Uses of Evidence Teaching Frame

HIGH-IMPACT PRACTICE	Disciplinary Uses of Evidence (DUE) **Element 1:** Foster students' ability to analyze textual and/or oral evidence for relevancy **Element 2:** Provide and support multiple opportunities for students to identify and use sufficient evidence to support claims in disciplinary writing and speaking		
CROSS-CUTTING PRACTICES	Facilitating Acquisition of Academic Language (FAAL) **Element 1:** Introduce and/or refer to the academic language demands of texts and tasks **Element 2:** Provide extended and supported opportunities for students to acquire and use the features of academic language	Fostering Metacognition for Disciplinary Learning (FM) **Element 1:** Visibly enact metacognitive processes and/or strategies students are expected to use in support of disciplinary learning **Element 2:** Deconstruct metacognitive processes and/or strategies that support disciplinary learning	Monitoring and Guiding Disciplinary Learning (MG) **Element 1:** Monitor learning and adjust instruction, supports, and/or disciplinary tasks to meet student needs **Element 2:** Provide written and/or oral feedback during lessons to promote disciplinary learning
FOUNDATIONAL PRACTICE	Designing Instruction for Disciplinary Thinking and Understanding (DI) **Element 1:** Set disciplinary learning targets that are aligned with ELA/Literacy CCSS and the target high-impact practice **Element 2:** Structure and connect tasks that support the learning targets **Element 3:** Establish high expectations that support the learning targets and maintain the intellectual rigor of classroom activities and tasks		

THINK BEFORE READING ACTIVITY

For students to develop arguments effectively, they need to identify textual and oral evidence and use that evidence with reasoning to support claims. Think about what needs to happen for students to be able to do both of these things. As you read the first part of this chapter, consider the supports Mr. O'Connor uses to help students identify evidence and support claims. Also, think about how you might use these ideas to develop supports for use with your students.

we will use the SOAR lens to compare two different approaches to planning a lesson that focuses on uses of evidence. Then you will read a classroom vignette that illustrates the alignment of the practices in the Teaching Frame and how the teacher enacts those practices in a lesson.

4th-Grade Non-Model Lesson

The teacher who created the non-model has been working with his students to engage in argument using relevant and sufficient evidence. He also wants students to be able to report on a topic with appropriate facts and relevant descriptive details. They have been studying structure and function in terrestrial animals and plants.

Let's think about why this is a non-model. The lesson lists the standards that will be addressed and the activities in which the students will be engaged. The High-Impact Practice of Disciplinary Uses of Evidence is the focus of the lesson. The students are working on making a claim and providing evidence to support the claim. However, it is unclear to what extent students are being fully supported to identify relevant evidence and use that evidence to support or refute the claim. The teacher could use the following guiding questions as he rethinks the lesson to help him zero in on these critical elements:

- What scaffolds can I provide to enable all my students to support or refute a claim using relevant evidence?
- What activities can my students engage in to help them understand what relevant and sufficient evidence means?
- Have I built in supported opportunities to allow students time to think about how to identify evidence and then use reasoning to link that evidence to a claim?

Now let's consider how the teacher addresses the three Cross-Cutting Practices. For Facilitating the Acquisition of Academic Language, this lesson

Standards

NGSS 4-LS1-1: Construct an argument that plants and animals have internal and external structures that function to support survival, growth, behavior, and reproduction.

CCSS.ELA-LITERACY.CCRA.SL.4.4: Report on a topic or text, recount a story, or recount an experience with appropriate facts and relevant descriptive details, speaking clearly at an understandable pace.

- Remind students that we are exploring different ecosystems, as well as plant and animal structures that help plants and animals survive in those ecosystems. Explain that students will be working on the connection among a claim, evidence, and reasoning.
- Tell students they will be creating an explanatory model, which includes the internal and external structures of their fictional animal, and explanations with evidence for how those structures help that animal survive in a specific environment.
- Provide each group with a Claim-Evidence-Reasoning (CER) poster and tell them that each group will use it to develop their arguments and present their thinking to the class.
- As students work in groups, ask for volunteers to share what they have completed so far, and ask if the groups have any questions.
- Students continue working on their CER posters in preparation for their presentations. Walk around and assist students who need help.
- When posters have been completed, ask student groups to share with the class.

does not address academic language explicitly. The teacher could refer to the academic language demands and support students in acquiring and using the academic language needed for the task. The teacher could ask the following questions as he plans the lesson:

- What are the academic language demands of this task, and where in the lesson might I draw students' attention to them?
- What supports can I provide to help students acquire and use academic language in an authentic and meaningful way?

In this lesson we see no evidence of metacognition. The teacher does not visibly enact or deconstruct metacognitive strategies or processes during the lesson. The teacher could ask the following questions as he plans the lesson for this Cross-Cutting Practice:

- What process or strategy do I need to demonstrate so that my students understand how to identify and evaluate relevant evidence?
- How can I help students understand the thinking process involved in identifying evidence, determining whether the evidence is relevant, and using the evidence to support or refute a claim?

In this lesson there is no explanation of how students will be monitored or ideas for the type of feedback the teacher might provide. It is always important to anticipate the types of misconceptions or gaps students might have and to plan for how to monitor the work and redirect students as needed. The teacher could ask the following questions as he plans the lesson:

- What misconceptions or gaps might my students have about identifying or using evidence?
- What questions can I ask to elicit and redirect student thinking and misconceptions?

We do see some evidence of the Foundational Practice. The standards are listed, but there is no explicit link to the High-Impact Practice. The connection between activities is unclear. The teacher could ask the following questions as he plans the lesson to ensure that the focus on the High-Impact Practice and learning targets remains consistent and purposeful across the lesson:

- How are the tasks I develop connected, and how do they build on one another?
- How will I establish and maintain high expectations and rigor for all my students?

4th-Grade SOAR Model Lesson With Annotations

Now we are going to look at this lesson again, only this time the teacher is aware of SOAR and has used guiding questions to reflect as he plans. We have identified where the teacher addresses each of the five practices in his planning. As you read the annotated lesson (see Table 4.2), note how much more intentional and thoughtful this lesson is and how each of the SOAR practices supports the High-Impact Practice of Disciplinary Uses of Evidence. The non-model lesson was structured in a way in which the teacher was doing all of the explaining and reminding. Notice the shift that takes place in this model lesson where the teacher actively engages the students' thinking about their learning by asking them questions about what they are doing at different points throughout the lesson. It is evident that the teacher has been more thoughtful and intentional in his planning and is using the SOAR Teaching Frame as a lens.

Table 4.2. 4th-Grade Annotated Model Lesson

Disciplinary Uses of Evidence (DUE) Teaching Frame Elements	Teacher Actions
Designing Instruction E1–Teacher aligns the High-Impact Practice to CCSS and NGSS	DUE-E1: Foster students' ability to analyze textual and/or oral evidence for relevancy DUE-E2: Provide and support multiple opportunities for students to identify and use sufficient evidence to support claims in disciplinary writing and speaking NGSS 4-LS1-1. Construct an argument that plants and animals have internal and external structures that function to support survival, growth, behavior, and reproduction. CCSS.ELA-LITERACY.CCRA.SL.4.4. Report on a topic or text, recount a story, or recount an experience with appropriate facts and relevant descriptive details, speaking clearly at an understandable pace.
Designing Instruction E1–Teacher explicitly states standards and learning targets to the students	Introduce the standards to the students and ask students to turn to their partner and talk about what we have been learning (different ecosystems and plant and animal structures that help them survive in those ecosystems). Explain that students will be working on the connection among a claim, evidence, and reasoning. Read the posted learning targets for today: • I can make a claim and support it with evidence. • I can explain why the evidence I gathered supports my claim. • I can explain, through an explanatory model, how structures work together as a system to allow an animal to survive in a specific environment. • I can critique my group's reasoning and provide supported, helpful, and specific feedback.

Table continues on next page

Table 4.2. 4th-Grade Annotated Model Lesson (continued)

Disciplinary Uses of Evidence (DUE) Teaching Frame Elements	Teacher Actions
Facilitating Acquisition of Academic Language E2–Students are given opportunity to acquire and use academic language in a meaningful way	Ask pairs of students to discuss what the terms "internal structure" and "external structure" mean, to think of an example of each structure, and to explain how one of these structures helps the animal survive.
Disciplinary Uses of Evidence E1–Teacher is fostering students' ability to analyze textual evidence for relevancy.	Post two of the claim and evidence cards from yesterday as a reminder. Have students discuss in pairs what a claim is and what evidence is.
Designing Instruction E2–Teacher has structured tasks that support the learning targets	Explain the group challenge. Tell students they will be creating an explanatory model, which includes the internal and external structures of their fictional animal. Their presentation will include an explanation with evidence on how those structures help that animal to survive in its specific environment.
Fostering Metacognition E1–Teacher is visibly enacting a metacognitive process by conducting a think-aloud to model the use of the poster	Display and distribute the CER (Claim-Evidence-Reasoning) poster and explain the elements of the poster. Model the use of the poster.
Facilitating Acquisition of Academic Language E1–Teacher refers to the academic language demands of the task	Point out the academic language used in the CER poster.
Facilitating Acquisition of Academic Language E2–Students are given opportunities to acquire and use academic language in a meaningful way	Read the sentence stems in the poster as added support.
Disciplinary Uses of Evidence E2–Teacher provides and supports opportunities for students to identify and use sufficient evidence to support claims in disciplinary writing	Students get into groups to design a fictional animal and explain how the animal's internal and external features work together to help the animal survive in the environment their group chose.
Monitoring & Guiding E1–Teacher monitors student work	Listen to group discussions and reasoning about the connections between the claim and the evidence.

Table 4.2. 4th-Grade Annotated Model Lesson (continued)

Disciplinary Uses of Evidence (DUE) Teaching Frame Elements	Teacher Actions
Monitoring & Guiding E2–Teacher provides oral feedback to promote disciplinary learning	Provide feedback and use prompts to help students go deeper or to redirect as needed (e.g., How do you know it is evidence? What does that structure mean for the chances of your animal surviving in that environment?).
Disciplinary Uses of Evidence E1–Teacher is fostering students' ability to analyze evidence for relevancy and gives them opportunities to acquire and use academic language in a meaningful way Fostering Metacognition E1–Teacher engages students in a think-aloud for the class	Pause the class and engage students in a think-aloud to share their thinking processes with the whole class. Specifically ask volunteer students to share the process they used to identify evidence showing that one of the internal or external structures of their animal would help it to survive in a particular environment. Facilitate the discussion to deepen students' understanding of the connection between evidence and claims and to address any misconceptions.
Facilitating Acquisition of Academic Language E2–Students are given an opportunity to acquire and use academic language	Ask students to share with a partner what the words "relevant" and "sufficient" mean.
Fostering Metacognition E1–Teacher is asking students to reflect on how the think-aloud helped them	Have students reflect on how listening to the group think-aloud helped them understand more about relevant and sufficient evidence.
Disciplinary Uses of Evidence E2–Teacher provides and supports opportunities for students to identify and use sufficient evidence to support claims in disciplinary writing and speaking DI3–Teacher establishes high expectations that support the learning targets	Remind students to use the sentence frames on the CER poster to help guide them in their presentations. Explain the expectations: • Make a claim, select supporting evidence, use scientific reasoning to develop their argument, and evaluate their use of evidence. • Include appropriate facts and relevant descriptive details. • Use full sentences. • Speak clearly at an understandable pace.
Monitoring & Guiding E1–Teacher monitors student work	Monitor students as they start to prepare their posters.

Table continues on next page

Table 4.2. 4th-Grade Annotated Model Lesson (continued)

Disciplinary Uses of Evidence (DUE) Teaching Frame Elements	Teacher Actions
Monitoring & Guiding E2–Teacher provides oral feedback to promote disciplinary learning	Provide feedback to students on the connections they are making between claims and evidence and also on their use of appropriate academic language.
Facilitating Acquisition of Academic Language E2–Students are given opportunities to acquire and use academic language in a meaningful way	Student groups present their completed posters to the class.
Disciplinary Uses of Evidence E1–Teacher is fostering students' ability to analyze evidence for relevancy	Provide students with a reflection guide. Ask them to use the guide during the presentations to highlight two things they have learned about identifying and using relevant evidence to support a claim. Tell students they will be asked to share one thing from their reflection guide with the entire class.

Now, let's see how the teacher takes this lesson and enacts it with his students. As you read this vignette, reflect on how the five practices of the Disciplinary Uses of Evidence Teaching Frame are being implemented and how they work in conjunction with one another during instruction. Try to answer the following guiding questions:

1. How does the teacher facilitate acquisition of academic language, foster metacognition, and guide the learning to support the High-Impact Practice of Disciplinary Uses of Evidence?
2. How do all five practices in the Teaching Frame work together to support the learning targets set by the teacher?

Step Inside Mr. O'Connor's Classroom

Mr. O'Connor wants his 4th-grade students to engage in argument using relevant and sufficient evidence. He also wants students to be able to report on a topic with appropriate facts and relevant descriptive details. He is integrating standards from the NGSS and CCSS for ELA and is focusing on the topic of Structure and Function in Terrestrial Animals and Plants. At the end of the unit, student groups will prepare and present an explanatory model to show how the animal's structures work together as a system to help the animal survive.

Mr. O'Connor asks the class to turn to their partner and explain to each other what they have been studying in science. Students share that they have been exploring different ecosystems as well as plant and animal structures that help them survive in those ecosystems. He points to the word wall with definitions and pictures and says, "Remember, we have been engaged in research and discussions about different ecosystems: tundra, grasslands, and deserts. And during those discussions you compared different features of those ecosystems. We also researched external and internal structures of animals and how those structures work together to help animals grow and survive. Today you will continue working in your groups, and the group challenge is to create an imaginary animal that has the specialized structures needed to live in a grassland, desert, or tundra ecosystem. So you will have to consider what special structures your animal will need in order to survive in that ecosystem."

> Mr. O'Connor explains how instructional tasks are connected to one another and support the learning target.

Mr. O'Connor asks students to read the posted learning targets and underlines the main tasks:

- I can make a claim and support it with evidence.
- I can explain why the evidence I gathered supports my claim.
- I can explain, through an explanatory model, how structures work together as a system to allow an animal to survive in a specific environment.
- I can critique my group's reasoning and provide supportive, helpful, and specific feedback.

> Mr. O'Connor is reinforcing the concepts of internal and external structures and monitoring students' understanding through the sorting activity.

Mr. O'Connor launches the day's lesson with a class brainstorming session about the structures that plants and animals could have that allow them to better survive in their environment as a way to activate students' prior knowledge. "Who can give us an example of an external and internal structure? . . . Yes, that is correct. Now who can explain why this structure helps the animal survive?" After brainstorming, students sort images of various structures into categories based on what they believe the purpose of each is.

Next, Mr. O'Connor tells students that they will be making a series of claims in their reports and will need to include evidence that supports their claims. He reminds the students of the activity they engaged in yesterday to distinguish between evidence and claims. "Remember, yesterday we looked at a set of cards, and we worked in groups to decide which of the statements was a claim and which was a piece of evidence." He puts two of the statements students had explored the day before on the whiteboard and asks them to identify which is the claim and which is the evidence, and to explain how they know.

"In this unit you are going to be examining how the internal and external structures of your fictional animal work together to help it survive and grow in a specific ecosystem. You will need to make a claim, find evidence relevant to your claim, and explain why this evidence supports or does not support your claim." He tells students that today they will be working on the connection among a claim, evidence, and reasoning. Mr. O'Connor then gives directions for the group challenge:

"Create an explanatory model that includes a drawing of your animal and its habitat. On your model, use annotations to show why the animal structures support survival in the environment that you selected. You should

1. include internal and external structures of your animal that help it survive, and
2. explain the function of these structures and how they work together as a system to support survival."

He explains that each group has a poster (see Table 4.3) it will be using to construct arguments. Mr. O'Connor reminds students that there are some sentence stems on their poster that they can use to address each of the questions in the CER structure.

> He thinks aloud to model how to fill out the chart.

Mr. O'Connor then models for students how to use the poster. "Let's use the CER poster to create our claim, evidence, and reasoning for why the snowshoe hare can live in the tundra. Look at the diagram of the snowshoe hare on the wall where we all labeled the internal and external structures together. Also look at the features on that diagram that we developed about the tundra. Now let's put it together to develop our argument."

> He provides supports for his students in the form of a poster with sentence stems reinforcing academic language.

1. First make a claim: *I designed a snowshoe hare with internal and external structures that work together so that the snowshoe hare will survive well in the tundra.*
2. Then select evidence: *The snowshoe hare has thick fur and flat teeth. The tundra is extremely cold, and shrubs and grasses are available to eat, but other food is limited.*
3. Next use the evidence and scientific reasoning to support the claim: "This is a very important part of your poster and where I find most of you need help. You are all very good at making a claim and selecting evidence, but you do not always explain how the evidence supports or justifies your claim. Let's see how we can do this better.

   "Because the snowshoe hare has thick, white fur, it can stay warm and be camouflaged in the snowy

> Mr. O'Connor points out an area that students need to improve upon and has them discuss it.

Table 4.3. Claim-Evidence-Reasoning (CER) Poster

<table>
<tr><td>Make a Claim</td><td colspan="2">What claim are you making about your fictional animal and specific environment?
I designed _______ (animal) with internal and external structures that work together so that the _______ (animal) will survive well in _______ (ecosystem).</td></tr>
<tr><td>Select Evidence</td><td colspan="2">What parts of your explanatory model will you use as evidence?
The _______ (animal) has _______ (internal structure[s]) and _______ (external structure[s]). The _______ (ecosystem) is _______ (feature) and _______ (feature).</td></tr>
<tr><td>Use Evidence and Scientific Reasoning to Support Claim</td><td>How are your animal's structures specifically designed for your ecosystem?
Because the _______ (animal) has _______ (internal/external structure) it can _______ (function), which helps it survive in the _______ (ecosystem).</td><td>How does your animal's structure work together as a system to support the animal's survival?
The _______ (animal's) structures help it to _______ and _______so it will have its needs met.</td></tr>
<tr><td>Evaluate Evidence</td><td colspan="2">Do you have enough evidence and strong reasoning to support the claim that your animal has the structures to help it survive? Why?
My evidence is related to my claim.
My evidence proves my claim.
I have multiple types of evidence.
I have enough evidence to support my claim.
My evidence that the _______ (animal) can survive in the _______ ecosystem) is strong because _______.</td></tr>
</table>

tundra. Notice how we just took the evidence—thick, white fur—and explained how it supports the claim. *Food is scarce in the tundra, but there are shrubs and grasses, and the hare has flat teeth to grind up plants.* Talk to your partner about how this evidence supports the claim: *So, the snowshoe hare will survive well in the tundra because it can get its needs for shelter and food met. Here is the conclusion."*

4. Finish by evaluating the evidence: Mr. O'Connor reads the four statements and explains to students that they are to check them to see if their evidence meets the criteria. "So, first, thumbs up if you think my evidence is related to my claim. . . . Yes, the fur and teeth support how the snowshoe hare can survive in the tundra. The second criterion states that my evidence supports my claim. . . . Yes, it does. The third statement asks for multiple types of evidence. Here we stated evidence for both the internal and external structures, so I would check this box. The last box is enough evidence. I can ask myself if I could add other

structures to support my claim. I might be able to. Then you write your statement: *My evidence that the snowshoe hare can survive in tundra is strong because the evidence explains both the internal and external structures necessary for the hare to live in the tundra. I could add more internal and external structures to make my claim even stronger."*

> Rather than telling students how to think, he uses questions as guidance and feedback.

When students are engaged in developing their explanatory models and making connections between their animal's structures and its chosen environment, Mr. O'Connor is walking around and monitoring their interactions. Mr. O'Connor is listening to one group as they discuss statements they have developed about their fictional animal. He asks the group some guiding questions: Which of these statements are evidence? How do you know they are evidence? What does that mean for the chances of survival of this animal in the specific environment? After the group has answered these questions, Mr. O'Connor asks the group if they would be willing to share their thinking process with the whole class. The group then uses a think-aloud to share the process they used to identify evidence that would show their animal would survive in one environment.

"We created a Snuggle with the following structure: It is cold-blooded. This keeps their temperature regulated by going in the sun to heat up and in the cold to cool down. Deborah said she thought that our animal, the Snuggle, could live in lots of different environments. We agreed, so our claim was that Snuggles can survive in the Arctic tundra. We talked about what we know about the Arctic tundra. It is a harsh environment without much precipitation. It is also so cold that the ground beneath the surface remains frozen all year. Jose said if the ground beneath the surface is frozen all year the Snuggle would not be able to regulate its temperature. We used the evidence about the Snuggle and about the Arctic tundra to decide that our claim was not true. We decided to change our claim to Snuggles would not survive in the Arctic tundra."

Mr. O'Connor asks the whole class to reflect on the thinking process that Deborah and her group just shared. "What were the two most important pieces of evidence for deciding the claim was not true?" Ally answers, "The fact that Snuggles are cold-blooded and that the Arctic tundra ground stays frozen." Mr. O'Connor tells students that this is an example of needing *relevant* and *sufficient* evidence. He asks students to look at the anchor chart and reread the definition of these terms.

The groups continue working on their models. Mr. O'Connor tells students to finish up their explanatory models and finalize their CER posters to present to the class. He tells them to use the sentence frames on the poster to help guide them. He reminds them that for the presentation he is expecting them to

1. report on their claim, supporting evidence, and reasoning;
2. include appropriate facts and relevant descriptive details;
3. use full sentences; and
4. speak clearly at an understandable pace.

Again Mr. O'Connor walks around monitoring students as they start to prepare their presentation posters. He provides feedback to students on their connections between claims and evidence and also on their use of appropriate academic language.

To launch the presentations, Mr. O'Connor says, "While groups are presenting, I want you to use the notetaking guide (see Table 4.4) that you have at your tables. Record the group number, their claim, the evidence they presented, and their reasoning." Mr. O'Connor demonstrates the notetaking guide using the snowball hare example.

Students are given a specific task that will strengthen their understanding of claims and evidence while listening to the presentations.

When the presentations are done, he asks the students to pair up and discuss each group's claim, evidence, and reasoning, answering two questions: (1) Was there sufficient and relevant evidence for the claim?, and (2) Did their reasoning support and justify the claim? Then he asks them to rate the presentation with a plus or minus. When the students have finished their discussions, Mr. O'Connor brings the class back together to debrief the presentations.

He has students reflect on each group's use of evidence and reasoning.

He then draws their attention to the bottom of the notetaking guide where it says *reflection*. He reads the prompts and gives the students time to think and write. He has a few students share. Brian states, "I understand that the evidence might support your claim, but it could also mean you need to change your claim." Then Lebron shares, "I learned that if you don't have sufficient evidence, you might make a wrong choice about the claim."

By stating examples of evidence and reasoning, Mr. O'Connor is providing feedback to the class.

Table 4.4. Notetaking and Reflection Guide

Group #	Claim	Evidence	Reasoning	Rating

Reflection: What have you learned about making a claim and identifying relevant evidence? What have you learned about justifying and supporting your claim with evidence?

Mr. O'Connor ends the class by complimenting his students on how well they did on creating a fictional animal with internal and external structures that help it survive in its ecosystem. He calls out specific examples of evidence and reasoning different students provided.

Think After Reading Activity

Mr. O'Connor constructed his lesson to engage and support his students in making claims, identifying evidence, and explaining their reasoning. The CER poster and his modeling of it helped students meet the learning targets. Reflect on the strategies and tasks he used in his lesson and identify the one you believe would be most relevant for your students. As you read the next section of this chapter, consider how the strategies we provide could be incorporated into lessons you teach.

IMPLEMENTING THE DISCIPLINARY USES OF EVIDENCE TEACHING FRAME

Next, we explain instructional strategies and tools that you can use to implement the Disciplinary Uses of Evidence Teaching Frame. Although many resources exist to help students identify evidence and use appropriate evidence to support claims, the strategies and tools we provide in the next section of this chapter address the specific elements of the SOAR practices in this Teaching Frame.

Instructional Strategy: Argument Evidence Scale

This strategy supports element 1, *Foster students' ability to analyze textual and/or oral evidence for relevancy.* The Argument Evidence Scale (Zwiers, O'Hara, & Pritchard, 2014b) (Figure 2.1), which you were introduced to in Chapter 2, engages students in a visual and hands-on process for prioritizing and weighing evidence on two sides of an issue. Students write each piece of evidence they find on different cards. They then place the cards on the appropriate side of the scale to determine which position is stronger.

Why Use This Strategy: Students need to understand that different types of evidence with different degrees of relevancy exist. The Argument Evidence Scale is an effective way to foster your students' ability to distinguish between those types and to evaluate their relative strength. Visually representing evidence also helps students notice holes in evidence and identify topics that need more investigation.

When to Use This Strategy: The visual and kinesthetic aspects of this strategy make it an effective way to introduce your students to the process of identifying evidence and analyzing it for relevancy.

How to Use This Strategy: Provide each pair of students with their own scale and a set of large and small blank cards. After they identify evidence for each side of the argument, students write each piece on the appropriately sized card and place them on the scale. Pairs of students then compare their evidence and try to determine which is more convincing.

Example Lesson

1. Explain to students that they are going to work on analyzing textual evidence for relevancy. Point to the anchor chart you created earlier and ask them to review the types of evidence (e.g., facts or statistical data, judgment or opinion, analogy, and testimony or anecdotal).
2. Begin by stating a claim to the class such as "Baseball is the best sport." Have student partners discuss evidence for that claim using the anchor chart. Have them share responses and name the type of evidence. With younger students you can just have them give reasons and then press them to make it evidence-based; for example, "Baseball is fun" or "Boys and girls can play baseball."
3. Next, provide the whole class with the same claim. An example could be a claim about a character in a book or a scientific or historical claim.
4. Now distribute varying evidence regarding that claim and the Argument Evidence Scale. Have students discuss the evidence and place it on either the pro or the con side.
5. Once the evidence is placed on either the pro or the con side of the scale, have students discuss the evidence in light of relevancy. Then have students discuss whether the evidence is sufficient.

Instructional Strategy: What Makes You Say That?

This strategy supports element 1, *Foster students' ability to analyze textual and/or oral evidence for relevancy.* What Makes You Say That? provides a specific set of prompts for students to use to share their ideas about a topic and support them with evidence. By facilitating a structured exchange of ideas among students, What Makes You Say That? promotes evidence-based reasoning and encourages students to consider different viewpoints and multiple perspectives.

Why Use This Strategy: This is an instructional strategy in which students prompt one another to justify their thinking and elaborate on their ideas. It helps students meet CCSS and NGSS expectations by having them demonstrate the ability to provide evidence for their claims and explain themselves using clear examples. It also provides support and structure that students can follow to practice these skills and engage in extended opportunities for purposeful explanations of the thinking behind their responses.

When to Use This Strategy: Because the prompts are relatively easy to teach and learn, this strategy can be adapted for use at any grade level and across a variety of content areas. However, you do need to identify topics that are most appropriate for the focus on claims and evidence.

How to Use This Strategy: Introduce this strategy with a visually interesting image, as it provides access for students who represent a wide range of academic abilities. Project the image for the class to see and model the prompts for students as a think-aloud. Encourage them to add to the prompt "What do you notice?" and to explain their reasoning. Introduce the students to another visual text and have them begin the protocol.

Example Lesson

1. Begin by selecting an image or piece of art that ties into your curriculum. We have used different types of images; for instance, Norman Rockwell's *The Problem We All Live With* and illustrations from Chris Van Allsburg's *The Mysteries of Harris Burdick*. Or you can use a historical painting, such as *Sunday Morning in the Mines* by Charles Christian Nahl, or Vincent van Gogh's *Café Terrace at Night*.
2. Project your image so that all students can see it. Create two columns on your whiteboard. On one side, write "What do you notice?" and on the other side, write "What makes you say that?" Begin by asking students the first question: "What do you notice?" Record one student's response and write it under that column and then ask the student, "What makes you say that?" Record that response. Repeat this process with other students. You are pushing students to think about evidence that supports their claim.
3. Add a row to your chart: "When do you think this is taking place?" and "What makes you say that?," repeating the same process as in step 2.
4. Add another row: "What can you say about the people?" and "What makes you say that?" as in step 2.
5. Once you have completed the demonstration, provide each pair of students with another visual text and have them respond to the prompts.
6. When students have completed their What Makes You Say That? responses, debrief with the students to check their claims and evidence.

Strategies for Enabling Beginning Readers to Identify Evidence

One approach you can use is to begin by having students identify evidence from visual texts like pictures or photographs. Engaging beginning readers in this way allows them to understand the concept of what we mean by evidence before having to find it in a written text. Start by engaging the whole class in the process by portraying a visual text and asking students questions like "How do we know . . . by looking at this picture? What evidence is in this picture that tells us . . . ?" Then have students work in pairs to look at other visual texts and answer similar questions. Another way to approach this would be to have students listen to a story and identify evidence about a key guiding question. It is a good idea to read the story more than once and make sure that the key guiding question is stated and posted for students to see. Model your thought process for the students and show how you would identify evidence to answer the key questions. These approaches also work well for struggling readers and English learners.

Instructional Strategy: Discussion Web

This strategy supports element 2, *Provide and support multiple opportunities for students to identify and use sufficient evidence to support claims in disciplinary writing and speaking.* The Discussion Web strategy (Alvermann, 1991) uses a specific type of graphic organizer for teaching your students to consider both sides of an argument or issue before drawing a conclusion. A Discussion Web (see Figure 4.1) helps students organize their thinking,

Figure 4.1. Discussion Web

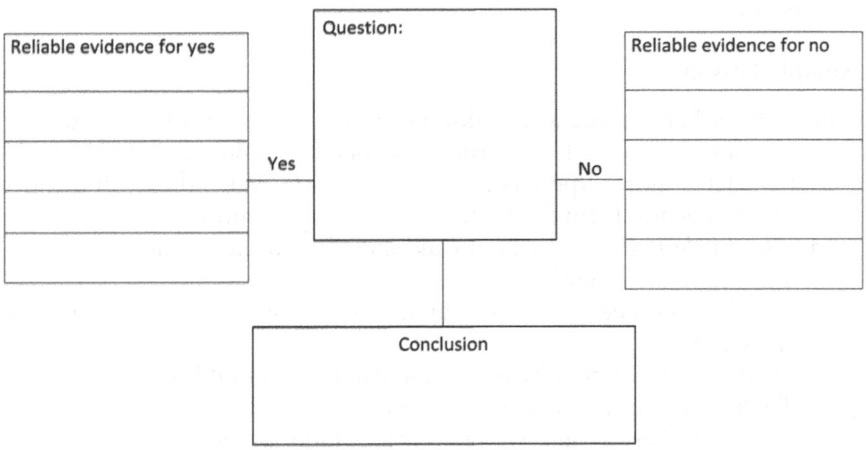

examine different perspectives, and weigh evidence about an issue, character, or situation that generates controversy or has no simple solution. For primary students, you can use a read-aloud and create a class Discussion Web that can be filled in together. For English learners, you can provide a few examples of evidence that they can place in the correct column to get them started.

Why Use This Strategy: Students need practice reading and discussing controversial and complex topics that require them to think critically. A Discussion Web provides students with a visual framework that will help them learn to make convincing arguments in support of a conclusion as well as to explain the thinking that connects their evidence to that conclusion.

When to Use This Strategy: The most appropriate time to use this strategy is when your students are studying a topic they can view from different perspectives and the learning target focuses on making claims and weighing evidence. The use of a Discussion Web will enable your students to clarify their thinking about ideas, activate their background knowledge about a topic, and set their own purposes for reading.

How to Use This Strategy: Identify a reading selection that presents conflicting opinions about a character or that deals with a controversial issue. Develop a focus question you want your students to consider and introduce the Discussion Web. After your students have read the selection, have them work in pairs or small groups to generate reasons for answering yes and then generate reasons for answering no. Finally, ask students to weigh the evidence on both sides of the issue and to attempt to reach consensus on a conclusion.

Example Lesson

1. Begin by either reading a text aloud or have students read the text.
2. Ask a question about the text that has opposing points of view. As students have more experiences with Discussion Webs, they will identify the main question from the text. Here are some examples:
    a. *The Little Red Hen* by Paul Galdone: Should the red hen have refused to share with her friends?
    b. *My Teacher Sleeps in School* by Leatie Weiss: Does Ms. Marsh sleep at school?
    c. *Bridge to Terabithia* by Katherine Paterson: Should Jess have gone back to Terabithia after the accident?
    d. Social Studies: Should we celebrate Columbus Day?
    e. Science: Should animals be kept in zoos?

3. Model with the class how to work with a partner to find evidence for the yes and no columns.
4. Have students think individually about the questions and jot down some evidence from the text on a piece of paper.
5. Ask students to pair up to identify and discuss evidence that supports the yes and no positions. They then record each piece of evidence under yes or no.
6. After they have exhausted all their evidence, ask students to join another pair to make a foursome. Pairs share all their evidence, come to consensus on a pro or con point of view, and share their responses with the class.
7. Have students write their own conclusion (i.e., claim) using the evidence and reasoning behind their decision.
8. Have students reflect on their learning using this strategy.

Instructional Strategy: Claim and Evidence Sort

This strategy supports element 2, *Provide and support multiple opportunities for students to identify and use sufficient evidence to support claims in disciplinary writing and speaking*. This is a strategy in which students practice using information as evidence to support a given claim. They focus on distinguishing between relevant and irrelevant evidence as related to the claim and then demonstrate their thinking by sorting the individual evidence cards. The card-sort activity facilitates your students' ability to explain the connections between the evidence and the claim as they use their conversation skills with a partner.

Why Use This Strategy: Considering claims, searching for sufficient evidence, and explaining their reasoning causes students to think critically about the connections between claims and evidence. Discussions of evidence also build student understanding of the concepts they are studying and encourage students to discuss and develop their own ideas while building on the ideas of others.

When to Use This Strategy: The CCSS and NGSS require students to support claims with logical reasoning and relevant data as well as to analyze different pieces of evidence in support of an argument. A Claim and Evidence Sort is an effective tool that you can use to address these standards. In our experience it is particularly useful when students need to move beyond simply identifying relevant evidence to explaining why that evidence is or is not relevant.

How to Use This Strategy: Create a set of claim and evidence cards related to a topic your students are studying. Then distribute one set of cards to each student pair. Students read the information on the evidence cards and decide whether or not each piece supports the claim, sorting the cards accordingly. As students discuss the information on the cards, they explain their reasoning about why the information is relevant or irrelevant to the claim. To make this more accessible to your early language learners, thoughtful pairing of those students with more proficient readers will enable them to participate in the card sort.

Example Lesson

1. Explain to students that they are going to work in pairs to sort for claims and evidence. In their sorts they will have two claims (e.g., "The Grand Canyon was created by erosion," "The Grand Canyon was created by weathering") and evidence. Have students discuss which evidence goes with which claim. When students complete the sort, have them explain their sorts and reasoning.
2. Have students do a second sort that has a claim (e.g., "*SpongeBob* is an educational TV show"), three subheadings (e.g., supports the claim, might support the claim, and does not support the claim), and evidence. Students discuss and decide where to place the evidence, and when they are done, they share their sort and reasoning.
3. Have students do a third sort that has a claim ("Kids should not be able to play the video game Fortnite") and six pieces of evidence. With their partner, have them read the evidence and rate it from relevant to not relevant. When students have completed the sort, have them share their reasoning.

Strategies for Teaching All Students to Support Claims with Evidence

We have three suggestions for addressing this challenge. First, use the model and non-model approach. Project a paper that represents the model and have student pairs identify the claim and evidence and share with the class. Then have them look at the reasoning while you deconstruct it to show them how the evidence is linked to and supports the claim. Now show your students the non-model (i.e., one that does not explain how the evidence is linked to the claim) and guide them through a collaborative process of constructing reasoning that supports the claim. Another approach would be to provide sentence frames for students to use in their papers, for instance: "This shows . . . because . . ." "The fact that . . . illustrates that . . . because . . ." "Based on the evidence, we know . . ." and "The evidence supports the claim because . . ." Finally, using the CER Checklist described in the Additional Implementation Considerations section on p. 121 reminds students of the importance of connecting the evidence to the claim.

Cross-Cutting Practice: Facilitating Acquisition of Academic Language

Building students' skills for identifying evidence and for using evidence to support claims relies heavily on their academic language proficiency. Effective teachers introduce the academic language demands of the texts and tasks and provide extended and supported opportunities for students to acquire and use the required academic language. The next set of instructional strategies and tools are designed to help you attend to the academic language needs of your students while working with them on disciplinary uses of evidence.

Instructional Strategy: Evidence Wall

This strategy supports element 1, *Introduce and/or refer to the academic language demands of texts and tasks.* An Evidence Wall is a collection of evidence and linguistic supports that are displayed on a wall, bulletin board, or other display surface in a classroom. The Evidence Wall is designed to be an interactive resource that students can use when identifying evidence, analyzing evidence for relevance, and using evidence to support a claim.

Why Use This Strategy: The Evidence Wall provides a place where students can centralize and organize evidence they collect while researching a claim. Collecting evidence is an important part of making a claim because it allows students to weigh different sides of an argument and eventually develop claims that they are able to defend. By organizing evidence in a central location, students are able to review the information they have collected and develop clear and relevant reasons to support their thinking.

When to Use This Strategy: You and your students should collaboratively build an Evidence Wall when they begin learning about the importance of claims, evidence, and reasoning. Creating a wall is also helpful when you introduce a unit's or lesson's essential question, because the wall will provide scaffolded support while your students research their responses.

How to Use This Strategy: Explain to students that as they identify pieces of evidence and use them to support a claim, they will be posting the pieces individually on the Evidence Wall for everyone to use as a resource. As the work continues, your students (and you if your support is needed) will work together to determine which evidence is most relevant and should continue to be displayed.

Example Lesson

1. Take a bulletin board and turn it into an Evidence Wall. Post the question you want students to use to create their claim, such as "Should plastic bags be banned?" "In *Stone Fox* by John Reynolds Gardiner, did Willy deserve to win?"
2. After discussing the academic language demands of writing a Claim, Evidence, and Reasoning paragraph or argumentative paragraph, introduce and post some sentence frames, transition words, and vocabulary that can be used as references as students begin working on their paragraphs.
3. With the students' help, identify and post graphs, photos, drawings, or realia that can be used as evidence for their claim.
4. Collaboratively create sentence frames or charts that show the connection between claim, evidence, and reasoning with your students.
5. It is important to keep the Evidence Wall alive. Co-create it with your students, reference content on it, and add to it as you see what students need.

Instructional Strategy: Rating Vocabulary

This strategy supports element 2, *Provide extended and supported opportunities for students to acquire and use the features of academic language.* Rating Vocabulary (Blachowicz, 1986) is a strategy in which students rate their knowledge of words at three different points in a lesson or unit: before they read the selection in which the words will appear, after they have read the selection, and after they have participated in a discussion of the selection. For young students still learning to read, this strategy can be used before and after they listen to you read a selection aloud or used with a guided reading group.

Why Use This Strategy: Rating Vocabulary encourages students to think metacognitively about their conceptual understanding of each word you introduce by helping them evaluate what they know and do not know about the specific terms. This process serves as a pre-reading or pre-listening activity to develop your students' metacognitive awareness about word meanings and as a post-reading or listening activity to help students assess their own learning.

When to Use This Strategy: This strategy can be used in any subject and at any grade level when students need scaffolding and support in acquiring the vocabulary feature of academic language. It is most effectively used at the beginning of a lesson or unit when you are introducing new terms to your students, who then return to these terms after reading and discussing the selection.

How to Use This Strategy: After identifying the most important words in an upcoming lesson or unit and giving students a Rating Vocabulary activity sheet (see Table 4.5), explain that they will be rating their knowledge of the words three different times, using a plus sign (+), a minus sign (–), or a question mark (?) to indicate how well they understand the words.

Example Lesson

1. Create a list of five to ten essential vocabulary words from the text the students are about to read.
2. Explain to students that they are going to be rating how well they know what the word means three different times: before they read the text, after they read the text, and after they have discussed the text.
3. Explain that they will enter a plus (+) if they know the meaning and can explain it to their partner; a minus (–) if they do not recognize the word; or a question mark (?) if they have heard the word before but are uncertain of what the word means.
4. Read each word aloud to the whole class and have students repeat it so that they pronounce the word correctly. Pause after each word and have the students rate the words in the Before Reading column of the activity sheet.
5. After rating is complete, ask students to share any predictions they may have about the selection.
6. Then have students silently read the selection, and when they have finished, rate the words again in the After Reading column.
7. Either in small groups or as a whole class, students then discuss the selection before completing the After Discussion column of the activity sheet.
8. With a partner or in a small group, students share their ratings by discussing what each word means; when in the process they figured out the meanings; and what, if any, words remain unknown.

Table 4.5. Rating Vocabulary

Word	Before Reading +, –, ?	After Reading +, –, ?	After Discussion +, –, ?	Definition

Cross-Cutting Practice: Fostering Metacognition

The skill of identifying evidence and then finding sufficient and relevant evidence to support claims is layered and complex. Students who do this effectively are generally more aware of their thinking processes and are capable of using strategies as needed to move forward with complex tasks. So effective teachers visibly enact and deconstruct metacognitive processes and strategies they expect students to use to help them become more independent learners. The following instructional strategies are designed to help you foster student metacognition to better equip them for disciplinary uses of evidence.

Instructional Strategy: Do Now

This strategy supports element 1, *Visibly enact metacognitive processes and/or strategies students are expected to use in support of disciplinary learning*. A Do Now is a strategy that engages students in a relatively brief, self-reflective process at the beginning and end of a lesson. It contains a list of actions related to the task students will be doing—in this case gathering evidence to support a claim—and helps make the learning targets and the purpose of learning activities clear. It also helps students reflect on which of the actions they need to improve upon.

Why Use This Strategy: Engaging your students in reflective processes is a critical step in developing their metacognitive knowledge of tasks, strategies, and themselves as learners. Establishing a Do Now routine at the beginning and end of lessons supports these goals and helps develop a culture of metacognition in your classroom.

When to Use This Strategy: As already noted, a Do Now is best done on a regular basis at the start of a lesson and again at the end. This strategy can be utilized across grade levels for any content area. For instance, in primary grades the Do Now could focus on different conventions of writing.

How to Use This Strategy: You should introduce your Do Now at the start of a lesson and ask students to mark which actions they will attempt to improve upon during the instructional activity. At the end of the lesson, students may return to their Do Now and reflect on how they improved in those areas.

Example Lesson

1. Begin the lesson by asking students to review what they have been studying and the learning targets for the day. For this example, we are using claims and evidence.

2. Distribute and read the Do Now sheet containing the following:
    - I will identify evidence that is connected to my claim.
    - I will identify enough evidence to support my claim.
    - I will choose the best evidence to support my claim.
    - I will explain how my evidence is connected to my claim.
3. Have students think about which item(s) they need to improve upon, check those items on the Do Now sheet, and then explain their choices to their partner.
4. After students have completed their task, they revisit their Do Now and discuss with their partner how they were able to improve in that area.
5. Debrief as a class. Which area did you work on? How did you approach the work differently?

Instructional Strategy: Model and Non-Model

This strategy supports element 2, *Deconstruct metacognitive processes and/or strategies that support disciplinary learning*. Virtually all teachers understand that explicitly modeling a strategy or work product helps students understand what is expected of them. However, in our experience, teachers often overlook the potential of non-models for helping their students learn. Showing models and non-models of a work product helps students differentiate between good ones and ones that need improvement, which in turn provides students with opportunities to see where changes need to be made.

Why Use This Strategy: While models help students see what it is that they are supposed to produce, teachers can create non-models that are specific to the areas students need to address to improve. Students learn to identify and diagnose problems, develop their own revision skills, and see how they could produce an acceptable product. In this way, non-models create opportunities for authentic revision, which increases the likelihood that the learning will transfer to your students' own work.

When to Use This Strategy: Model and Non-Model can be used across disciplines and in all grade- and ability-level classrooms. Nearly everything that you want students to accomplish, whether a thought process, strategy, or work product, can have some kind of model and non-model incorporated into your instruction. Models and non-models are particularly useful for students who you think might struggle or fail and for students who are learning about a particular element (e.g., distinguishing between relevant and irrelevant evidence) for the first time.

How to Use This Strategy: You must first identify or create a model and non-model appropriate for your instructional focus. Sometimes anonymous examples from former students are the most authentic samples. Show students the one that models what you want them to do or produce. Have students discuss with a partner what makes this a good model. Write those ideas on the whiteboard. Next, show them the non-model. Ask students to work with a partner to identify differences between the two examples and to work collaboratively to make the necessary changes to the non-model. Finally, make sure you provide opportunities to discuss and compare the revisions the student pairs made so that they learn what is and is not appropriate about the model and non-model.

Example Lesson

1. Explain to students that they are going to look at a Claim-Evidence-Reasoning paragraph or an argumentative paragraph written by a student. Project it on the whiteboard and read the entire paragraph aloud. If you are working with students who have not had much experience looking for claims, evidence, and reasoning, you would identify each piece for the students as a think-aloud. Then you can move into having students identify them together (gradual release of responsibility), as in steps 2–4.
2. Ask students to work with their partner and identify the claim. Call on students to explain why they think it is the claim. Ask if anybody has another idea. Confirm the claim and underline it.
3. Ask partners to identify the evidence. Call on students to explain why they think the information is evidence. Circle the evidence.
4. Ask partners to identify the reasoning. Call on students to explain their thinking. Be sure to point out how the evidence is tied to and justifies the claim. Highlight the reasoning. You should also point out academic language and transition words that are used.
5. Give students another model paragraph and have them underline the claim, circle the evidence, and highlight the reasoning. Have students share and debrief as a class.
6. Then project a non-model paragraph, have the students identify the claim, and ask them what can be done to it to make it better. Collaboratively rewrite the claim with your students. Ask them to identify the evidence, discuss what is wrong with it—not enough, not relevant—and have them come up with some solutions. Next, ask them to share and debrief their ideas and collaboratively rewrite them. Finally, follow the same process for the reasoning.
7. Next, give pairs of students another non-model paragraph and have them rewrite it. Choose some students to project their rewrites and discuss how and why they changed the original to make it better. Debrief as a class.

Cross-Cutting Practice: Monitoring and Guiding

In order for students to effectively identify oral and textual evidence and build arguments using relevant and sufficient evidence, they need in-the-moment guidance and feedback as they work on relevant tasks. It is very important that teachers monitor students' thought processes and provide feedback to address any misconceptions or information gaps. Teachers should also adjust their instruction and tasks as needed. The instructional strategies that are described next are designed to help you monitor and guide your students' learning as they identify evidence and use that evidence to support claims.

Instructional Strategy: Fist to Four

This tool supports element 1, *Monitor learning and adjust instruction, supports, and/or disciplinary tasks to meet student needs*. Fist to Four is a rating scale for which students use the fingers on one hand to indicate their understanding of a topic or readiness for a task. For instance, four fingers indicate deep understanding; no fingers indicate a lack of understanding. In the context of Disciplinary Uses of Evidence, we recommend you use Fist to Four to have students rate the relevancy of evidence, thus serving as a tool for you to monitor their understanding of the claim and evidence they are investigating.

Why Use This Strategy: Fist to Four provides you with a quick formative assessment as to where your students are with the lesson. The formative nature of this information allows you to consider other ways to present the material or clarify student understanding as you proceed. It also gives you a sense of who may need individual assistance.

When to Use This Strategy: This strategy should be used when you want to provide your students with a simple, nonthreatening, formative way for them to indicate their level of understanding or to express an opinion.

How to Use This Strategy: Create a rating scale with students. At the appropriate point(s) in the lesson, ask students to use the Fist to Four rating as a way for you to monitor their understanding.

Example Lesson

1. Ask students to remind you of the strategy Fist to Four. Explain to students that for this unit they are going to use Fist to Four as a way to rate the relevancy of their evidence. It is also a way for you to check their understanding.

2. Define relevancy or point to the anchor chart, stating that relevant evidence is evidence that directly relates to the claim.
3. Create a Fist to Four evidence rating anchor chart with your students. Here is an example:
   0: Not relevant at all. It has nothing to do with the claim.
   1: A little bit relevant. It is superficially related to the claim.
   2: Somewhat relevant. Good to know but not clearly connected to the claim.
   3: Very relevant. Connects to the claim.
   4: Extremely relevant. Specific and connects to the claim.
4. Model the process for students. For instance, state the claim: "Eating too much candy causes a stomachache." Read the evidence and have students use Fist to Four to rate it (e.g., "I ate all of my Halloween candy and nothing happened," "My dog ate my Halloween candy and threw up," "My sister ate her Halloween candy and had a stomachache for two days," "I ate some of my Halloween candy and didn't feel great," "I ate my Halloween candy and it was really good.") Note the ratings of your students to see which ones need further instruction. After each statement, have students explain to their partner why they choose that rating.

Instructional Strategy: Peer Feedback

This tool supports element 2, *Provide written and/or oral feedback during lessons to promote disciplinary learning.* Peer Feedback is the practice of students giving and receiving constructive information from one another about their performance on a learning task. The primary goal, as it is with all types of feedback, is to help students understand what they have done well and what steps to take for improvement. Peer Feedback also provides students with opportunities to learn from one another.

Why Use This Strategy: The interaction between students who give feedback and those who receive it helps both giver and receiver develop as learners. Peer Feedback encourages collaborative learning as students learn to listen to one another, teach one another about the learning tasks, and respond thoughtfully rather than emotionally to constructive criticism. In addition, learning to detect errors and provide suggestions for improvement helps students take more responsibility for their own learning.

When to Use This Strategy: While Peer Feedback should always supplement rather than substitute for teacher feedback, it is a way in which students can receive personalized feedback when it is impossible for you to provide it. In our experience, however, one of your biggest challenges will be getting students to make specific suggestions instead of just saying, "Good job!" So Peer Feedback should be used only after you have explained the criteria, modeled the process, and given students the opportunity to practice.

How to Use This Strategy: Begin by explaining that giving feedback to other students is a way to help their peers improve and grow while also helping themselves. When introducing the process to your students, we recommend starting small by asking students to review something short and simple. This can be done whole-class or in small groups.

Example Lesson

1. Explain to your students the purpose of Peer Feedback: It is not used to judge or evaluate one another's work but to help one another improve. Feedback is specific and actionable. It must be tied to a rubric or set of criteria. It should inform the student's partner what they need to do to meet the criteria. It also helps students improve their own work by thinking more deeply about the rubric or learning targets.
2. Project different examples of feedback and discuss with students which are effective (e.g., "Did you consider a way to connect this evidence to your claim?," "Is there another way you could explain your reasoning?") and which are not effective (e.g., "Good job," "I like your paper").
3. Model giving effective feedback to a sample student work product. As you model, ask students to identify what you are saying and doing that makes it effective. When you have finished, have students discuss your model with a partner. For younger students, you could pause during your modeling and point out the type of language you used based on the criteria, rubric, or learning target.
4. Next, model feedback that is not effective and have students discuss how to improve it.
5. Then provide pairs of students with a sample work product and ask them to develop feedback on one specific area such as, "Was the evidence relevant and sufficient?" or "Were there enough details?" You may distribute feedback sentence stems for them to use as support (e.g., "Did you consider . . . ?," "What if . . . ?," "Maybe try . . . ," "I noticed . . . ," "I wondered . . ."). Have students share examples of their feedback.
6. As students gain confidence, you can have them provide feedback to their partner's work.

Foundational Practice: Designing Instruction

Like the foundation of a house, the Foundational Practice needs to be the strong basis on which the High-Impact and Cross-Cutting Practices are constructed. You have to deconstruct the standards and the High-Impact Practice that is being addressed in the lesson or unit to truly understand what it is the students are expected to understand and do. Once there is a deep understanding of the standards and learning targets, you can address how you are going to structure your lesson so that the tasks and activities are connected. You also need to know how you are going to have your students demonstrate their learning and how the tasks and activities will scaffold that learning. The instructional strategy that follows will help you understand what element 2 would look like when planning your unit or lesson.

Instructional Strategy: Backward Design

This strategy supports element 2, *Structure and connect tasks that support the learning target.* Backward Design (Wiggins & McTighe, 2005) (see Figure 4.2) is a process for developing curricula and learning experiences by setting goals before choosing instructional methods and assessment tools. The process begins with a consideration of the alignment of the CCSS, the High-Impact Practice, and learning targets of your lesson or unit and proceeds backward to the creation of lessons that support your students in achieving those goals.

Figure 4.2. Structuring of Lessons and Connecting Tasks

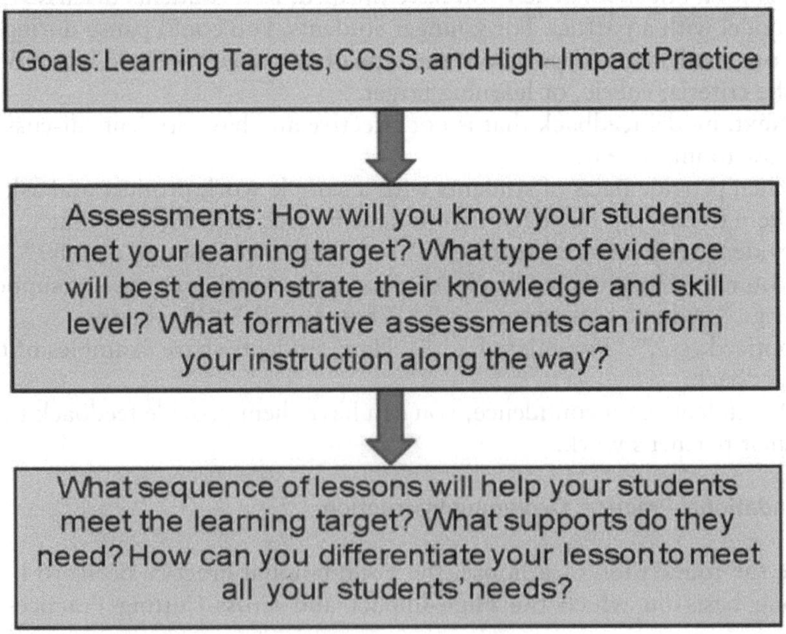

Why Use This Strategy: Starting your instructional planning with the end goal in mind, rather than with the first lesson you plan to teach, enables you to design a series of lessons, learning tasks, and assessments that have a coherent and achievable focus. This beginning-with-the-end approach provides you with a structure you can follow when designing your lessons and increases the likelihood that your students will reach the learning target.

When to Use This Strategy: Because this strategy is a process for designing curricula and learning experiences, you use Backward Design when you begin planning your unit or lesson to clarify your own thinking about what it is you want students to know and be able to do. You also use it when you want to reexamine your instructional tools and activities to ensure that they are coherent and will help students meet the learning goal.

How to Use This Strategy: You begin by reviewing the content standards you expect your students to meet during a lesson or unit and by considering how those standards are aligned with the High-Impact Practice. Then you identify the essential knowledge and skills that students will need to learn, and you determine the most appropriate way(s) for students to demonstrate that learning. In other words, how will you assess whether and to what degree your students have met the learning targets? Based on this planning, you create a lesson or series of lessons that contain structured and connected learning tasks that support the learning targets.

Example Lesson

1. Begin by articulating what it is you want your students to know and be able to do at the end of the lesson or unit. In other words, what knowledge and skills do you want them to learn? This should be based on the standards and High-Impact Practice.

   Example:
   First grade W1.2—Write informative or explanatory texts in which they name a topic, supply some facts about the topic, and provide some sense of closure.
   RI1.2: Identify the main topic and retell key details of a text.
   High-Impact Practice: Disciplinary Uses of Evidence foster students' ability to identify textual evidence.
2. Next, think about how the students will demonstrate the knowledge and skills they have attained. What will be acceptable evidence? What formative assessments can you have students do along the way to show their progress so that you can make any needed adjustments to your plan? Will you ask students to write an essay, create a model, respond to short response questions, or create a portfolio?

Example:
Students highlight details, facts, and evidence in a text.
Teacher uses a checklist of the details and facts students are using in their discussion as a formative assessment.
Students draw a picture and write an explanatory sentence about a bird.

3. Knowing what the end product or demonstration of learning will be will guide you in planning structured and connected tasks to help students be successful in reaching those goals. If you are asking students to write an essay, you have to ask yourself, "What do my students need to know in order to be able to write that essay successfully? What scaffolds or supports do they need? What do I need to model? How will I introduce the rubric? How can I differentiate so that I reach all of my students?"

Example of Sequenced Lesson

1. Explain what facts are. Give some examples. Read text about birds. Have students discuss facts they heard. Chart them on the whiteboard.
2. Read a poem about birds. Model how to highlight facts. Have students share the facts with their partners.
3. Project pictures of different birds. Have students discuss the details and facts about each bird. Use a checklist to monitor students' progress. Write their facts on the whiteboard with the picture of the bird.
4. Have student pairs read a text and highlight facts. Use as a formative assessment to see if students are ready to draw and write their sentence.
5. Have students draw a picture and write their sentence using facts about birds. Students can use the facts on the whiteboard.

ADDITIONAL IMPLEMENTATION CONSIDERATIONS

Developing arguments to support claims with clear reasoning and relevant evidence is a performance expectation across content areas at all grade levels. For example, the NGSS expect students in kindergarten through 2nd grade to engage in argument from evidence by building on prior experiences and comparing ideas about the natural and designed worlds. With the flow of information coming from social media and the Internet, it is important for students to develop these 21st-century skills and become critical consumers of knowledge. In this section we provide additional resources you can use in your classroom to support students in Disciplinary Uses of Evidence.

Claim-Evidence-Reasoning (CER) Checklist

CER Checklists (see Table 4.6) are powerful tools to help students attain autonomy by internalizing the steps to create a finished product. First, use the checklist as a think-aloud, demonstrating how to use it to confirm that all the steps are included in the work and what to do if any are missing. Then have students use the checklist themselves to verify that they have included all the steps and to make any necessary corrections. Checklists can also be used with peers to check one another's work. Shifting responsibility to students helps them understand the expectations.

Table 4.6. Claim-Evidence-Reasoning (CER) Checklist

Name______________________ Date______________________

Claim	Underline your claim My claim answers the question. My claim can't be answered with a yes or no answer. My claim doesn't include the word because. There are no pronouns (I, you, me, we, they, us, him, her, them) in my claim.
Evidence	Highlight your evidence Each piece of evidence or data supports the claim. Each piece of evidence is relevant (appropriate) to the claim. There is sufficient (enough) evidence to support the claim.
Reasoning	Put a box around your reasoning Explains why your evidence supports the claim. Some of my evidence has a different justification for why it supports the claim. My reasoning explains how the evidence connects to the claim.

Claim-Evidence-Reasoning (CER) Rubric

CER Rubrics (see Table 4.7) are another powerful tool for you and your students. Like a checklist, it helps students understand what is expected of them. Begin by explaining the rubric and projecting a sample paper to the class. Do a think-aloud to deconstruct the paper, using the rubric and assigning a point value for each criterion to help students understand what the rubric means. Write a modeled or shared writing piece with the class, referencing the rubric as you write. Have students use the rubric to score themselves or to provide peer feedback.

Table 4.7. Claim-Evidence-Reasoning (CER) Rubric

	1 point	2 points	3 points
Claim	Makes an inaccurate claim.	Makes an accurate, but incomplete or vague claim.	Makes an accurate and complete claim.
Evidence	Evidence is inappropriate or it does not support the claim.	Provides appropriate, but insufficient evidence. May include some inappropriate evidence.	Provides appropriate and sufficient evidence to support claim.
Reasoning	Reasoning is not appropriate or does not link the claim to the evidence.	Provides reasoning that links some of the evidence to the claim and explains how it supports the claim.	Provides accurate and complete reasoning that links all or most of the evidence to the claim and explains how the evidence supports the claim.

CONCLUSION

The purpose of this chapter has been to deepen your understanding of the Disciplinary Uses of Evidence Teaching Frame by unpacking the language of and rationale for the instructional practices that comprise it. The model lesson and associated classroom vignette provide additional insight into these practices by illustrating the dynamic and interdependent ways in which they work together in the context of a Teaching Frame to drive both teacher and student growth. Supporting students' ability to develop arguments using appropriate evidence requires developing the academic language of argumentation, providing constructive feedback on their use of evidence, and ultimately equipping them to find and use evidence independently.

Finally, the instructional strategies and tools are designed to deepen your understanding of the Disciplinary Uses of Evidence Teaching Frame and to provide you with concrete examples of approaches teachers are currently using in their classrooms to implement it. These strategies will equip you to develop your students' analytical thinking and argumentative writing skills.

CHAPTER 5

Disciplinary Communication

This chapter introduces you to Disciplinary Communication, the final Teaching Frame of the four SOAR frames. The goal of Disciplinary Communication is to have students talk and write as a way to process the content they are learning. Examples of oral communication are asking and answering questions, think-pair-share, interviews, debates, and oral reports. Examples of written communication are emails, blogs, reflective journals, letters, and essays. The High-Impact Practice focuses on structuring, strengthening, and supporting the quantity and quality of students' oral and written communication using academic language. Two essential elements make up this practice: Effective teachers provide opportunities for students to produce and fortify both oral communication (element 1) and written communication (element 2). Please take a few minutes to review the Disciplinary Communication Teaching Frame in Table 5.1.

USING THE SOAR LENS TO PLAN AND REFLECT

We will now take a deeper look at the Disciplinary Communication Teaching Frame by examining a non-model of a lesson, considering why this is a non-model and how we can use SOAR guiding questions to strengthen the lesson. Then we will analyze an annotated model of the lesson and step into a classroom with an illustrative vignette.

Think Before Reading Activity

Disciplinary Communication empowers students with critical speaking and writing skills that help them develop more language and deepen content understanding. As you read the model lesson and vignette in this chapter, consider how Ms. Alvarez addresses the language needs of her students to support their communication. How could you utilize these ideas with your students to increase the quantity and quality of their oral and written communication?

Table 5.1. Disciplinary Communication Teaching Frame

HIGH-IMPACT PRACTICE	Disciplinary Communication (DC) **Element 1:** Provide multiple and supported opportunities for students to produce and fortify original disciplinary oral communication appropriate to task, purpose, and audience **Element 2:** Provide extended and supported opportunities for students to produce and fortify original disciplinary written communication appropriate to task, purpose, and audience		
CROSS-CUTTING PRACTICES	Facilitating Acquisition of Academic Language (FAAL) **Element 1:** Introduce and/or refer to the academic language demands of texts and tasks **Element 2:** Provide extended and supported opportunities for students to acquire and use the features of academic language	Fostering Metacognition for Disciplinary Learning (FM) **Element 1:** Visibly enact metacognitive processes and/or strategies students are expected to use in support of disciplinary learning **Element 2:** Deconstruct metacognitive processes and/or strategies that support disciplinary learning	Monitoring and Guiding Disciplinary Learning (MG) **Element 1:** Monitor learning and adjust instruction, supports, and/or disciplinary tasks to meet student needs **Element 2:** Provide written and/or oral feedback during lessons to promote disciplinary learning
FOUNDATIONAL PRACTICE	Designing Instruction for Disciplinary Thinking and Understanding (DI) **Element 1:** Set disciplinary learning targets that are aligned with ELA/Literacy CCSS and the target high-impact practice **Element 2:** Structure and connect tasks that support the learning targets **Element 3:** Establish high expectations that support the learning targets and maintain the intellectual rigor of classroom activities and tasks		

Kindergarten Non-Model Lesson

The teacher who created the non-model has been working with her kindergarten students on identifying key details in a story, asking and answering questions, and retelling stories. They have been reading books by Dr. Seuss.

Let's think about why this is a non-model. The teacher plans to have students engage in oral communication during the lesson, and we can see the standards clearly stated in the lesson plan. Certainly, it appears from the plan that students will have different opportunities to communicate orally. The teacher does supply the students with picture cards to help them in sequencing. However, it is unclear what supports or guidance the teacher will offer to strengthen the quality of students' oral communication skills. Furthermore, we do not see any stated plan to integrate written activity of any type into the lesson. The teacher could use the following questions as she plans the lesson to help her address these key elements and elevate instruction:

- How might I structure my lesson to include both oral and written communication activities to engage all students?
- What supports or guidance can I provide to increase the quality of my students' oral and written communication?

Now let's consider how she addresses the three Cross-Cutting Practices. For Facilitating the Acquisition of Academic Language, this lesson plan does

Standards

CCSS.ELA-LITERACY.RL.1.3 Describe characters, settings, and major events in a story, using key details.
CCSS.ELA-LITERACY.RL.1.2 Retell stories, including key details, and demonstrate understanding of their central message or lesson.
CCSS.ELA-LITERACY.SL.1.2 Ask and answer questions about key details in a text read-aloud or information presented orally or through other media.

- Launch the lesson by providing a brief biography of Dr. Seuss and explain to students why we are studying this author.
- Ask students what they do when it is rainy outside and have them discuss it with their partner.
- Read the book *The Cat in the Hat* to the class. Then ask students to sit knee to knee with their elbow partner and ask and answer these questions: Who is the story about? What happens in the story? Where does it take place?
- Reread the story to the class. Then engage student pairs in an activity to sort and arrange pictures and sentence strips into an appropriate story sequence. Walk around and monitor students as they are engaged in this activity.
- Ask pairs to retell each other the story in the correct sequence. Listen to the pairs and correct them as needed.
- When they have finished, lead a whole-class discussion about the moral of the story.

not address academic language explicitly. Since there are multiple academic language demands reflected in the standards for this lesson (e.g., asking and answering questions, sequencing and retelling a story), it is very important that the teacher explicitly helps students acquire and understand the academic language needed to engage in these tasks. Younger students especially need language supports to assist them in engaging in these types of tasks. The teacher could ask the following questions as she plans the lesson:

- What language supports can I design, adapt, or adopt to help my students acquire and use the academic language needed to complete the tasks successfully?
- Where in the lesson could I provide examples of both oral and written communication as a guide for my students' use of academic language?

In the lesson plan it is not clear that the teacher will visibly enact metacognitive strategies or processes during the lesson. Fostering student metacognition is very central to fortifying their oral and written output. The teacher could ask the following questions as she plans the lesson for this Cross-Cutting Practice:

- What process or strategy should I model for my students so they can successfully ask and answer questions?
- What process or strategy do I need to demonstrate so that my students understand how to sequence the events in a story?

In the non-model we do see a stated intention to monitor students. However, there is no specific information on the type of feedback or redirection students might need. It is always important to anticipate the types of feedback students might need and to generate in advance ideas for providing it. This can include planning for specific questions that could be used during the lesson. The teacher could ask the following questions as she plans this lesson:

- How will I monitor and track students as they are engaged in pair work?
- What kind of feedback can I give my students to help them meet the learning target?

We do see evidence of the Foundational Practice. The standards are listed, although there is no explicit link to the High-Impact Practice, Disciplinary Communication. The teacher could ask the following questions as she plans the lesson:

- How do the tasks I developed connect and work together to help students reach the learning targets?
- Where in the lesson can I remind students of the learning targets?
- How can I maintain high expectations for my students throughout the lesson?

Kindergarten SOAR Model Lesson With Annotations

Now we are going to guide you through a process that will deepen your understanding of how SOAR can be used as a lens to plan. Let's look at this lesson again, only this time the teacher has planned her lesson using the SOAR Teaching Frame. As in previous chapters we have annotated the model lesson for the five practices in the Disciplinary Communication Teaching Frame to explicitly indicate where they appear.

As you read the annotated lesson (see Table 5.2), note how intentional and thoughtful this lesson is and how all the practices in the Teaching Frame work together to support the learning targets.

Table 5.2. Kindergarten Annotated Model Lesson

Disciplinary Communication (DC) Teaching Frame Elements	Teacher Actions
Designing Instruction E1–Teacher aligns the High-Impact Practice to CCSS and NGSS	DC-E1: Provide multiple and supported opportunities for students to produce and fortify original disciplinary oral communication appropriate to task, purpose, and audience DC-E2: Provide extended and supported opportunities for students to produce and fortify original disciplinary written communication appropriate to task, purpose, and audience CCSS.ELA-LITERACY.RL.1.3. Describe characters, settings, and major events in a story, using key details. CCSS.ELA-LITERACY.RL.1.2. Retell stories, including key details, and demonstrate understanding of their central message or lesson. CCSS.ELA-LITERACY.SL.1.2. Ask and answer questions about key details in a text read aloud or information presented orally or through other media. CCSS.ELA-LITERACY.W.1.1. Write opinion pieces in which they introduce the topic or name the book they are writing about, state an opinion, supply a reason for the opinion, and provide some sense of closure. ELD Standard: Offering and supporting opinions and negotiating with others in communicative exchanges.
Designing Instruction E1–Teacher explicitly states standards and learning targets to the students	Introduce the standards to the students. Remind students that they are spending time reading Dr. Seuss books. Ask students to read aloud the learning targets for today: • I can retell the story. • I can use full sentences to ask and answer questions about a story. • I can write about my opinion.

Table continues on next page

Table 5.2. Kindergarten Annotated Model Lesson (continued)

Disciplinary Communication (DC) Teaching Frame Elements	Teacher Actions
Disciplinary Communication E1–Teacher provides opportunity for students to produce disciplinary oral communication	Launch the lesson by providing a brief biography of Dr. Seuss. Have students look at the cover of the book and tell their neighbor what they notice.
Facilitating Acquisition of Academic Language E2–Students are given opportunity to acquire and use academic language in a meaningful way	Ask students what the word "rhyme" means and how rhyming works in a Dr. Seuss story.
Disciplinary Communication E1–Teacher provides opportunity for students to produce disciplinary oral communication Designing Instruction E3–Teacher establishes high expectations that support the learning targets	Ask students what they do when it is rainy outside and say to the students: "Turn and talk to your partner and tell them some things you do at home when it is raining."
Facilitating Acquisition of Academic Language E1–Teacher refers to the academic language demands of the task by reminding students to use complete sentences	Remind students to always use full sentences when answering questions.
Disciplinary Communication E1–Teacher provides opportunity for students to produce disciplinary oral communication Fostering Metacognition E1–Teacher is visibly enacting a metacognitive process by conducting a think-aloud to model the process of asking questions	Read the book to the class and model the process of asking questions by stopping to ask questions and providing time for students to respond.
Designing Instruction E2–Teacher has structured tasks that support the learning targets Facilitating Acquisition of Academic Language E2–Students are given opportunity to acquire and use academic language in a meaningful way Designing Instruction E3–Teacher establishes high expectations that support the learning targets	Then ask students to sit knee to knee with a partner and ask and answer the questions, "Who is the story about? What happens in the story? Where does it take place? What is one crazy thing you think the cat did?" Remind students to answer using full sentences and provide sentence frames for them.

Table 5.2. Kindergarten Annotated Model Lesson (continued)

Disciplinary Communication (DC) Teaching Frame Elements	Teacher Actions
Monitoring & Guiding E1–Teacher monitors student work	Monitor pairs as they ask and answer questions.
Monitoring & Guiding E2–Teacher provides oral feedback to promote disciplinary learning	Provide feedback to students on their use of full sentences.
Fostering Metacognition E1–Teacher is visibly enacting a metacognitive process by conducting a think-aloud to model the process of sequencing	Reread the story to the class. Then engage student pairs in an activity to sort and arrange pictures into an appropriate story sequence. Use one picture to model for students the thinking process involved in deciding where in the sequence it belongs.
Monitoring & Guiding E1 Teacher monitors student work	Walk around and monitor students as they work in pairs to sequence the pictures.
Monitoring & Guiding E2–Teacher provides oral feedback to promote disciplinary learning	Ask questions to help students move through the activity and provide direction as needed.
Fostering Metacognition E2–Teacher deconstructs a metacognitive strategy to support learning	When pairs are stumped, remind students of a strategy they can use if they are stuck deciding what comes next in the sequence. Explain, "Sometimes when I am stuck, I think about which ones cannot come next in the story because those come at the very end. Getting rid of some in this way allows me to have fewer to choose from and makes the sequencing easier for me."
Disciplinary Communication E1–Teacher provides opportunity for students to produce disciplinary oral communication	Ask students to retell the story to each other using the picture cards as a support.
Facilitating Acquisition of Academic Language E2–Students are given opportunity to acquire and use academic language in a meaningful way Designing Instruction E3–Teacher establishes high expectations that support the learning targets	Remind them to use the sequencing words below in the retelling and to use the structure: First ____________. Next ____________. Then ____________. Last ____________.

Table continues on next page

Table 5.2. Kindergarten Annotated Model Lesson (continued)

Disciplinary Communication (DC) Teaching Frame Elements	Teacher Actions
Monitoring & Guiding E1 & E2–Teacher monitors student work and provides feedback	Monitor the students as they do this and provide feedback by either reminding them to use the sequencing words or praising them for doing so.
Disciplinary Communication E1–Teacher provides opportunity for students to produce disciplinary oral communication	Explain there is a moral to this story. A moral to a story is the lesson the story is trying to teach. Ask the class, "What do you think Dr. Seuss is trying to teach us?" Have students share their ideas.
Disciplinary Communication E1–Teacher provides opportunity for students to produce disciplinary oral communication	Ask students if they would let the cat come to their house. Give them some time to think about the answer and tell them to also think about why or why not.
Facilitating Acquisition of Academic Language E2–Students are given opportunity to acquire and use academic language in a meaningful way	Tell students to interview three friends and ask them, "Would you let the cat come to your house? Why or why not?" Remind students to ask and answer using complete sentences.
Fostering Metacognition E1–Teacher is visibly enacting a metacognitive process by conducting a think-aloud to model the process of asking and answering questions	To model the process, select a student volunteer to ask the question: "Would you let the cat come to your house? Tell me why or why not." Respond, "I would not let the cat come to my house because cats make me sneeze."
Disciplinary Communication E2–Teacher provides an opportunity for students to produce disciplinary written communication Facilitating Acquisition of Academic Language E2–Students are given an opportunity to acquire and use academic language in a meaningful way	Ask the students to go back to their seats. Explain they will now write one sentence explaining why they would want the cat to come to their house and one sentence explaining why they would not want the cat to come to their house. Ask them to use the sentence stems: ▪ I would let the cat come to my house because________. ▪ I would not let the cat come to my house because________. Remind them of the words on the word wall that might help them complete the writing task.

Now, let's see how the teacher enacts this lesson with her students. As you read this vignette, reflect on how the five practices of the Disciplinary Communication Teaching Frame are being implemented. Try to answer the following questions:

- How does the teacher facilitate acquisition of academic language, foster metacognition, and guide the learning to support Disciplinary Communication?
- How do the High-Impact, Cross-Cutting, and Foundational Practices work together to support the learning targets?

Step Inside Ms. Alvarez's Classroom

Ms. Alvarez has a high percentage of English learners in her kindergarten class and has considered this in her teaching by giving them many opportunities to talk (oral communication) and use academic language. Her kindergarten students will be reading Dr. Seuss books all week to celebrate Read Across America Day. Ms. Alvarez asks the class to read aloud the student-friendly learning targets on the board:

- I can retell details from the story.
- I can use full sentences to ask and answer questions about the story.
- I can discuss and write about my opinion.

Ms. Alvarez starts the unit by providing a brief biography of Dr. Seuss, describing his writing style and explaining why they are doing an author study on him. She tells the class, "Today we are going to read *The Cat in the Hat*. I love reading this book because, like all of Dr. Seuss's books, he uses rhyming to tell the story. Can someone remind us what rhyming means?" Sonya raises her hand and answers, "It is words that sound the same." "Yes. Let's look at our rhyming word wall. We have been using it to help us read our word families. Now, let's look at the cover of the book. Tell your neighbor what you notice and say 'I notice'. . . . I heard some of you say, 'I notice the cat has a hat.' 'I notice the cat has a bowtie.' Did anyone notice the cat is standing up? Do cats wear hats, bowties, or stand up and walk? No, so is this story real, which we call nonfiction, or is it make-believe, which we call fiction? Yes, it is fiction."

> Ms. Alvarez builds students' knowledge of fiction and nonfiction.

Next, Ms. Alvarez explains that the book is about Sally and her brother, Sam, who are home alone on a rainy day. "What do you do when you are home and it is raining, and you can't go outside? Turn and talk to your partner and tell them some things you do." She records a few of the student responses on the whiteboard, sounding out the words as she writes them. Then she says, "For Sally and her brother, a cat comes to the door telling them they can still have lots of fun that is funny. And this is no ordinary cat. This is the Cat in the Hat."

Ms. Alvarez reads the book, stopping at times to ask questions, "Why are they stuck indoors? What is happening now? Who just came into the house? Why does the fish think it's a bad idea for the Cat in the Hat to be in the house? What do you think about Thing 1 and Thing 2? What happens when the fish says their mother is on her way home?" When she is done, Ms. Alvarez asks students to sit knee to knee with one of their learning partners and ask and answer these questions: "Who is the story about?" "What happens in the story?" "Where does it take place?" "State one crazy thing you think the cat did." She reminds them to add on to one another's details since so many things happen in the story.

> Students have multiple opportunities for oral communication.

She listens to different pairs as they ask and answer the questions and notices that some pairs are giving one-word answers. She pauses the pair work and reminds the class, "Remember that we need to answer in complete sentences. Molly, can you please ask me the same question you asked Caitlin?" Molly responds, "Who is the story about?" Ms. Alvarez replies, "The story is about Sally and Sam and the Cat in the Hat." She then goes on to explain, "Notice that I did not just say 'Sally and Sam and the Cat.' I answered with a complete sentence." The pairs go back to asking and answering questions.

> Ms. Alvarez models speaking in complete sentences.

Ms. Alvarez has a class discussion about whether Sally and Sam should or should not tell their mother what happened. First, she asks students to raise their hands if they think they should tell their mom. Then she asks how many think they shouldn't. She counts the number of hands and writes it on the whiteboard next to the sentence starters. She says, "Use this sentence starter, 'I think they should tell their mom because . . . ' if you think they should. Use this sentence starter if you think they shouldn't: 'I think they should not tell their mom because . . . .'"

> She provides supported opportunities to communicate orally by offering sentence starters.

The next day Ms. Alvarez explains that she is going to reread the story and that, when she is done, they will retell the story. She rereads the story to the class and distributes picture cards depicting different events of the story. She tells the students that they are going to use the picture cards to retell the story, but the important thing is to put the cards in the order that they occurred in the story. She explains how sequencing is a key to understanding the text. She asks students what the sequence of a story means. After some students share, she states, "Sequencing means putting things in the order that they happen. It helps you recall the important events in the story. This is something we will continue to work on all year. You start by thinking about what comes in the beginning of the story, what comes in the middle, and what comes at the end. I want you to use the words 'beginning,' 'middle,' and 'end.' Watch me do that." Next, Ms. Alvarez models by thinking aloud how to sequence the pictures using beginning, middle, and end.

Ms. Alvarez gives students, working in pairs, the picture cards and has them sequence them according to what happened in the story. She monitors students as they are working. She notices two students who are talking about what would come next and asks them what strategy they could use to figure that out. They look at each other and are unsure. Ms. Alvarez shares, "Sometimes when I am stuck, I think about which ones come at the very end of the story. Which one happens last?" The students point to a picture and Ms. Alvarez replies, "Good, so maybe you could set this one aside for now because we know that happens last. See if there are others you can put aside for now."

> She supports students' retellings and academic language by providing picture cards and sequencing words.

After the students have grouped the cards by beginning, middle, and end, she then has students retell the story to each other using their picture cards and sequencing words in the retelling.

First ______________________.
Next ______________________.
Then ______________________.
Last ______________________.

As they are doing so, she monitors the interactions and provides feedback to various pairs.

When the students are done, she asks them why they think Dr. Seuss wrote this story. She calls on some students to share their ideas. She then explains, "There is a moral to this story. A moral to a story is the lesson the story is trying to teach. What do you think Dr. Seuss is trying to teach us?" Students share their ideas.

Next, Ms. Alvarez asks the students if they would let the cat come to their house and why. She says, "I want you to think about this for a minute. Put on your thinking cap. The thinking is in answering the why. So no matter if you say yes or no, I really want to know why." After their think time, she tells them they will go around the classroom and interview three friends about whether they would let the cat in their house and why. They need to be sure to use complete sentences and to say why. She models for them by saying, "For example, I might reply, 'I would not let the cat into my house because cats make me sneeze.'" After students complete that task, she asks for two volunteers—one who said yes, and one who said no—to come to the front of the class and explain why they said yes or no. She reminds them to speak clearly and loudly so everyone can hear them.

> Ms. Alvarez provides another opportunity for extended use of academic language and oral communication.

Ms. Alvarez then has everyone go back to their seats and distributes a paper to her students telling them to write two sentences, one explaining why they would want the cat to come to their house and one explaining why they would not want the cat to come to their house. She has differentiated the amount of support she is giving to her students based on their needs by providing different sentence stems. Some students' sentence stems will be (a) I would . . . because . . . , or (b) I would not . . . because . . . . Other students receive (a) I would let the cat come to my house because . . . , or (b) I would not let the cat come to my house because . . . . Ms. Alvarez has a small group of students meet her at the back table to give them more one-on-one support in their home language. She also points to words on the word wall that might help them complete the writing task.

She supports written communication by having students discuss before writing and by providing differentiated sentence frames.

To close out the lesson, she returns to the standards and asks students to give a thumbs-up if they retold the story, if they used complete sentences to discuss the story, and if they discussed and wrote about their opinion.

THINK AFTER READING ACTIVITY

Providing supported opportunities for students to create authentic messages as Ms. Alvarez did increases the quality and quantity of their oral and written communication and helps them retain more language and content. Ms. Alvarez supported her students by giving them many opportunities to think and talk about the tasks with their partners, which fortified their responses. She also differentiated the supports based on her students' needs. Think about ways you strengthen your students' content knowledge by supporting their ability to communicate orally and in writing. As you read the remainder of this chapter, consider how the instructional strategies and example lessons we provide could be used in your classroom to better support oral and written output.

IMPLEMENTING THE DISCIPLINARY COMMUNICATION TEACHING FRAME

There are many different instructional strategies and tools that you can use to help students produce and fortify their oral and written communication. In the next section of this chapter, we share strategies and example lessons to help you engage your students in this work.

Instructional Strategy: Inside-Outside Circle

This strategy supports element 1, *Provide multiple and supported opportunities for students to produce and fortify original disciplinary oral communication appropriate to task, purpose, and audience.* Inside-Outside Circle (Kagan, 1994) is a strategy that facilitates short oral exchanges between students by giving them opportunities to respond to prompts with a variety of classmates in a structured manner. Students form two concentric circles, with the inside group facing out and the outside group facing in. Students share their response to the prompt with their partner (i.e., the person facing them in the other circle) until you cue one of the circles to move to the right or to the left. When the circle stops, each student has a new partner with whom to talk.

Why Use This Strategy: All students, especially English learners, need as many opportunities as possible to speak English and to hear it modeled. Inside-Outside Circle accomplishes this by engaging all students simultaneously in sharing information in a short time and in a structured way. Furthermore, by pairing students with a variety of classmates—some of whom they may rarely work with—it also addresses the CCSS emphasis of having students work with diverse partners.

When to Use This Strategy: Inside-Outside Circle can be easily incorporated into a lesson or unit, in part because no specific materials are needed for it. It can be used during a lesson to share opinions on an issue, before a test to review information, or as a way to practice solving problems with help from a partner. Whatever the learning target, this strategy works best when used with your whole class or a large group of students.

How to Use This Strategy: Divide your class into inside and outside circles, and model how students are to show they are actively listening to their partner, how to move in the circle, and how to respond in complete sentences.

1. Provide an oral communication task (e.g., ask a question, describe an event, or ask for an idea where students exchange viewpoints) to either the inside or the outside circle. Give students a moment to think about a response before answering.
2. After that set of students responds, have their partners respond.
3. Once each student pair has responded to each other, tell students to move. You can be creative about this. For instance, the inside circle can move two persons to their left, or the outside circle can move three persons to their right.

4. Ask a new question, explaining whether the inner or outer circle goes first, and have students respond to one another.
5. Your job is to monitor student responses and provide support and feedback as necessary.
6. At the end of the Inside-Outside Circle, bring students back together for a quick debrief.

Instructional Strategy: I Am . . . Monologue

This strategy supports element 1, *Provide multiple and supported opportunities for students to produce and fortify original disciplinary oral communication appropriate to task, purpose, and audience.* I Am . . . Monologue (Zwiers, O'Hara, & Pritchard, 2014a) is a strategy in which students choose or are assigned a person or object to be the focus of an oral monologue. In the monologue, students assume a first-person point of view and describe who or what they are and what they do. Students work individually or with others to prepare their monologues, gathering information from instructional materials if necessary, and then present them to other students.

Why Use This Strategy: Creating and communicating the oral output required by this strategy supports students' content learning and their ability to articulate clearly what they have learned. Organizing and articulating ideas for this type of authentic communication also provides students with opportunities to practice and develop complex language that goes beyond vocabulary and syntax—to the academic discourse required for communicating more sophisticated messages.

When to Use This Strategy: I Am . . . Monologues are most effectively used as a culminating activity at the end of a unit of study. By carefully selecting the people and objects on which students should focus, you can ensure that the preparation and presentation of the monologues will result in a review of the most important concepts in the unit.

How to Use This Strategy: Hand each student a card with a picture or name of a person or object on it. Students pick key traits, concepts, or distinguishing characteristics to use for their oral output: What I am like (physical or personality traits); What I do (or did) that makes me important. Students practice with one to two partners. They may use notes or sentence frames at this point, but not when they present to their group or whole class.

Example Lesson

1. Explain to students that they are going to be using a strategy called I Am . . . Monologues. "This is a strategy that we will be using as a

way to practice our oral communication and demonstrate our content knowledge. When we create our monologues, it is important to include as many details as possible."

2. Demonstrate an I Am . . . Monologue by projecting and reading it to the class. Here is an example: "I am the equator. I am halfway between the North and the South Pole. I divide the earth into two hemispheres, the Southern Hemisphere and the Northern Hemisphere. I am at 0 degrees of latitude. I am the widest part of the earth."
3. Ask students what they noticed about your presentation (e.g., you looked at the class, you did not read from your notes, you spoke with expression). Have students identify all the details you included in your monologue and explain that they need to do the same.
4. The first time you have students create an I Am . . . Monologue, have them work in pairs. Once each student has a partner, distribute pictures or names of people or things to each pair and ask them to create their monologues.
5. Once the monologues have been created, have students rehearse their monologues with another pair of students. Then have students present their I Am . . . Monologues to the whole class. Listeners take notes and have the opportunity to ask questions.

Strategies for Designing and Implementing Language Supports

Providing your students with language supports is a very important way to help them use appropriate academic language during oral communication. To do this effectively, you should always identify the language demands of the texts and tasks for a lesson and design language supports to help students to meet those demands. But just providing the students with language supports is not enough. It is very important to ensure that students are using them effectively. For example, if you have developed sentence stems for them to use when speaking, model the use of those sentence stems and monitor that students are actually using them appropriately. It is also important to explicitly refer to the academic language you want students to use, which you can do when modeling and as you are guiding and monitoring activities. Another idea is to ask students to revise your oral communication to include appropriate academic language. You can produce a statement or an answer to a question that is a non-model and ask the whole class how to strengthen the oral output using appropriate academic language.

Instructional Strategy: Varying Sentences

This strategy supports element 2, *Provide extended and supported opportunities for students to produce and fortify original disciplinary written communication appropriate to task, purpose, and audience.* Varying

Sentences (Hoyt, 2000) is a writing strategy that is based on the 6+1 Writing Traits' concept of sentence fluency—the way individual words and phrases sound together within a sentence, and how groups of sentences sound when read one after the other (Education Northwest, 2012). In our adaptation of this strategy, you teach students to analyze the sentence fluency of their writing by focusing on sentence beginnings (Do my sentences start the same way? Are they repetitive and boring?) as well as sentence length and structure (Do my sentences vary in length? Do I use different sentence constructions?).

Why Use This Strategy: The way in which students construct sentences and weave them together in a paragraph affects not only the overall tone and flow of their writing but also its clarity and meaning. Varying Sentences teaches students the importance of monitoring and revising the beginnings, lengths, and structures of their sentences to ensure that there is a variety of each in any piece of writing they produce. Developing this type of reflective stance enables students to be more effective and independent writers.

When to Use This Strategy: You can use this strategy at any time during the writing process. It can be modeled for the whole class, during shared writing, or when conferencing with individual students. For younger students, you can also demonstrate Varying Sentences through mentor texts and modeled writing.

How to Use This Strategy: Teachers typically introduce this strategy by projecting an exemplar paragraph or two and asking students to write the first four words of each sentence on a blank piece of paper. Students then count the total number of words in each sentence and write that number in parentheses after the four words. Then students work in pairs to answer these questions: Is there a variety of sentence beginnings? Does the length of the sentences vary? The Example Lesson below unfolds over time. Steps 1 through 3 can be used with primary students to help them grow as writers. Using mentor text and anchor charts helps support students' writing.

Example Lesson

1. Bring students' attention to sentences that begin the same way in a paragraph by projecting and reading it aloud. Non-model Example: We went camping. We put up a tent. We made a campfire. We had fun.
2. Now project a model. Model Example: We were excited to go camping. Putting up the tent was a struggle. A crackling campfire is my favorite part of camping. I can't wait to go camping again.
3. Ask students to comment on the two paragraphs. What did they notice? Which sounded better?

4. Project another non-model example and ask students to help you rewrite it. Have students work with partners to think about the rewrite and then have them share some possibilities. Point out different ways students thought about beginning the sentences (e.g., with a gerund; with an adverb; with a clause; with an adjective; using a time phrase opening, such as "later that afternoon," or a place phrase opener, such as "under the window").
5. Create an anchor chart with different ways to start a sentence and use examples so that students can see what they look like.
6. Use mentor texts to demonstrate the different ways an author begins a sentence. With the students' help, select examples from the book and add them to the anchor chart.
7. Distribute another non-model and have students work in pairs to add variety to the beginning of their sentences using the examples from the anchor chart.
8. Have students look at an older piece of their writing and edit it for sentence variety.
9. Now have students look at sentences of different lengths. Take a short sentence and have students stretch it. It might be accomplished by adding adjectives, adverbs, phrases, or clauses or by asking where, when, how, and why.
10. Point out how adding to the sentence gives the reader a clearer picture and better understanding of what you are saying.
11. Use a checklist so that students can check their own writing.
    - My sentences begin in different ways.
    - Some sentences are long, and some are short.
    - It sounds good when I read it aloud.

Extension: Sentence Combining

1. Begin by explaining to students that combining two or more simple sentences is an easy way to make your writing more interesting.
2. Project two to three simple sentences on the board. Here are examples of simple sentences: "I parked my car." "The meter is running." "My car is yellow."
3. Now combine the simple sentences; for instance: "I parked my yellow car while the meter was running." "The meter was running while I parked my yellow car." For younger grades you might use: "I love my mom." "I love my dad." Combine these to make "I love my mom and dad."
4. Project more examples for students to combine and then share with the class.
5. Remind students to look at their own writing for opportunities to combine sentences.

Instructional Strategy: 3-2-1 Bridge

This strategy supports element 2, *Provide extended and supported opportunities for students to produce and fortify original disciplinary written communication appropriate to task, purpose, and audience.* The 3-2-1 Bridge strategy (Ritchhart, Church, & Morrison, 2011) activates prior knowledge before beginning a unit of study or a lesson and provides students with opportunities to produce original written output related to the topic. Students first brainstorm three words or thoughts that come to mind when they think about the topic being studied. Then they write two questions about the topic and one metaphor, simile, or analogy. After completing the unit or lesson, students respond to the same prompts and reflect on what they have learned. The bridging part of the strategy is designed to help students synthesize their prior knowledge, questions, and understandings with new ideas they develop as the lesson progresses.

Why Use This Strategy: 3-2-1 Bridge (Table 5.3) is an instructional strategy in which students generate ideas, ask questions, and elaborate on ideas using writing as the primary means of communication. By helping students recognize and reflect on their own learning, it fosters the development of the metacognitive processes and strategies all learners need to be successful.

When to Use This Strategy: This written communication strategy can be used in all subject areas to develop student understanding of a new topic or to uncover surprising or new knowledge about a familiar topic. It can also be used in primary grades, as illustrated in the Example Lesson below. The bridging aspect of this strategy is most effective when your instruction takes student thinking in a new or different direction.

Table 5.3. 3-2-1 Bridge Graphic Organizer

Initial Response	New Response
3 Thoughts ▪ ▪ ▪	3 Thoughts ▪ ▪ ▪
2 Questions ▪ ▪	2 Questions ▪ ▪
1 Metaphor/Simile/Analogy	1 Metaphor/Simile/Analogy

Bridge: Explain how your new responses connect to your initial response.

How to Use This Strategy: Distribute the graphic organizer for students to record their responses. Ask students to generate three words or thoughts that come to mind when they think of the topic. Tell students not to overthink it! You are looking for their initial reactions. Then ask students to generate two questions that quickly come to mind as well as their own metaphor, simile, or analogy for the topic. (You decide which of the three is most appropriate for your students.) Teach the lesson or unit of study. Have students return to their graphic organizer and repeat these steps. Students can then work individually or with a partner to identify the bridge between their initial learning and new learning; for instance: "First, I thought firefighters just put out fires but now I know they perform CPR, rescue people who are trapped in car accidents, and get cats out of trees." Facilitate whole-class sharing of the bridges.

Example Lesson

1. To teach metaphors to your students, you can use mentor texts like *Owl Moon* by Jane Yolen; *Wilfrid Gordon McDonald Partridge* by Mem Fox; *Black Is a Rainbow Color* by Angela Joy; or *Amber on the Mountain* by Tony Johnston. To teach similes, you can use *Quick as a Cricket* by Audrey Wood; *My Heart Is Like a Zoo* by Michael Hall; or *My Best Friend Is as Sharp as a Pencil* by Hanoch Piven. Books like *Animology: Animal Analogies* by Marianne Berkes, and *Beach Is to Fun: A Book of Relationships* by Pat Brisson, are great for teaching analogies.
2. Explain to your students that their next science unit is on bridges and that they will be sketching a bridge to show how it functions.
3. Distribute the 3-2-1 Bridge graphic organizer (Table 5.3). Project a number of pictures of different bridges for students to see. In the left-hand column, have students write three words that come to mind when they think of a bridge.
4. Under that, have them write two questions about bridges.
5. Finally, ask students to write a simile: A bridge is like a ________. For students who cannot write independently, you can create a class 3-2-1 Bridge and record student responses on the class chart.
6. Teach your unit on bridges, and then ask students to repeat the three steps on the right side of the graphic organizer.
7. Students read their responses in both columns, think about all they have learned from this unit, and share their reactions with a partner or the class. Record responses on the whiteboard.
8. Have students write their bridge.

Instructional Strategy: CSI: Color, Symbol, Image

CSI: Color, Symbol, Image (Ritchhart, Church, & Morrison, 2011) is a strategy that engages students in identifying and distilling the essential ideas from reading, viewing, or listening by using a color, symbol, and image to represent the ideas. It is an effective tool for supporting synthesis of big ideas and provides a structured protocol for oral and written communication, thus addressing both elements 1 and 2.

Why Use This Strategy: Using visuals as a way to represent the big ideas students identify helps them think, speak, and write metaphorically about those big ideas. It also enables students to make deeper connections with the content, and promotes oral and written communication skills as students explain and support their representations of the big ideas. These nonlinguistic representations also enable students who are less proficient in English to demonstrate their understanding more easily.

When to Use This Strategy: This strategy can be used after reading, viewing, or listening as a way to promote oral and written communication, facilitate the discussion of a text or event, and increase comprehension. It can also be used to reflect on previous learning.

How to Use This Strategy: Distribute the CSI: Color, Symbol, Image graphic organizer (see Figure 5.1). Ask students to think about what they read, listened to, or viewed, and then choose three things they found interesting, important, or insightful. (For this example, we will assume students read a text.) For one of those things, students choose a color that they feel best represents or captures the essence of that idea. Using crayons or colored pencils, students color the top half of the Color column of the graphic organizer. Under their color, students write an explanation of why they chose it.

Figure 5.1. CSI: Color, Symbol, Image Graphic Organizer

Depending on grade level and language proficiency, the explanations may be a word or two, or up to a paragraph in length. Then students choose a symbol and an image to represent the other two ideas, sketch them in the Symbol and Image columns, and write an explanation under each. With a partner or in groups, students share their thinking, citing evidence from the text.

Example Lesson

1. Project the CSI graphic organizer (Figure 5.1) and explain to students that this is the strategy they are going to use after they have read a text.
2. Begin by teaching students about how colors and symbols can represent feelings or ideas.
3. Create an anchor chart to teach your students the meaning of colors that represents mood or tone. Begin with a few basic ones:
   - red: anger, love, heat,
   - green: jealousy, money, environment,
   - blue: sad, wisdom, loyalty, and
   - white: pure, cleanliness, safety.

   Add to the chart throughout the year as students come across other examples. You could also read *My Many Colored Days* by Dr. Seuss, as a way to see how color sets mood.
4. Create another anchor chart to teach your students about symbols. Begin with symbols they know, such as a stop sign, peace sign, or heart, and have students tell you what they represent. For example, a heart is often used as a symbol of love. You can also have them use emojis or symbols that are found on a keyboard.
5. Discuss with your students how they will also need to think about an image or snapshot that they visualize when they are reading the text. For example, in *Goldilocks and the Three Bears* it might be the image of Goldilocks in the bed with the three bears looking at her, or it could be Goldilocks running away from the three bears' house. Explain to students that their drawings do not need to be perfect; stick figures are fine. The important part will be their explanation of what it is and why they chose it.
6. Choose a text. It can be an historical speech, picture book, short story, movie, piece of music, or piece of art. Have students create their CSI by identifying a color, symbol, and image that represents the text and noting their reasoning for choosing what they did. To elicit responses from students who may need additional support, prompt with questions such as: How does your color represent the tone or mood? How does your symbol represent the big idea? How does your image capture the essence of the theme?
7. With a partner or in a group, have students discuss their choices, explain why they chose them, and share with the class.

Strategies for Scaffolding Writing to Support All Students

It is very important to maintain the intellectual challenge and rigor of tasks for all students, which means providing more scaffolding and supports for those who need that level of assistance. One approach to helping those students who struggle to persevere is to scaffold the writing process by designing a sequence of connected tasks that build on one another and support student engagement throughout the process. Integrating oral and written communication tasks within a lesson can be a powerful way to do this. This approach can provide students with opportunities to talk about the content, discuss what they have written, give one another feedback, and support one another through iterations of a piece of written work. Remember that providing students with detailed and actionable feedback will also help them take their writing to the next level because it gives them something specific to respond to.

Cross-Cutting Practice: Facilitating Acquisition of Academic Language

Academic language development is critical to both written and oral communication. Effective teachers attend to the language demands of oral and written tasks during instruction (element 1). They also plan lessons to provide supported opportunities for students to acquire and use academic language during oral and written communication tasks (element 2). Next, we provide instructional strategies you can use in your classroom to ensure that students are developing the academic language needed to be successful in oral and written communication.

Instructional Strategy: Sentence-Strip Paragraphs

This strategy supports element 1, *Introduce and/or refer to the academic language demands of texts and tasks*. This strategy helps students organize their writing into logically sequenced introductory, body, and concluding paragraphs. Each sentence of an exemplar paragraph that you have chosen is written on its own strip of paper, and students have to determine which slip is the introductory sentence, the concluding sentence, and the supporting details.

Why Use This Strategy: Many students struggle to write a well-organized paragraph, let alone the multi-paragraph essays expected of students as they progress as writers. The Sentence-Strip Paragraphs strategy provides an engaging way to help students understand the basic structure of a well-organized paragraph and use that understanding to write their own paragraphs.

When to Use This Strategy: Providing your students with sample paragraphs to analyze for basic structure is a preparatory process that should precede the challenge of writing their own paragraphs. This strategy can be used at any time during the writing process.

How to Use This Strategy: Identify an appropriate paragraph or write your own and create the necessary number of sentence strips for your class.

Example Lesson

1. Do a think-aloud to model for students how to lay out the sentence strips, read them, and figure out the order in which they go. Demonstrate how to add transition words to connect the sentences using the anchor chart you and your students have created.
2. In primary grades, you can use a familiar text like a nursery rhyme, a fable, or a fairy tale, or a rebus with transition words. You can also begin with a "How to" paragraph (e.g., how to make a peanut butter sandwich, how to ride a bike, how to blow a bubble).
3. Cut the paragraph into sentence strips and distribute a set to each pair of students.
4. Students read the sentence strips, put them in the correct order, and add transition words from the anchor chart to connect the sentences.
5. When finished, students share their completed paragraph.
6. Explain that the first sentence is the topic sentence, the last sentence is the concluding sentence, and the rest are details.
7. As students progress, you can cut a multi-paragraph essay into paragraph strips and have students read the paragraphs and decide on the sequence.

Instructional Strategy: Sentence Dissecting

This strategy supports element 2, *Provide extended and supported opportunities for students to acquire and use the features of academic language.* The Sentence Dissecting strategy (Hartung-Cole, 2015) requires students to break up (i.e., dissect) compound or complex sentences containing key information on the topic being studied into simple sentences. This process, which is typically done in small groups, helps students develop academic language and literacy skills as well as an understanding of content.

Why Use This Strategy: Literary and informational texts used in CCSS classrooms consist largely of sentences with multiple clauses. Sentence Dissecting can be used across content areas to support student comprehension of these texts. Because this strategy supports the academic language development of students—especially English learners—it also promotes oral communication using academic vocabulary and sentence structures.

When to Use This Strategy: You can use this strategy when students need instructional support to understand the structure and meaning of linguistically rich and complex sentences. The teachers with whom we work have found that this strategy is particularly useful with students who are intimidated by complex sentences because they lack confidence in their ability to unpack and understand them.

Example Lesson

1. Begin by projecting a complex sentence on the board. Model how to dissect it into many smaller sentences. Here is an example of a complex sentence: "Because it was raining, he ran as fast as he could to his friend's house because it was closer than his own." Dissecting it into simpler sentences would look like this: "It was raining. He ran. He ran fast. He ran to his friend's house. His friend's house was closer. His friend's house was closer than his own."
2. After you have modeled Sentence Dissecting, project another complex sentence and have students work together in small groups to dissect the sentence on chart paper.
3. Explain that one student in each group writes a simpler sentence on the chart paper and writes their initials after it. The rest of the group is responsible for checking that it comes directly from the original sentence, is not a fragment, and is spelled correctly.
4. Pass the chart paper to the next student, who writes another simple sentence and initials it. Students continue doing this until you call time or until they cannot think of any other simple sentences.
5. Groups post their charts and the class circulates, reading each chart and circling any sentences they think are not valid.
6. Bring the class back together and discuss why the circled sentences are or are not valid.

Extension: Dissecting and Assimilating

1. Divide the class into two groups and give each group a different complex sentence.
2. Have pairs of students dissect their sentence, finding as many simple sentences as possible.
3. When they have finished, pairs switch their simple sentences with a pair in the other group and try to re-create that group's original complex sentence on chart paper.
4. Select a few students to share their complex sentence with the class, comparing it to the original, and debrief with your students.

Cross-Cutting Practice: Fostering Metacognition

In order to produce and fortify oral communication, students need to persevere through a number of iterations where they revise and strengthen their work. Often students will struggle with this, becoming stuck and unsure of how to move forward. Students who can persevere and produce strong oral and written communication are generally strategic learners. To help all students become strategic learners, teachers should visibly enact and deconstruct metacognitive processes and strategies they expect students to use. Below are instructional strategies that you can use to help you foster student metacognition to better equip your students to produce high-quality oral and written output.

Instructional Strategy: Exit Ticket

This strategy supports element 1, *Visibly enact metacognitive processes and/or strategies students are expected to use in support of disciplinary learning.* An exit ticket is a written student response to a prompt you pose at the end of a lesson—in effect, a "ticket out the door." Although an exit ticket can be used as a quick assessment that enables you to evaluate the effectiveness of your instruction, we present it here as a way for students to reflect on their learning once you have completed a lesson.

Why Use This Strategy: An exit ticket helps students reflect on what they have learned by prompting them to express their thoughts about the lesson, such as whether they have any questions about the content or what they thought was most interesting. When used regularly, exit tickets contribute to the development of a metacognitive culture in your classroom. In addition, written student responses at the end of class, even brief ones like an exit ticket, provide opportunities for your students to produce original disciplinary written communication.

When to Use This Strategy: An exit ticket is done at the end of a lesson on a regular basis.

How to Use This Strategy: At the end of a lesson, ask students to respond to a prompt. Fisher, Brozo, Frey, and Ivey (2011) recommend three categories of prompts: those that document learning (e.g., "Write one thing you learned today"), those that emphasize the process of learning (e.g., "Write one question you have about today's lesson"), and those that evaluate the effectiveness of instruction (e.g., "Did you enjoy working in small groups today?"). Some teachers find that asking students to write their responses on 3" x 5" index cards is a convenient way to collect their exit tickets.

Example Lesson

1. Create exit tickets based on your learning target and have each student complete one. Focus the exit ticket on one particular skill or concept for the day.
2. Distribute the exit tickets just before the end of class, and have students write their name on their tickets. Stand at the door and collect them as the students leave. (Students could also complete their exit ticket electronically.)
3. Read the responses and put them in like piles. Look for trends and patterns. What needs to be clarified due to misconceptions? What needs to be retaught to the whole class versus what needs to be taught to a small group?
4. Share patterns in the responses with the class the following day, explaining how the patterns affect your next instructional steps.

Instructional Strategy: Think-Aloud

This strategy supports element 2, *Deconstruct metacognitive processes and/or strategies that support disciplinary learning*. A think-aloud is a way to model what students should do when asked to produce oral or written communication. Think-alouds do not just explain the procedural steps students should follow. You must verbalize your own thought processes to help your students examine and develop their own metacognitive processes and strategies. Thus, this strategy helps students develop their ability to monitor the oral and written processes in which they are engaged and improve on them.

Why Use This Strategy: It is critical that students develop a range of strategies for remaining actively engaged in oral and written communication. Many, if not most, students need these strategies modeled and explained before they can consciously and deliberately employ them, especially English learners. The challenge teachers face is how to enact invisible mental processes. A think-aloud provides a way for you to reveal the internal thinking processes that normally go on in the minds of engaged learners, giving students an opportunity to observe how they can utilize their own metacognitive processes and strategies.

When to Use This Strategy: The Think-Aloud strategy is based on research indicating that if teachers model and describe their own thoughts about a task, students will realize how and when to do the same (Pritchard & O'Hara, 2007). This research supports their use in any content area or grade level to provide students with a glimpse into expert thinking. Think-alouds also contribute to creating a culture of metacognition in your classroom.

How to Use This Strategy: Focus your think-aloud on an area of either oral or written communication that you want to make visible to your students. Rehearse and take notes on decision points you want to make explicit. Use first-person language when you explain your thinking process.

Example Lesson

1. For oral communication, students are developing questions for their interviewee.
2. Explain that as an interviewer, it is important to be a good listener because you might need to ask a clarifying question or paraphrase something the interviewee said. Write the four things that you need to do as a listener on chart paper:
   - Listen to the words and try to picture what the speaker is saying.
   - Be patient and give the speaker time to articulate their thinking.
   - Do not interrupt.
   - Be aware if you are listening or thinking about other things.
3. Explain that you are going to think aloud as you interview a student and you want everyone to notice what you are doing.
   Sample: You say, "'What do you want to be when you grow up?' Notice that the question I asked is open-ended, so I need to be patient and give the interviewee some time to think and put their thoughts into words." The student responds: "I want to be an astronaut and go to Mars." You say, "Notice I didn't ask another question yet. I paused to see if the interviewee wanted to add anything else before I asked another question. Now, did you notice I looked at them and nodded? I want to understand more about them wanting to be an astronaut, so I'll ask another open-ended question. 'What is it about being an astronaut that interests you?'" The student responds: "I like the idea of going into space. I think being weightless would be cool." You say, "I am picturing them up in space being weightless and I'm thinking about what question I want to ask now. What do I want to know now? 'What is it about being weightless that you think is cool?'"
4. Debrief with your students. What did they notice you did and why? What seemed most important and why? Chart what the students saw you do.

Example Lesson

1. For written communication, choose an area of writing that students need to improve on. Demonstrate how to sound out words as you write, use transitions, write an introduction, or write a report.
2. Explain what you will be demonstrating and why. Tell your students that you will be verbalizing what is going on in your head as you write. Have students pay attention to your decisions and why you make

them. Explain to them that they will be working on the same thing in their own writing and that, by watching you, they will know how to approach it.

Sample: "Today for our modeled writing I am going to show you opinion writing, which is what we are going to be working on next. The topic that we will write about is 'Which kind of pet is better, a cat or dog?' I don't want to just say a dog is the better pet. That is a boring way to start my paragraph. I could start with a question. How about, 'Do you know what pet is known as man's best friend?' Yes, that is so much better. I think I have hooked my reader to want to read on. Now I can write, 'It is a dog.' Next, I need to give some reasons why a dog is the better pet. I am going to brainstorm some ideas and then decide which ones are the best. Let's see. They are loyal. You can play with them. They can be trained. They bark and wag their tails when they are excited. They can protect you. They love to be affectionate. Okay, now I have to decide which three are the best. Let me reread what I written so far. 'Do you know what pet is known as man's best friend? It is a dog.' Okay, I'll add, 'They are loyal.' I need to expand on that more. I need it to be clearer to my reader. I can add the part about barking and wagging their tails. 'They are loyal and recognize their owner by barking and wagging their tails.'"

3. Debrief with your students. What did they notice you did and why? What seemed most important and why? Chart what the students saw you do.

Cross-Cutting Practice: Monitoring and Guiding

Monitoring and providing feedback are critical to helping students improve the quantity and quality of their oral and written communication. Monitoring and guiding the production and fortification of disciplinary communication requires teachers to provide both oral and written feedback that is constructive and actionable. In addition, closely monitoring student communication tasks allows teachers to know when to adjust instruction or tasks, which may include providing more supports and scaffolds or reducing the amount of scaffolding. Below we provide an instructional strategy and an instructional tool that have been designed to help you monitor and guide your students as they work through the process of producing and fortifying their written and oral communication.

Instructional Strategy: Placemat

This strategy supports element 1, *Monitor learning and adjust instruction, supports, and/or disciplinary tasks to meet student needs*. Placemat is a

Figure 5.2. Placemat Template

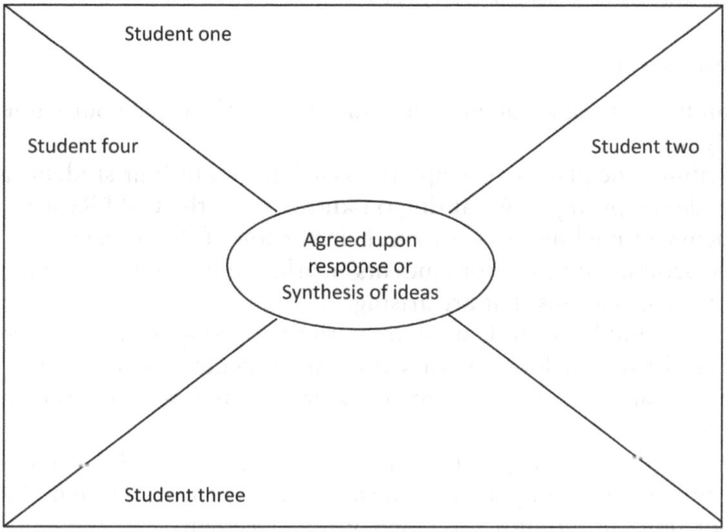

strategy where individual students brainstorm their own ideas on a topic and then write them in their designated section of a group placemat (see Figure 5.2). Once individual brainstorming and writing are complete, ideas are shared and synthesized by the group and are written in the center of the placemat. In our adaptation of this strategy, you use the written product and the group discussions as tools to monitor student understanding of the topic.

Why Use This Strategy: The Placemat process and products provide a formative window into how well your students understand the topic or issue your prompt asks them to consider. It also allows you to monitor the dynamics and findings of each student group and provide feedback when necessary.

When to Use This Strategy: You can use Placemat at different points in a lesson or unit. At the beginning, the Placemat process helps students generate background knowledge about the topic at hand. Toward the end, it can be used to organize student thinking and knowledge prior to a formative or summative assessment.

How to Use This Strategy: Pose an open-ended prompt, the answers to which will give you insight into your students' understanding of a topic your class is studying. Allow time for individual thinking and writing, followed by time for group sharing. As students write, circulate around the room to monitor and offer assistance as necessary.

Example Lesson

1. Begin by creating an open-ended question on the topic your students are studying.
2. Distribute one placemat template to each group of four students and provide the prompt "What do you know about the Gold Rush?" Give students a time limit to write on their portion of the placemat.
3. Walk around and monitor students' work. Note who knows what and any misconceptions that are arising.
4. Call time and have students share with their group what they wrote in round-robin fashion. As they do that, students cross out any duplications on their placemat. Walk around and monitor students' responses.
5. Explain that now groups are going to reach consensus by synthesizing the information and placing it in the middle of their placemat. Take the opportunity to monitor this stage of the placemat.
6. Have groups share their ideas and take this opportunity to address any misconceptions.
7. Collect the placemats to check for trends and patterns that can inform your instruction.

Instructional Tool: Formative Assessments of Student Talk—DC

This tool supports element 2, *Provide written and/or oral feedback during lessons to promote disciplinary learning.* Formative Assessments of Student Talk—Disciplinary Communication, or FAST-DC (see Appendix E), provides a three-dimensional monitoring and evaluation tool that enables you to analyze oral communication. You can use the information derived from FAST-DC to provide students with in-depth, constructive feedback that will enhance their oral communication, academic language, and metacognitive strategies.

Why Use This Tool: FAST-DC contains three dimensions, each of which can be scored individually using a four-point rubric (Appendix E). The first dimension, Communicating Understanding, focuses on the clarity of the claim or idea being communicated, the extent to which it is effectively organized and connected, and whether or not it is supported by evidence. The second dimension, Using Academic Language, focuses on which academic language features are used in the communication and on whether or not the discourse feature is used to communicate understanding. The third dimension, Applying Metacognitive Strategies, focuses on whether or not students are monitoring their own interactions and, when needed, applying strategies appropriately and independently.

When to Use This Tool: As mentioned above, FAST-DC is a tool that you can use when you want to monitor or evaluate oral communication and provide constructive feedback to students. You can use it effectively to assess all three dimensions or to focus on one dimension at a time, depending on your specific learning targets and your students' needs.

How to Use This Tool: You can use FAST-DC to monitor oral communication in one of two ways. During a lesson in which students are engaged in disciplinary communication, you can listen to a student or pair of students for evidence of one or more dimensions and use that to provide in-the-moment guidance. You can also use FAST-DC to analyze a written transcript or recording of student communication and provide targeted feedback to help strengthen the next exchange. As with other one-on-one assessment tools, the more you use FAST-DC, the better you will be at analyzing oral communication and providing effective feedback to your students.

Foundational Practice: Designing Instruction

At their most basic level, oral and written language are about communicating with other people, and to do that effectively students need your support and guidance. Your ability to set disciplinary learning targets that are aligned with the appropriate CCSS and the High-Impact Practice of Disciplinary Communication play a vital role in enabling your students to communicate effectively, both orally and in writing. The instructional tool that follows is a resource for you to use when designing lessons that target the development of the different types of oral communication and the language skills students need for each type.

Instructional Tool: Oral Communications Matrix

This tool supports element 1, *Set disciplinary learning targets that are aligned with ELA/Anchor Literacy CCSS and the target high-impact practice.* Designing lessons to support oral language development and communication between students is an essential facet of the CCSS and elementary school curricula. The Oral Communications Matrix (see Table 5.4) provides you with a comprehensive and structured approach for determining the types of oral communication on which to focus and for identifying the language skills each type requires.

Why Use This Tool: At an early age, children begin to learn how language can be used to serve many purposes, and as a result, they enter school with some pragmatic knowledge of how to use language to communicate. Teachers need to build on this knowledge base by providing opportunities for different types of communication as well as instruction in the specific language skills needed to support them. The Oral Communications Matrix (Table 5.4) is a tool you can use when designing lessons to support these learning targets and the High-Impact Practice of Disciplinary Communication.

Table 5.4. Oral Communications Matrix

Type of Oral Communication	What It Is	Language Skills	Examples
Oral Report a) planned b) unplanned	Sharing of new information that can include multimedia Planned: introduction, body, and conclusion Unplanned: organized by reconstructing information or explanation	❑ Select and organize information ❑ Identify key facts ❑ Use clear and precise language ❑ Include subject-specific concepts and words	Personal topics, book report, topic report Spontaneous reporting of group work
Storytelling	Telling stories, retelling events, and relating personal anecdotes	❑ Retell a series of events ❑ Include descriptive vocabulary ❑ Speak with appropriate tone of voice and volume ❑ Use expressive body language	Community stories, family stories, puppetry, reader's theater
Partner or small-group work	Developing speaking and listening skills	❑ Use language to interact ❑ Listen and respond to what others say ❑ Summarize or evaluate ❑ Initiate ideas	Think-Pair-Share, Literature Circles, Jigsaw

Table 5.4. Oral Communications Matrix (continued)

Type of Oral Communication	What It Is	Language Skills	Examples
Giving instructions	Explaining a series of steps	❑ Describe using facts ❑ Include details for how, when, and where ❑ Use sequence words appropriately	Barrier games (example: Battleship), How to . . .
Questioning and Inquiry	Encouraging higher-order thinking; dialogue between students and teachers; probing, speculative inquiry questions	❑ Ask and answer questions ❑ Pose multilevel questions (literal, inferential, and evaluative) ❑ Paraphrase responses ❑ Question yourself	Hot Seat, Socratic Questions, Question Matrix, Six Thinking Hats
Arguments and formal/informal debates	Persuading someone to a particular point of view	❑ Use persuasive tone and body language ❑ Use data or evidence ❑ Understand contrasting points of view ❑ Give and justify opinions ❑ Gather accurate and relevant information	Four Corners, Take a Stand, Formal Debate
Interviews	Questioning in an authentic context	❑ Ask open and closed questions ❑ Clarify others' ideas ❑ Acknowledge others ❑ Listen critically ❑ Paraphrase	Hot Seat, Who Am I?, Interviews
Interest Talks	Sharing topics of personal interest	❑ Explain or describe ❑ Organize appropriately for audience ❑ Draw on background knowledge or experiences ❑ Use subject-specific vocabulary ❑ Include descriptive and sequencing words ❑ Pace your speech and use appropriate tone of voice ❑ Include visual aids	Show and Tell, small-group or whole-class presentation

When to Use This Tool: Across all grade levels and content areas, teachers must identify and teach the language skills students need to engage in the eight different types of oral communication. Using this tool when planning and structuring your lessons will enable your students to meet these learning targets.

How to Use This Tool: Using the Oral Communications Matrix when designing your lesson involves five steps:

1. Reflect on the learning target(s) of your lesson and the type of oral communication in which you want your students to engage. Consult the Oral Communications Matrix to identify the specific language skills they need to develop.
2. Create an anchor chart with your students, explaining the purpose, audience, and context for the oral communication chosen.
3. Model the type of speaking you expect your students to engage in, focusing on the appropriate language structures, concepts, and vocabulary.
4. Provide an opportunity for students to practice and apply the skills.
5. Monitor student progress and provide feedback as necessary.

ADDITIONAL IMPLEMENTATION CONSIDERATIONS

Students, particularly those from diverse backgrounds, often need to develop and navigate bridges between their cultural and linguistic resources and the academic expectations of school. The implementation considerations that follow will further inform your Disciplinary Communication instruction and help your students achieve this goal.

Distinguishing Between Oral Communication and Discussions

In our work with teachers on the SOAR Teaching Frames, a question that often arises is, "How do I distinguish between oral communication and discussions?" Oral communication involves individual students exchanging or presenting feelings, thoughts, and ideas about disciplinary content. Examples include responding to a teacher's question, giving an oral presentation, or participating in a Think-Pair-Share. For instance, you might ask students to share one of the causes of the American Revolution using the Think-Pair-Share or Round-Robin structure. The goal of oral communication is to support individual students' ability to use their oral language in a manner appropriate to task, purpose, and audience.

Discussions are extended conversations in which two or more students work together to co-construct meaning. Examples include tasks like face-to-face interactions, online dialogues, or written conversations. For instance, you might ask students to decide which of the causes of the American Revolution was most important, with students proposing ideas, clarifying fuzzy concepts, encouraging one another to elaborate, and building on others' ideas. The goal of a discussion is to have students develop conversation skills and use them to strengthen their disciplinary learning.

The Writing Process and Written Communication

Teaching the writing process to students is critically important. Writing is a complex skill, so students must understand and engage in the progression of steps—prewriting, drafting, revising, and editing—that will enable them to become effective writers. For instance, helping students understand that their initial draft is exactly that—a piece of writing that needs to be revised and edited—is an important concept for students to learn. In addition, some of the written communication strategies we have explained in this chapter—Varying Sentences, Sentence Combining, Sentence Dissecting, and Sentence-Strip Paragraphs—are ones you can incorporate into your teaching of the writing process. Still others—CSI, Placemat, and 3-2-1 Bridge—result in drafts that students can revise and expand. Nonetheless, not every piece of student writing can or should go through the entire writing process. Our SOAR experience has taught us that the more writing students do, the better writers they become, even when the writing tasks produce shorter written products.

Third Spaces

The writing process, like the reading process, occurs in dynamic sociocultural contexts that shape and are shaped by the learner. Consequently, you must understand and respond to the writing needs and interests of your culturally and linguistically diverse students, especially English learners, through the social networks and linguistic resources they bring to school. Third spaces provide insight into how you and your students can integrate the personal, social, and cultural experiences of home (first space) with the academic expectations of school (second space) by creating a third space that recognizes and values the culturally and linguistically diverse backgrounds of your students. Assaf (2014) describes three kinds of third spaces:

> 1) as bridges built between home and school literacies, 2) as navigational, in which students learn to navigate their literacies with those of school, 3) as transformational, where the intersection of home and school literacies leads to new knowledge and new ways of learning. (p. 3)

Creating a third space in your classroom ensures that all your students can fully engage in academic writing tasks. You play a critical role in this process by establishing meaningful contexts for writing, providing relevant options for topics, encouraging students to share their culturally developed funds of knowledge (Moll & Gonzalez, 1994), and in general offering students the opportunity to draw on their cultural and linguistic backgrounds to express themselves. Not only does utilizing this approach provide support and scaffolding for your students' written communication, it also fortifies their writing skills by allowing them to bridge prior linguistic and cultural knowledge with the new academic language and content they are learning. Furthermore, when students can tap into different funds of knowledge that they bring to the classroom, their ability to produce original and authentic written communication is enhanced.

CONCLUSION

The purpose of this chapter has been to deepen your understanding of the Disciplinary Communication Teaching Frame by unpacking the language of and rationale for the instructional practices that comprise it. The model lesson and associated classroom vignette provide additional insight into these practices by illustrating the dynamic and interdependent ways in which they work together in the context of a Teaching Frame to drive both teacher and student growth. When teachers help students develop the language needed for both oral and written communication, explicitly teach metacognitive strategies, and provide feedback to students on oral and written output, they fortify student communication. Finally, the instructional strategies and tools are designed to deepen your understanding of the Disciplinary Communication Teaching Frame and to provide you with concrete examples of approaches teachers are currently using in their classrooms to implement it. These strategies will equip you to strengthen both the quality and quantity of student communication, a key skill as they advance in school and as productive citizens.

CHAPTER 6

Supporting Teachers to Build Literacy Classrooms That SOAR

In Chapters 2–5, we introduced you to four SOAR Teaching Frames, and you explored how each Frame can be used as a lens to plan, teach, reflect on, and elevate instruction. We provided classroom examples and instructional strategies to help you consider how to implement the High-Impact, Cross-Cutting, and Foundational Practices in your own classroom. Although each chapter dealt with a separate Teaching Frame to allow for a deep dive into those practices, the Teaching Frames do not work in isolation.

Typically, we suggest that teachers and schools adopt the Teaching Frames in a specific sequence, starting with Disciplinary Discussions. Supporting students to engage in conversations about content is key to everything students need to do to be successful. By starting with the Disciplinary Discussions Teaching Frame, you provide your students with essential skills needed to interact with complex text, use evidence appropriately, and fortify their communication effectively.

Our work in the field has shown us that moving from Disciplinary Discussions to Disciplinary Interactions With Complex Text helps teachers and students learn how to integrate the skills from both of these Teaching Frames during instruction. So helping your students better interact with complex texts will lead to deeper discussions, and building your students' ability to engage in discussion can facilitate their interactions with complex text. Disciplinary Uses of Evidence is a natural next step, since we often expect students to find relevant and sufficient evidence when they are interacting with texts. Finally, having students engage in discussion, interact with text, and learn how to find evidence to support claims are all critical to improving the quality and quantity of their oral and written communication. Furthermore, although communication skills are integral to most classroom tasks, very often we use either oral or written communication as a culminating task or assessment. As such, we suggest Disciplinary Communication as the last frame in the sequence.

So, the Teaching Frames are mutually reinforcing, and when they are adopted as a framework by schools and districts where all teachers are using them and sharing their ideas, they have a powerful impact on professional growth and, as a result, on student learning. Improving student outcomes is the ultimate purpose of schooling. Identifying those practices that can drive student learning and providing teachers with the tools to implement those practices are important to elevating instruction. An effective professional-growth culture relies on collaborative peers, support from instructional coaches, and effective instructional leaders (Reyes et al., 2020). Professional learning needs to be grounded in the day-to-day practice of teaching, where teachers reflect, assess, and collaboratively find ways to elevate instruction as a part of a cycle of continuous improvement. Teachers need dedicated time to engage in this reflection both individually and with peers. When the expectation is on all teachers within a school and across a district to collaborate at this level, there is a profound impact on teaching and learning (O'Hara et al., 2018; Reyes et al., 2020). In this chapter we describe how the SOAR Teaching Frames can be systematically applied to foster metacognition of individual teachers, support the collective professional growth of teachers at the school level, and drive improvements in teaching and learning across districts. We also share additional tools that teachers and leaders can use individually and with peers to observe and elevate instruction using the SOAR Teaching Frames as a lens.

FOSTERING AN ABILITY TO TEACH WITH METACOGNITION

Teaching with metacognition enables teachers to gain awareness about and control over how they think and teach by planning, monitoring, evaluating, and adjusting their instructional goals and teaching strategies in accordance with their students' needs and the sociocultural context. Through our professional-development work with partner schools and districts across the United States, we have identified four stages of awareness and action that teachers typically go through when using SOAR Teaching Frames to teach with metacognition:

- The first stage represents a teacher who is not familiar with SOAR and, therefore, is unable to use it as a lens to plan, teach, and reflect.
- A teacher at the second stage has been introduced to SOAR but is still learning how to use a Teaching Frame and the instructional practices that support the metacognition of learners engaged in a High-Impact Practice. Teachers at this stage of the continuum tend to equate SOAR with the use of certain instructional strategies (e.g., Layering Texts, Juicy Sentences) rather than a specific High-Impact, Cross-Cutting, or Foundational Practice.
- Teachers at the third stage of the continuum have developed a deeper understanding of SOAR as evidenced by their ability to

use a High-Impact, Cross-Cutting, or Foundational Practice as a lens to plan, teach, and reflect. However, because their focus is at the practice level and not at the level of the Teaching Frame, the metacognitive impact of the planning-reflecting process is limited.

- Finally, teachers at the last stage have developed an understanding of how all the practices of the SOAR Teaching Frame work together and can be used as a lens to plan, monitor, evaluate, and adjust their instructional goals and teaching strategies in accordance with their students' needs and the sociocultural context. Helping teachers understand which stage they are at is an important first step in helping them to teach with metacognition.

It is important to support teachers in consistently using the SOAR Teaching Frames as the lens to plan, teach, and reflect on their instructional practice (O'Hara, Pritchard, & Pitta, 2019). This helps teachers gain awareness about and control over how they think and teach by using the High-Impact, Cross-Cutting, and Foundational Practices to plan, monitor, evaluate, and adjust their instructional goals and teaching strategies. To support teachers through this process, we have developed a set of implementation rubrics that are aligned with each SOAR Teaching Frame. Table 6.1 contains the rubric that is aligned with the High-Impact Practice Disciplinary Discussions. The full rubric for the Disciplinary Discussion Teaching Frame and the rubrics for Disciplinary Interactions With Complex Text, Disciplinary Uses of Evidence, and Disciplinary Communication are all provided in Appendices F-I.

Each rubric is used as a guide for teachers to help them reflect on planning and teaching and to ultimately elevate their practice. Moving along the rubric from no implementation to full implementation enables teachers in the planning stage to focus specifically on what they need to include in their lessons. For instance, if their students are still developing the conversation skills necessary to engage in disciplinary discussions (element 1, or E1 in the rubric), the implementation rubric will help teachers recognize the need to introduce and refer to those skills as well as provide support for students to use them in tasks and activities. Then, when the lesson is over and teachers are reflecting on how successful it was, the rubric can help them recognize what worked and what did not work. For instance, they may realize that the supports they used enabled some students to use the conversation skills to engage in a discussion but that other students clearly needed something more. This insight will help the teachers adjust their instruction during the next lesson.

Table 6.1. Disciplinary Discussions Implementation Rubric

		No Implementation	→ →	→ →	→ → Full Implementation
Disciplinary Discussions	E1	Teacher does not introduce or refer to disciplinary conversation skills.	Teacher introduces and/or refers to disciplinary conversation skills, but does not provide support for students to use them during tasks and activities.	Teacher introduces and/or refers to disciplinary conversation skills and provides support to enable most students to use them during tasks and activities.	Teacher introduces and/or refers to disciplinary conversation skills and provides support to enable all students to use them during tasks and activities with diverse partners.
	E2	Teacher does not provide opportunities for disciplinary discussions.	Teacher provides limited and/or unsupported opportunities for students to engage in disciplinary discussions. Routines for disciplinary discussions are not evident, or students are not required to use them during tasks and activities.	Teacher provides supported opportunities for students to participate in disciplinary discussions. Routines for disciplinary discussions are evident, and teacher provides support to enable most students to use them during tasks and activities.	Teacher provides extended and supported opportunities for students to participate in disciplinary discussions. Routines for disciplinary discussions are evident, and teacher provides support to enable all students to use them during tasks and activities.

SUPPORTING THE COLLECTIVE GROWTH OF TEACHERS THROUGH PROFESSIONAL LEARNING COMMUNITIES

Supporting individuals to teach with metacognition and engage in reflective practice can have a positive impact on student learning. The impact we see on teaching and learning is even greater when teachers, instructional coaches, and instructional leaders engage together in cycles of observation and reflection. One approach to establishing and sustaining a collaborative professional-growth model is to cultivate professional learning communities (PLCs) at each school site. This type of professional-growth initiative at the school level requires a commitment to building trust, instructional capacity, and professional relationships.

A PLC is not a program but a continuous process (Figure 6.1) in which "educators work collaboratively in recurring cycles of collective inquiry and action research to achieve better results for the students they serve" (DuFour, DuFour, Eaker, & Many, 2006, p. 2). Research clearly shows that the most significant impact on school improvement and student achievement happens when school personnel function as a PLC (Fullan, 2005), as long as the PLC is truly designed to foster collaborative discussions about teaching and learning. Therefore, for a PLC to be effective, teachers, instructional coaches, and administrators all need to collaborate around student achievement.

One essential component of effective collaboration is establishing a shared vision and a common language for teaching and learning. Colleagues enact this shared vision and work interdependently, whereas leadership

Figure 6.1. A Process to Guide SOAR-Focused Professional Learning Communities (PLCs)

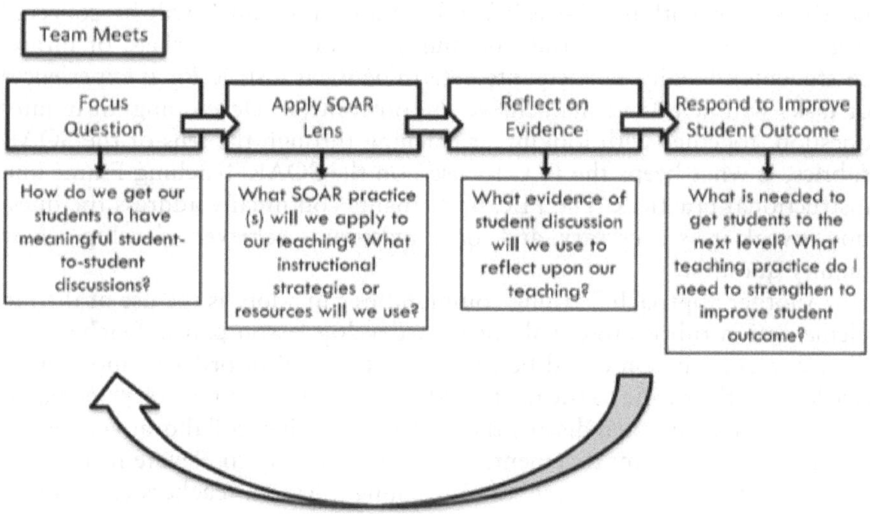

creates new structures and approaches for working together that are focused on the continuous improvement of teaching practices and student learning. They make adjustments to instruction based on shared data and are guided by key questions: What is working and for whom? What do we need to do for those who aren't getting it? In our work with schools and districts, we have used the following approach to guide the work of SOAR PLCs.

Inquiry Questions

PLCs are data-driven. To maintain a laser-like focus on the instructional practices articulated in a SOAR Teaching Frame, data are examined through the lens of inquiry questions that are derived from these guiding questions:

- What do we expect students to learn?
- How will our students demonstrate their new knowledge and skill?
- How will we use the SOAR lens to identify which teaching practices we need to strengthen or adjust to help students achieve the outcomes?
- What instructional experiences or tasks will help me strengthen that practice and help students achieve the outcomes?

Addressing the first guiding question involves establishing learning targets that are aligned with the CCSS and the target High-Impact Practice. Next, PLC participants consider how they will know when students have learned it. In other words, how will students demonstrate their new knowledge and skills, and what type of data (e.g., written work, transcripts, anecdotal evidence, or video) will provide evidence of student learning? Participants must also decide when they will collect data (e.g., tomorrow, next week, or within a 2-week window) and how much will be collected (e.g., a snapshot of two students, multiple groups, whole class, or targeted students). Finally, participants determine what instructional experiences or tasks will help students achieve the outcome(s). Developing an inquiry question, together with looking at teaching through the lens of the SOAR rubrics, is what keeps the PLC focused on the SOAR Teaching Frame and instructional practices. The PLC participants continually address the question, tweak it as necessary, and, once mastery is achieved, develop a new inquiry question.

Another approach learning communities can adopt is the use of the implementation rubrics to collaboratively develop lesson plans. Teachers can discuss ways a lesson could be revised and refined in order to move from one level of the rubric to the next. Additionally, asking a peer or principal to watch a lesson and then discuss the evidence together, collaboratively brainstorming areas for improvement, is an excellent way to elevate instruction across a school. For example, after teaching a lesson, teachers can look at the implementation rubric together and see where they believe their lessons could be elevated, similar to the example we saw in Chapter 1 with Ms. Aguirre and Ms. Rahim. Teachers could also share videos of their teaching with peers in the PLC setting. The following vignette describes how one school used the SOAR Teaching Frames and instructional resources to foster professional growth within a PLC structure.

Step Inside Rockville School

Rockville School (pseudonym) is in transition. It has a new principal who understands the necessity of building relationships and creating a collaborative culture. This is a school that has had very little professional development over the years. Teachers worked independently, and grade levels had little shared understanding of who was teaching what. In his first year, the principal implemented a two-day professional-learning session around the SOAR Disciplinary Discussions Teaching Frame. During the professional learning, teachers had time to collaborate and talk about what they could do to get their migrant population of students engaged in more disciplinary discussions. They also had opportunities to unpack the language of the teaching practices and view video examples of these practices in action. The principal shared his belief that if students were engaged in deeper discussions, they would improve their academic language, deepen their content knowledge by co-constructing meaning, and be more engaged in learning. The school already had established early release days throughout the year. The expectation was that teachers and administrators would meet once a month on those days in the library to work in PLCs to extend their learning and develop a culture of collaboration.

At the first PLC of the year, teachers discussed what the indicators of successful collaboration would be. They also reviewed four guiding questions:

1. What do we expect students to learn?
2. How will our students demonstrate their new knowledge and skills?
3. How will we use the SOAR lens to identify which teaching practices we need to strengthen or adjust to help students achieve the outcomes?
4. What instructional experiences or tasks will help us strengthen that practice and help students achieve the outcomes?

Then the teachers agreed to a set of norms, developed their inquiry question around the targeted Teaching Frame using the template provided by the facilitator, and created an agenda for the next meeting. The inquiry question they developed was: How do we facilitate lengthier and more authentic discussions among students that demonstrate critical thinking and processing? Teachers came to consensus regarding the student data they would collect, planned lessons using the SOAR Teaching Frame, and selected the instructional strategies they would use in those lessons. These professional conversations were very powerful, as participants began to share different ideas on how to engage their students in discussions guided by the language in the SOAR Teaching Frame. The principal shared what he had seen as he visited classrooms.

Teachers began the second PLC by discussing their inquiry question and looking at student data and evidence of teaching through the SOAR lens. All the grade levels decided to use transcripts from three sets of students before they began focusing on student discussions as baseline data. Then they began reflecting on their teaching and using the SOAR Teaching Frame to analyze areas that could be strengthened. They discussed concerns for those students who were reluctant to talk. Teachers asked one another how they introduced the conversation skills. Others shared how they started with baby steps, just giving their students one response question such as, "Can you tell me more?" There was energy in the room as teachers nodded their heads and asked one another clarifying questions. Teachers decided that they needed to spend more time focusing on facilitating students' use of appropriate academic language to engage in the conversation, and they discussed additional sentence frames and support they could provide to students. They collaboratively used the SOAR Teaching Frame to develop the next lesson they would implement.

Across the school year, teachers and instructional leaders engaged in strategic cycles of inquiry. They engaged in peer-to-peer observations and self-reflection using the SOAR Teaching Frames and rubrics. Teachers video-recorded lessons and uploaded them to an online platform where coaches could access the videos and provide feedback through the lens of the SOAR tools, using the rubrics as evidence of current instruction and the Teaching Frame to give feedback on how to enhance lessons. During subsequent PLC sessions, teachers, instructional coaches, and administrators debriefed this process, shared video examples, and discussed improvements and adjustments they had made to move from one level of teaching to the next for all practices in the Frame. In addition, they tracked changes they were seeing in student disciplinary discussions.

In this vignette, we see how cross-school adoption of the SOAR Frames can shift a culture to one of professional collaboration with impact on teaching and learning. This case also reflects the important role instructional leaders play in putting conditions in place that allow such a culture to flourish. The SOAR Teaching Frames provide the common language and thread that leads to a cohesive approach to improvements in instruction, targeting those practices we know drive student learning (Reyes et. al, 2020). The structures that were put in place at Rockville School, like the PLCs and dedicated time for collaboration, were key to supporting deep implementation of the SOAR practices in every classroom.

BUILDING A CULTURE OF PROFESSIONAL GROWTH DISTRICTWIDE

We know that when it comes to the academic achievement of students, among school-related factors, teaching matters most. Therefore, it is imperative that schools and districts understand that supporting teachers' professional growth must be one of their highest priorities and that effective professional-growth experiences require much more than a one- or two-day seminar. All professional-growth initiatives within a district should be built on three key principles (O'Hara, Pritchard, & Zwiers, 2016; Reyes et al., 2020):

1. Focus consistently on the teaching practices that we know drive learning for all students.
2. Cultivate learning communities where teachers, instructional coaches, and instructional leaders engage together in cycles of strategic observation and reflection and develop the ability to teach with metacognition.
3. Create the conditions districtwide for supporting professional growth of teachers to drive improvements in teaching and learning.

The success of professional-growth initiatives depends on district leadership embracing these principles and ensuring that they are the focus of teachers and leaders at all schools across the district. Louis, Leithwood, Wahlstrom, Anderson, Michlin, and Mascall (2010) defined leadership as "establishing agreed-upon and worthwhile directions for the organization in question and doing whatever it takes to prod and support people to move in those directions" (pp. 9–10). In the executive summary of their report, these authors concluded that "leadership effects on student learning occur largely because leadership strengthens professional community; teachers' engagement in professional community, in turn, fosters the use of instructional practices that are associated with student achievement" (p. 10). One large urban district in California illustrates how district leadership enacted these principles to implement the SOAR Teaching Frames for Literacy.

Step Inside South End School District

Among the largest in the nation, the South End School District (pseudonym) is a diverse urban district serving a high proportion of students classified as ELs (36%). The district's journey began with South End teachers and coaches enrolling in a massive open online course (MOOC) focused on the SOAR Teaching Frames. The MOOC sought to establish a common vision of instruction targeting the needs of ELs and appealed to district administrators who were interested in fostering professional growth across the district to implement the California ELA/ELD Framework. The charge for the cross-role district design team was to implement the ELD Standards in tandem with the California Content Standards. Their approach to this was to

- establish and expand collaboration,
- develop resources, and
- align curriculum, instruction, and assessment.

> "Our story began with a desire to move action research into classroom practice with the aim of improving instruction for English learners. We wanted to build the capacity in the district to meet the needs of our EL students and to focus on language as a driver for content learning."
> —South End Design Team Member

Together, South End teachers and coaches engaged in professional learning through participation in the MOOC, and in spring 2016 they worked with the SOAR developers to design and implement a SOAR Fellowship, the district's term for a professional learning program. The program was implemented with 70 district administrators over five Fridays and with 100 teacher-principal pairs over five Saturdays.

The South End design team wanted to implement a common vision of instruction that would drive learning as articulated in the California ELA/ELD Framework and would also prioritize the importance of language for learning. They selected the SOAR Teaching Frames as their shared set of high-impact instructional practices.

Once the team made the decision to focus work on the SOAR Teaching Frames, they began to determine how best to develop the professional capital needed for ongoing facilitation of professional growth around those practices. They developed curriculum support materials and unit plans aligned with the practices for different grade spans. In addition, they developed a suite of videos and online tools to support this work. They had principal and teacher pairs from schools within each local district participate in a SOAR Fellowship Program, and they also had district administrators and Title III coaches participate in their own SOAR professional learning to prepare them to support teachers' implementation of the SOAR practices.

> "We need to be all learning together, so we want to build the knowledge and skills of teachers, coaches, and administrators together. We've done professional development around constructive conversations and we know that speaking and listening around the content area is important. SOAR furthers that work and will benefit my staff and it will benefit every child in my school—not just the ELs—every student."—South End Administrator

The South End design team understood the importance of building a professional culture that would promote ongoing collaboration and feedback. They recognized that this professional culture included building relationships internally and also with external partners.

> "We see the importance of building relationships to facilitate this work. We have focused on building teacher-principal reflective teams, relationships among administrators across different departments within South End, and building relationships with university intermediaries as we co-develop the professional-growth work."—South End Design Team Member

They focused time on building a community of trust and strengthening relationships between and among teachers, administrators, management, and labor. They also recognized the importance of structuring the collaboration to allow teachers and leaders to have an equal voice.

> "We see the importance of bringing in teacher-principal pairs to learn about SOAR together as reflective partners in the work. Working in reflective pairs, teachers and principals have had the same learning. They can see together what they need to strengthen, and it also helps principals to think about how to provide the best support for teachers."
> —South End Design Team Member

The South End team put a number of structures in place to facilitate peer-to-peer collaboration and feedback across the district using the SOAR Teaching Frames as their common vision of instruction. These structures were designed to (a) support individual teachers and improve their ability to teach with metacognition, (b) foster collective teacher growth through PLCs at each school, and (c) facilitate ongoing professional dialogue across the district about instructional improvement using the SOAR Teaching Frames as a lens.

When you read the case of Rockville School earlier in the chapter, you saw the power of adopting the SOAR Teaching Frames schoolwide. The vignette above shows how the impact is amplified when SOAR is adopted by an entire district. Leaders at South End School District understood that adopting the framework and providing professional-learning experiences focused on SOAR is just one step in an approach to improve teaching and learning. Structures and conditions should also be in place to allow principals, instructional coaches, and teachers to engage in regular, strategic cycles of observation and reflection using the SOAR Teaching Frames as a lens. With a common instructional framework like SOAR in place, teachers can share ideas and lessons based on the Teaching Frames that can be more easily adopted by their peers and implemented in all classrooms.

CONCLUSION

Improvement of teaching practice through any school- or district-level effort relies on teachers and instructional leaders using common language to discuss teaching practices and make suggestions for improvement. Furthermore, it relies on consistent, dedicated time for communities to come together, reflect on teaching, and collaborate to elevate instruction. The common language used should be aligned to the teaching practices that we know drive student learning.

You have now been introduced to all four SOAR Teaching Frames, and you have explored strategies, tools, and lesson examples to provide you with illustrations for how the practices can be implemented in your classroom. As we stated in Chapter 1, the frames were developed to support the disciplinary language and literacy development of all students and are designed to meet the needs of a wide range of students. Implementing these practices in your classroom will elevate your instruction and support you in ensuring that your students can meet the challenge of being college and career ready.

As an individual teacher adopting these frames and using them to plan, teach, reflect upon, and elevate your practice, you will see a difference in student outcomes. Working collaboratively with peers at your grade level, school, or district to use the Teaching Frames for dialogue about teaching and learning will yield even greater results. The Teaching Frames and rubrics are a research-based framework to help you and your colleagues build literacy classrooms that SOAR.

Appendixes

Appendix A. Conversation Prompts and Responses

CREATE: 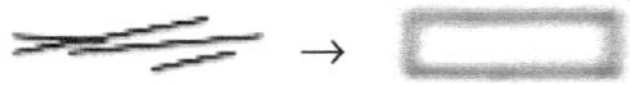 (Put hands over head, open and close them, as if an idea is coming out of your head)		**CLARIFY:** 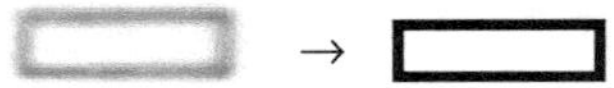 (Place hands over eyes as if focusing binoculars)	
Prompt Starters:	*Response Starters:*	*Prompt Starters:*	*Response Starters:*
• What is your idea? • What do you think about . . . ? • Why? How? I wonder . . . • What are other points of view?	• One idea could be . . . • My hypothesis is . . . • I think . . . • I noticed the pattern of . . .	• Can you elaborate on the . . . ? • What do you mean by . . . ? • Can you clarify the part about . . . ? • Say more about . . . • Does that make sense?	• I think it means . . . • In other words, . . . • It is important because . . . • It sounds like you think that . . . • A different way to say it is . . .
NEGOTIATE: 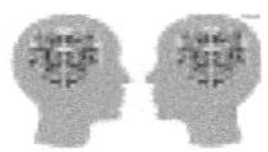 (Put your hands out by your shoulders, palms up. Move them up and down like a scale)		**FORTIFY:**  (Place your hand palm down as if putting an idea on the table, and use the fingertips of the other hand to support the palm)	
Prompt Starters:	*Response Starters:*	*Prompt Starters:*	*Response Starters:*
• What is your opinion? • Where do you disagree? • How might we take the best from both ideas?	• I see it a different way. • On the other hand, . . . • I agree with you on . . . • I disagree . . .	• Can you give an example from the text? • Where does it say that? • Are there any cases of that in real life?	• For example, . . . • In the text it said that . . . • Remember in the other story, we read that . . . . • An example from my life is . . .

Adapted from *Common Core Standards in Diverse Classrooms*, by J. Zwiers, S. O'Hara, and R. Pritchard, 2014a. Copyright 2014 by Stenhouse. Adapted with permission.

American Symbols

The American Flag: Our flag has 50 stars, one for each state, and 13 stripes for each of the original colonies. Red stands for bravery. Blue represents justice. White stands for goodness. It is often called "Stars and Stripes" and "Old Glory."

Statue of Liberty: This statue stands in New York Harbor. She welcomed many people to the United States. She stands for freedom. She was a gift for America's 100th birthday. The people of France gave her to us.

Bald Eagle: The Bald Eagle is our national bird. It has been a patriotic symbol since 1782. It represents courage, strength, and freedom. The eagle is on many coins, the dollar bill, and the presidential flag.

Liberty Bell: The Liberty Bell is located in Philadelphia, Pennsylvania. It cracked the first time someone rang it. It was named the Liberty Bell by the abolitionists who fought slavery. It is a symbol of America's Independence.

Washington Monument: The Washington Monument was built to honor George Washington. He commanded the army that fought the British and was our first president. It is the tallest structure in the city limits of Washington, DC.

Constitution of the United States: The Constitution was completed in 1787. It says how government works. It created the three branches of government: Executive (President), Legislative (Senate and House of Representatives), and Judicial (Supreme Court and lower courts). It also lists important rights that all people have.

Capitol Building: This is the building where U.S. Congress meets. Congress is made up of the House of Representatives and the Senate. Congress's job is to make laws. It represents the American people's government.

Buffalo Soldiers

Origin of the Buffalo Soldiers

After the Civil War, Congress established six all African-American army regiments: the 9th and 10th Cavalries and the 38th, 39th, 40th, and 41st Infantries. Several years later, the four infantry units were reorganized into the 24th and 25th Infantries, and the cavalry and infantry often fought together. Each of these regiments contained approximately 1,000 men, who became known as Buffalo Soldiers. Although we cannot be sure how they got their name, most people believe that Native Americans first called the troops Buffalo Soldiers because of their dark curly hair, the buffalo-skin coats they wore, and their bravery in battle.

Life as Buffalo Soldiers

Many of the original members of these segregated units were former slaves who had served in the United States Colored Troops during the Civil War. Although the pay was low (about $13 a month), many African American men enlisted because they could make more money in the army than by doing anything else. They were also given food, shelter, and medical help. So for many of the men who had been slaves, being a soldier offered dignity and a way to start a new life. In fact, for most African American citizens at the time, the Buffalo Soldiers were a symbol of hope for a better future.

On the Western Frontier

During the early years of their history, the Buffalo Soldiers' primary responsibilities were to help rebuild the country after the Civil War and to patrol the western frontier. They protected settlers, built forts, and mapped the wilderness. In 1885, some Buffalo Soldiers were sent to the Indian Territory to remove White settlers who were illegally claiming Native American land. During the same period, Buffalo Soldiers helped control the Native American tribes of the plains and the Southwest, escorted stagecoaches and payrolls, and fought cattle rustlers.

The Legacy of the Buffalo Soldiers

African-American soldiers performed exemplary service in segregated units from the time Buffalo Soldier regiments were first formed until 1948, when President Harry Truman ordered the army to integrate. These soldiers earned many Medals of Honor and Certificates of Merit despite often being issued older horses, undependable equipment, and less ammunition than other regiments. At a time when many soldiers suffered from alcoholism, Buffalo Soldiers were rarely drunk. In addition, they were court-martialed less frequently than White soldiers were, and they deserted less often than White soldiers did. In fact, from 1880 to 1886, Buffalo Soldiers had the lowest desertion rate in the entire army.

Appendix D. Formative Assessments of Student Talk—Disciplinary Discussions

Score	Building Up an Idea	Score	Using Academic Language	Score	Applying Metacognitive Strategies
4	The discussion is clear and focused, effectively addresses the prompt or task, and leads to co-construction of new ideas. The discussion includes the following: • Creates a clear initial idea • Builds on others' ideas • Fortifies others' ideas with evidence • Combines and connects ideas to strengthen the discussion		This discussion demonstrates the use of discourse feature language to effectively convey co-constructed ideas. This discussion includes the following: • Uses vocabulary appropriately • Uses syntax appropriately • Uses the language of the discourse feature to strengthen the discussion		In this discussion, metacognition (awareness and action) is appropriately and independently applied. This discussion includes the following: • Clear and well-connected turns demonstrate monitoring • When needed, strategies are applied appropriately and independently
3	The discussion is clear but not consistently focused, addresses the prompt or task, and leads to co-construction of new ideas. The discussion includes the following: • Creates a clear initial idea • Builds on others' ideas • Fortifies others' ideas with evidence • Combines and connects ideas, but they don't consistently strengthen the discussion		This discussion demonstrates the use of discourse feature language to convey co-constructed ideas. This discussion includes the following: • Uses vocabulary appropriately • Uses syntax appropriately • Uses the language of the discourse feature, but not in ways that consistently strengthen the discussion		In this discussion, metacognition (awareness and action) is appropriately applied with support. This discussion includes the following: • Clear and well-connected turns demonstrate monitoring • When needed, strategies are applied appropriately with support

Score	Building Up an Idea	Score	Using Academic Language	Score	Applying Metacognitive Strategies
2	This discussion is somewhat unclear, irrelevant, or incomplete. This discussion includes the following: • Creates a clear initial idea • Demonstrates limited attempts to build on others' ideas • Provides evidence but it is irrelevant or inappropriate		The discussion demonstrates use of vocabulary and syntax, but does not demonstrate use of discourse feature language. This discussion includes the following: • Uses vocabulary appropriately • Uses syntax appropriately		In this discussion, metacognition is partially applied (awareness only). This discussion includes the following: • Clear and well-connected turns demonstrate monitoring • Strategies are not applied when the conversation stalls or gets off track
1	This discussion is unclear and lacks central purpose. The discussion includes the following: • Does not create a clear initial idea • Expresses only simplistic or random ideas		This discussion does not demonstrate appropriate use of academic language. This discussion includes the following: • Uses vocabulary inappropriately • Uses syntax inappropriately		In this discussion, metacognition is not applied. This includes the following: • There are no clear or well-organized turns that demonstrate monitoring • Strategies are not applied

Appendix E. Formative Assessments of Student Talk—Disciplinary Communication

Score	Communicating Understanding	Score	Using Academic Language	Score	Applying Metacognitive Strategies
4	The oral communication is clear and focused. There is a clear initial claim or idea that is supported by evidence through logical and connected supporting statements. The oral communication includes the following: • First sentence clearly helps listeners understand what the claim or idea will be • Next sentences effectively clarify and/or use evidence to support the claim or idea • Sentences are effectively organized and connected (e.g., using transitions)		This oral communication demonstrates the use of discourse feature language to effectively communicate disciplinary understanding. This communication includes the following: • Uses vocabulary appropriately • Uses syntax appropriately • Uses the language of the discourse feature to strengthen the communication		In this oral communication, metacognition (awareness and action) is appropriately and independently applied. This communication includes the following: • Active listening and/or recognizing flaws or gaps in the communication demonstrate monitoring • When needed, strategies are applied independently
3	The oral communication is clear and somewhat focused. There is a clear initial claim or idea that is supported by some evidence. Supporting statements are logical but not consistently connected. The oral communication includes the following: • First sentence satisfactorily helps listeners understand what the claim or idea will be, with some lack of clarity • Next sentences satisfactorily use evidence to support the claim or idea, with some lack of clarity • Sentences are organized but are not consistently connected (e.g., using transitions), which results in some lack of clarity		This oral communication demonstrates the use of discourse feature language to communicate disciplinary understanding. This communication includes the following: • Uses vocabulary appropriately • Uses syntax appropriately • Uses the language of the discourse feature, but not in ways that consistently strengthen the communication		In this oral communication, metacognition (awareness and action) is appropriately applied with support. This communication includes the following: • Active listening and/or recognizing flaws or gaps in the communication demonstrate monitoring • When needed, strategies are applied appropriately with support

Score	Communicating Understanding	Score	Using Academic Language	Score	Applying Metacognitive Strategies
2	The oral communication is clear but not focused. There is a clear initial claim or idea, but it is not supported by limited evidence and/or supporting statements are not logical or connected. The oral communication includes the following: The student does most or all of the following: • First sentence communicates what the claim or idea will be • Next sentences are unclear and/or use limited evidence to support the claim or idea • Sentences are somewhat organized but not connected (e.g., using transitions), which results in a lack of clarity		The oral communication demonstrates use of vocabulary and syntax but does not demonstrate use of discourse feature language. This communication includes the following: • Uses vocabulary appropriately • Uses syntax appropriately		In this oral communication, metacognition is (awareness only). This communication includes the following: • Active listening and/or recognizing flaws or gaps in the communication demonstrate monitoring • Strategies are not applied when needed
1	The oral communication is unclear and not focused. There is no clear initial claim or idea. There is no use of supporting evidence. The oral communication includes the following: • Sentences are unclear • No use of evidence to support the claim or idea • Sentences are not organized or connected (e.g., using transitions)		The oral communication does not demonstrate appropriate use of academic language. This communication includes the following: • Uses vocabulary inappropriately • Uses syntax inappropriately		In this oral communication, metacognition is not applied. This communication includes the following: • No active listening and/or no recognizing flaws or gaps in the communication which demonstrates a lack of monitoring • Strategies are not applied

Appendix F. Implementation Rubric—Disciplinary Discussions Teaching Frame

		No Implementation	→ →	→ →	→ → Full Implementation
Disciplinary Discussions	E1	Teacher does not introduce or refer to disciplinary conversation skills.	Teacher introduces and/or refers to disciplinary conversation skills, but does not provide support for students to use them during tasks and activities.	Teacher introduces and/or refers to disciplinary conversation skills and provides support to enable most students to use them during tasks and activities.	Teacher introduces and/or refers to disciplinary conversation skills and provides support to enable all students to use them during tasks and activities with diverse partners.
	E2	Teacher does not provide opportunities for disciplinary discussions.	Teacher provides limited and/or unsupported opportunities for students to engage in disciplinary discussions. Routines for disciplinary discussions are not evident, or students are not required to use them during tasks and activities.	Teacher provides supported opportunities for students to participate in disciplinary discussions. Routines for disciplinary discussions are evident, and teacher provides support to enable most students to use them during tasks and activities.	Teacher provides extended and supported opportunities for students to participate in disciplinary discussions. Routines for disciplinary discussions are evident, and teacher provides support to enable all students to use them during tasks and activities.

		No Implementation	→ →	→ →	→ → Full Implementation
Facilitating Acquisition of Academic Language	E1	Teacher does not introduce or refer to the academic language demands of texts or tasks.	Teacher introduces and/or refers to the academic language demands, but does not explain how the demands are connected to the disciplinary texts and/or tasks.	Teacher introduces and/or refers to the academic language demands, and explains how the demands are connected to the disciplinary texts and/or tasks. The explanation is structured to be accessible to most students.	Teacher introduces and/or refers to the academic language demands, and explains how the demands are connected to the disciplinary texts and/or tasks. The explanation is structured to be accessible to all students.
	E2	Teacher provides unsupported opportunities for students to acquire academic language.	Teacher provides supported opportunities for students to acquire and use academic language, but these opportunities only address vocabulary and/or syntax.	Teacher provides supported opportunities for students to acquire and use academic language of the discourse feature, and these opportunities are structured to engage most students.	Teacher provides extended and supported opportunities for students to acquire and use academic language of the discourse feature, and these opportunities are structured to engage all students.

Table continues on next page

Appendix F. Implementation Rubric—Disciplinary Discussions Teaching Frame (continued)

		No Implementation →	→ →	→ → →	Full Implementation
Fostering Metacognition for Disciplinary Learning	E1	Teacher does not enact metacognitive processes and/or strategies students are expected to use in support of disciplinary learning.	Teacher partially enacts metacognitive processes and/or strategies students are expected to use, and/or it is not clear how these support disciplinary learning.	Teacher clearly and completely enacts metacognitive processes and/or strategies students are expected to use in support of disciplinary learning.	Teacher clearly and completely enacts metacognitive processes and/or strategies students are expected to use in support of disciplinary learning. Teacher overtly makes enactment visible to all students.
	E2	Teacher does not draw attention to metacognitive processes and/or strategies that support disciplinary learning.	Teacher draws attention to metacognitive processes and/or strategies that support disciplinary learning, but does not explain how, why, or when to use them.	Teacher deconstructs metacognitive processes and/or strategies that support disciplinary learning by explaining how, why, or when to use them.	Teacher deconstructs metacognitive processes and/or strategies that support disciplinary learning by explaining how, why, or when to use them. The deconstruction is structured to enable all students to use strategies independently.

		No Implementation	→ →	→ →	→ → Full Implementation
Monitoring and Guiding Disciplinary Learning	E1	Teacher does not monitor student learning.	Teacher monitors student learning but does not adjust instruction or disciplinary tasks as needed to meet student needs.	Teacher monitors student learning and adjusts instruction, supports, and/or disciplinary tasks as needed to meet the needs of most students.	Teacher monitors student learning throughout instruction and adjusts instruction, supports, and/or disciplinary tasks as necessary to meet the needs of all students.
	E2	Teacher does not provide feedback during lessons or provides only evaluative feedback.	Teacher provides feedback that is vague and/or nonspecific.	Teacher provides constructive feedback during lessons. Suggestions for how to improve disciplinary learning are specific and substantive.	Teacher provides constructive feedback during lessons. Suggestions for how to improve disciplinary learning are specific and substantive. Feedback is constructed to meet the specific needs of all students.

Table continues on next page

Appendix F. Implementation Rubric—Disciplinary Discussions Teaching Frame (continued)

		No Implementation →	→ →	→ → →	Full Implementation
Designing Instruction for Disciplinary Thinking and Understanding	E1	Learning targets are not apparent and/or do not align with the ELA/Literacy CCSS.	Learning targets are apparent and align with ELA/Literacy CCSS, but do not support the target High-Impact Practice.	Learning targets are apparent, align with ELA/Literacy CCSS, and support the target High-Impact Practice.	Learning targets are apparent, align with ELA/Literacy CCSS, and support the target High-Impact Practice. Teacher strategically attends to the learning targets during the lesson.
	E2	Teacher structures tasks that do not support learning targets.	Teacher structures discrete tasks that support learning targets, but the tasks do not work in conjunction with one another.	Teacher structures tasks that support the learning targets. The tasks work in conjunction with one another.	Teacher structures tasks that support the learning targets, and the tasks work in conjunction with one another. The teacher makes explicit to students how tasks are connected to one another and to the learning targets.
	E3	Teacher does not establish high expectations.	Teacher establishes high expectations, but designs activities and tasks that are almost entirely rote or routine.	Teacher establishes high expectations and designs activities and tasks that are intellectually rigorous. These activities and tasks are structured to enable most students to meet these expectations.	Teacher establishes high expectations and designs activities and tasks that are intellectually rigorous. These activities and tasks are structured to enable all students to meet these expectations.

Appendix G: Implementation Rubric—Disciplinary Interactions With Complex Text

		No Implementation	→ →	→ → →	Full Implementation
Disciplinary Interactions With Complex Text	E1	Teacher does not refer to language, text features, and/or literary devices used in text.	Teacher refers to language, text features, and/or literary devices used in text, but does not engage students in an analysis of how these are used to convey meaning and/or purpose.	Teacher engages students in an analysis of text to examine how language, text features, and/or literary devices are used to convey meaning and/or purpose. The analysis is structured to be accessible to most students.	Teacher engages students in an analysis of text to examine how language, text features, and/or literary devices are used to convey meaning and/or purpose. The analysis is structured to be accessible to all students.
	E2	Teacher does not provide opportunities for students to interact with complex text.	Teacher provides opportunities for students to interact with complex text. However, these opportunities are unsupported and/or not structured to build academic language and disciplinary literacy.	Teacher provides supported opportunities for students to interact with complex text to build academic language and disciplinary literacy. These opportunities are structured to be accessible to most students.	Teacher provides supported and extended opportunities for students to interact with complex text to build academic language and disciplinary literacy. These opportunities are structured to be accessible to all students.

Appendix H: Implementation Rubric—Disciplinary Uses of Evidence

		No Implementation	→ → →	→ → →	Full Implementation
Disciplinary Uses of Evidence	E1	Teacher does not engage students in an analysis of evidence.	Teacher engages students in an analysis of evidence that is unclear and/or inaccessible to most students.	Teacher engages students in a complete and accurate analysis of evidence for relevancy. The analysis is clear and structured to be accessible to most students.	Teacher engages students in a complete and accurate analysis of evidence for relevancy. In addition, the teacher deconstructs the evidence by explaining why and how it is or is not relevant. The analysis is structured to be accessible to all students.
	E2	Teacher does not provide opportunities for students to identify and/or use evidence.	Teacher provides opportunities for students to identify and/or use evidence, but the opportunities are not structured to enable students to understand how the evidence supports the claims.	Teacher provides and supports opportunities for students to identify and use sufficient evidence to support claims. These opportunities are structured to enable most students to understand how the evidence supports the claims.	Teacher provides and supports multiple opportunities for students to identify and use sufficient evidence to support claims. These opportunities are structured to enable all students to understand how the evidence supports the claims.

Appendix I: Implementation Rubric—Disciplinary Communication

		No Implementation → →	→ →	→ →	Full Implementation
Disciplinary Communication	E1	Teacher does not provide opportunities for students to produce disciplinary oral communication.	Teacher provides limited and/or unsupported opportunities for students to produce disciplinary oral communication, and/or there are limited opportunities for original production.	Teacher provides supported opportunities for students to produce original disciplinary oral communication appropriate to task, purpose, and audience. These opportunities are structured to engage most students.	Teacher provides multiple and supported opportunities for students to produce and fortify original disciplinary oral communication appropriate to task, purpose, and audience. These opportunities are structured to engage all students.
	E2	Teacher does not provide opportunities for students to produce disciplinary written communication.	Teacher provides limited and/or unsupported opportunities for students to produce disciplinary written communication, and/or there are limited opportunities for original production.	Teacher provides supported opportunities for students to produce and fortify original disciplinary written communication appropriate to task, purpose, and audience. These opportunities are structured to engage most students.	Teacher provides extended and supported opportunities for students to produce and fortify original disciplinary written communication appropriate to task, purpose, and audience. These opportunities are structured to engage all students.

References

Alvermann, D. E. (1991). The Discussion Web: A graphic aid for learning across the curriculum. *The Reading Teacher, 45*, 92–99.

Andrews, R., Torgerson, C., Low, G., & McGuinn, N. (2009). Teaching argument writing to 7- to 14-year-olds: An international review of the evidence of successful practice. *Cambridge Journal of Education, 39*(3), 291–310.

Anstrom, K., DiCerbo, P., Butler, F., Katz, A., Millet, J., & Rivera, C. (2010). *A review of the literature on academic English: Implications for K–12 English language learners*. The George Washington University Center for Equity and Excellence in Education. https://nysrti.org/files/resources/ells/litreviewacademicenglish.pdf

Assaf, L. C. (2014). Supporting English language learners' writing abilities: Exploring third spaces. *Middle Grades Research Journal, 9*, 1–17.

August, D., Branum-Martin, L., Cardenas-Hagan, E., Francis, D., Powell, J., Moore, S., & Haynes, E. (2014). Helping ELLs meet the Common Core State Standards for literacy in science: The impact of an instructional intervention focused on academic language. *Journal of Research on Educational Effectiveness, 7*, 54–82.

Bernabei, G., & Reimer, J. (2013). *Academic writing for serious learning*. Corwin Literacy.

Blachowicz, C. L. Z. (1986). Making connections: Alternatives to the vocabulary notebook. *Journal of Reading, 29*, 643–649.

Board of Regents of the University of Wisconsin System. (2012). *WIDA's 2012 amplification of the English language development standards, kindergarten–grade 12*. https://wida.wisc.edu/sites/default/files/resource/2012-ELD-Standards.pdf

California Department of Education. (2014). *English language arts/English language development framework for California Public Schools*. https://www.cde.ca.gov/ci/rl/cf/documents/elaeldfwintro.pdf

Cook, H. G., Boals, T., & Lundberg, T. (2011). Academic achievement for English learners: What can we reasonably expect? *Phi Delta Kappan, 93*(3), 66–69.

Cummins, S. (2013). *Close reading of informational texts: Assessment-driven instruction in grades 3–8*. Guilford Press.

Curtis, R. (2013). *Finding a new way: Leveraging teacher leadership to meet unprecedented demands*. The Aspen Institute. https://www.aspeninstitute.org/publications/finding-new-way-leveraging-teacher-leadership-meet-unprecedented-demands

DuFour, R., DuFour, R., Eaker, R., & Many, T. (2006). *Learning by doing: A handbook for professional learning communities at work*. Solution Tree USA.

Duke, N. K., & Pearson, P. D. (2009). Effective practices for developing reading comprehension. *Journal of Education, 189*(1/2), 107–122.

Education Northwest. (2012). *What are the traits?* https://educationnorthwest.org/traits/trait-definitions

Fisher, D., Brozo, W. G., Frey, N., & Ivey, G. (2011). *50 instructional routines to develop content literacy* (2nd ed.). Pearson.

Fisher, D., & Frey, N. (2014). *Close reading and writing from sources*. International Reading Association.

Fisher, D., Frey, N., & Lapp, D. (2012). *Text complexity: Raising rigor in reading*. International Reading Association.

Fogo, B. (2011). Making and measuring the California History Standards. *Phi Delta Kappan, 92*(8), 62–67.

Fullan, M. (2005). Professional learning communities writ large. In R. DuFour, R. Eaker, & R. DuFour (Eds.), *On common ground: The power of professional learning communities* (pp. 209–223). Solution Tree.

Gronn, P. (2002). Distributed leadership. In K. Leithwood, P. Hallinger, K. Seashore-Louis, G. Furman-Brown, P. Gronn, W. Mulford, & K. Riley (Eds.), *Second international handbook of educational leadership and administration* (pp. 653–696). Kluwer.

Grossman, P. (2018). *Teaching core practices in teacher education*. Harvard Education Press.

Grossman, P., & Davis, E. (2012). Mentoring that fits. *Educational Leadership, 69*(8), 54–57.

Hartung-Cole, E. (2015). Complex sentences: Independent access for your ELLs. *TESOL Connections*, November 1–4. http://newsmanager.commpartners.com/tesolc/issues/2015-11-01/4.html

Hattie, J. (2012). Feedback in schools. In R. Sutton, M. Hornsey, & K. Douglas (Eds.), *Feedback: The communication of praise, criticism, and advice* (pp. 265–278). Peter Lang.

Hoyt, L. (2000). *Snapshots: Literacy lessons up close*. Heinemann.

Hunzicker, J. (2013). Attitude has a lot to do with it: Dispositions of emerging teacher leadership. *Teacher Development, 17*(4), 538–561.

Kagan, S. (1994). *Kagan Cooperative Learning*. Kagan Publishing.

Kazemi, E., & Hintz, A. (2014). *Intentional talk: How to structure and lead productive mathematical discussions*. Stenhouse Publishers.

Kibler, A., Walqui, A., & Bunch, G. (2015). Transformational opportunities: Language and literacy instruction for English language learners in the Common Core era in the United States. *TESOL Journal, 6*(1), 9–35. https://doi.org/10.1002/tesj.133

Kolic-Vehovec, S., & Bajsanski, I. (2006). Metacognitive strategies and reading comprehension in elementary-school students. *European Journal of Psychology of Education, 21*, 439–451.

Louis, K. S., Leithwood, K., Wahlstrom, K., Anderson, S., Michlin, M., & Mascall, B. (2010). *Learning from leadership: Investigating the links to improved student learning. Final report of research*. Center for Applied Research and Educational Improvement, University of Minnesota & Toronto: Ontario Institute for Studies in Education at the University of Toronto. https://www.wallacefoundation.org/knowledge-center/Documents/Investigating-the-Links-to-Improved-Student-Learning-Executive-Summary.pdf

Marzano, R., & Heflebower, T. (2011). *Teaching & assessing 21st century skills.* Marzano Research. https://eric.ed.gov/?id=ED539069

Marzano, R. J., & Simms, J. A. (2013). *Vocabulary for the Common Core.* Marzano Research.

Marzano, R., Yanoski, D., Hoegh, J., & Simms, J. (2013). *Using Common Core standards to enhance classroom instruction and assessment.* Marzano Research.

McDonald, M., Kazemi, E., & Kavanagh, S. (2013). Core practices and pedagogies of teacher education: A call for a common language and collective activity. *Journal of Teacher Education, 20*(10), 1–9.

McKenna, M. C. (2002). *Help for struggling readers: Strategies for grades 3–8.* Guilford.

Minero, E. (2016). *Talking in class: Strategies for developing confident speakers who can share their thoughts and learning.* Edutopia. https://www.edutopia.org/practice/oracy-classroom-strategies-effective-talk

Moll, L. C., & Gonzalez, N. (1994). Lessons from research with language-minority children. *Journal of Reading Behavior, 26,* 439–456.

Nagy, W., & Townsend, D. (2012). Words as tools: Learning academic vocabulary as language acquisition. *Reading Research Quarterly, 47*(1), 91–108. https://doi.org/10.1002/RRQ.011

Ness, M. (2011). Explicit reading comprehension instruction in elementary classrooms: Teacher use of reading comprehension strategies. *Journal of Research in Childhood Education, 25*(1), 98–117.

O'Hara, S., Bookmyer, J., Martin, R., & Newton, R. (2018). Theory of action for resourcing professional growth. *Journal of Professional Capital and Community, 4*(1), 52–65.

O'Hara, S., & Pritchard, R. (2016). Framing teaching for Common Core literacy standards: SOAR Teaching Frames for literacy. *Psychology Research, 6*(2), 92–101. https://doi.org/10.17265/2159-5542/2016.02.004

O'Hara, S., Pritchard, R., & Pitta, D. (2019). Teaching with and for metacognition in disciplinary discussions. In N. Feza (Ed.), *Metacognition in learning* (pp. 17–35). IntechOpen. https://www.intechopen.com/books/metacognition-in-learning/teaching-with-and-for-metacognition-in-disciplinary-discussions

O'Hara, S., Pritchard, R., & Zwiers, J. (2014). The academic language development program: A capacity-building approach to supporting secondary teachers of English learners. *Proceedings of the Adult Education Research Conference, 2014,* pp. 349–354. https://newprairiepress.org/aerc/2014/papers/59

O'Hara, S., Pritchard, R., & Zwiers, J. (2016). Academic language and literacy in every subject (ALLIES): A capacity building approach to supporting teachers in grades 4–8. In P. Proctor, A. Boardman, & E. Hiebert (Eds.), *English learners and emergent bilingualism in the Common Core era* (pp. 197–214). Guilford Press.

O'Hara, S., Zwiers, J., & Pritchard, R. (2014). Cutting to the Common Core: Changing the playing field, part 1. *Language Magazine: The Journal of Communication & Education, 13*(5), 24–27.

Pritchard, R., & O'Hara, S. (2007). Using think alouds to identify and teach reading comprehension strategies. *The CATESOL Journal, 18*(1), 151–159.

Pritchard, R., & O'Hara, S. (2016). Framing the teaching of academic language to English learners: A Delphi study of expert consensus. *TESOL Quarterly, 51*(2), 418–428. https://doi.org/10.1002/tesq.337

Reyes, R., Bookmyer, J., O'Hara, S., Pitta, D., & Pritchard, R. (2020). Rebuild and reboot: California district's teacher-driven approach focuses on equity. *The Learning Professional 41*(1), 52–56.

Ritchhart, R., Church, M., & Morrison, K. (2011). *Making thinking visible: How to promote engagement, understanding, and independence for all learners.* Jossey-Bass.

Schoenbach, R., Greenleaf, C., & Murphy, L. (2012). *Reading for understanding: How reading apprenticeship improves disciplinary learning.* Jossey-Bass.

Stahl, S. A., & Kapinus, B. A. (1991). Possible sentences: Predicting word meaning to teach content area vocabulary. *The Reading Teacher, 45*, 36–45.

Steurer, J. (2011). The Delphi method: An efficient procedure to generate knowledge. *Skeletal Radiology, 40*(8), 959–961.

Strong, R., Silver, H., & Perini, M. (2001). *Teaching what matters most: Standards and strategies for raising student achievement.* Association for Supervision and Curriculum Development.

Thompson, J., Windschitl, M., & Braaten, M. (2013). Developing a theory of ambitious early-career teacher practice. *American Educational Research Journal, 50*(3), 574–615.

Wiggins, G. (2012). Seven keys for effective feedback. *Feedback for Learning, 70*(1), 10–16.

Wiggins, G., & McTighe, J. (2005). *Understanding by Design* (2nd ed.). ASCD.

Wilson, H. W., Sztajn, P., Edington, C., & Myers, M. (2015). Teachers' uses of a learning trajectory in student-centered instructional practices. *Journal of Teacher Education, 66*(3), 227–244.

Windschitl, M., Thompson, J., & Braaten, M. (2011). Ambitious pedagogy by novice teachers? Who benefits from tool-supported collaborative inquiry into practice and why? *Teachers College Record, 113*(7), 1311–1360.

Wong Fillmore, L., & Fillmore, C. (2012). *What does text complexity mean for English learners and language minority students?* Stanford University. https://ell.stanford.edu/sites/default/files/pdf/academic-papers/06-LWF%20CJF%20Text%20Complexity%20FINAL_0.pdf

Zwiers, J., & Crawford, M. (2011). *Academic conversations.* Stenhouse.

Zwiers, J., O'Hara, S., & Pritchard, R. (2014a). *Common Core Standards in diverse classrooms: Essential practices for developing academic language and disciplinary literacy.* Stenhouse.

Zwiers, J., O'Hara, S., & Pritchard, R. (2014b). Conversing to fortify literacy, language, and learning. *Voices from the Middle, 22*(1), 10–14.

Bibliography

Berkes, M. (2011). *Animalogy: Animal analogies.* Arbordale Publishing.

Bernard, G. (2011). An argument for zoos: Extinction and endangered animals. In T. Snead & J. Ballester (Eds.), *Should there be zoos? A persuasive text* (pp. 7–8). Mondo Publishing.

Branley, F. (2015). *What makes day and night.* HarperCollins.

Brett, J. (1992). *Goldilocks and the three bears.* G. P. Putnam's Sons.

Brisson, P. (2004). *Beach is to fun: A book of relationships.* Henry Holt Co.

Carney, E. (2011). *Cats vs. dogs.* National Geographic Society.

Crow, R. (2020, April 18). *Mean girls.* YouTube. https://www.youtube.com/watch?v=nTIBDuTxzUw

DiCamillo, K. (2000). *Because of Winn-Dixie.* Candlewick Press.

Fox, M. (1989). *Wilfrid, Gordon, MacDonald, Partridge.* Kane/Miller Book Publishers.

Fritz, J. (1996). *And then what happened, Paul Revere?* Puffin Books.

Galdone, P. (1973). *Little red hen.* Clarion Books.

Gardiner, J. R. (1980). *Stone fox.* HarperCollins.

Geisel, T. (1985). *The cat in the hat.* Random House.

Hall, M. (2013). *My heart is like a zoo.* Greenwillow Books.

Johnston, T. (1998). *Amber on the mountain.* Penguin Books.

Joy, A. (2020). *Black is a rainbow color.* Roaring Brook Press.

Kolar, R. (2011). Zoochosis. In T. Snead & J. Ballester (Eds.), *Should there be zoos? A persuasive text* (pp.12–13). Mondo Publishing.

Marley, B. & King, S. (1983). *Buffalo Soldier.* https://www.azlyrics.com/lyrics/bobmarley/buffalosoldier.html

Munsch, R. (1980). *Paper bag princess.* Annick Press.

Munson, D. (2000). *Enemy pie.* Chronicle Books.

Nahl, C. (1872). *Sunday morning in the mines* [Oil on canvas]. Crocker Art Museum, Sacramento, CA, United States.

National Museum of African American History & Culture (2020, April 18). *Buffalo Soldiers: Legend and legacy.* https://nmaahc.si.edu/explore/manylenses/buffalosoldiers

Nelson, K. (2020). *American Revolution: American allies (The French).* Ducksters. https://www.ducksters.com/history/american_revolution/american_allies_french.php

Patterson, K. (1977). *Bridge to Terabithia.* HarperCollins.

Piven, H. (2010). *My best friend is as sharp as a pencil.* Random House.

ReadWorks. (2015). *Non-colonists in the American Revolution*. https://www.readworks.org/article/Non-Colonists-in-the-American-Revolution/d3cceb2f-5813-4060-80d9-9b707e8764f0#!articleTab:content/

Rockwell, N. (1964). *The problem we live with* [Oil on canvas]. Norman Rockwell Museum, Stockbridge, MA, United States.

Sachar, L. (1997). *There's a boy in the girls' bathroom*. Yearling Press.

Spilsbury, L. (2011). *Octopus (A day in the life: Sea animals)*. Heinemann Library.

TIME for Kids. (2020). *Bring the world to your classroom*. www.timeforkids.com

Van Allsburg, C. (1984). *The mysteries of Harris Burdick*. Houghton Mifflin.

Van Gogh, V. (1888). *Café terrace at night* [Oil on canvas]. Kröller-Müller Museum, Otterlo, Netherlands.

Waber, B. (1975). *Ira sleeps over*. Houghton Mifflin Harcourt.

Wallace, K. (1998). *Gentle giant octopus*. Candlewick Press.

Warren, H. *Sticks and stones may break my bones*. As cited in Johnston, P. (2004). *Choice words*. Stenhouse.

Weiss, L. (1985). *My teacher sleeps at school*. Puffin Books.

Wood, A. (1990). *Quick as a cricket*. Child's Play International.

Yolen, J. (1987). *Owl moon*. Philomel Books.

Index

About the Authors

Dr. Susan O'Hara is co-founder of *EPF for Teaching*. She was formerly a Center Director at University of California, Davis and a faculty director at Stanford University. Susan's research and partnership work with districts is focused on building instructional capacity and implementing integrated professional-growth systems, with specific attention to meeting the needs of linguistically and culturally diverse populations. Her work in this area has spanned 22 years, and she is specifically interested in partnerships that translate into actions and improvements in practice. She served as principal investigator on a grant from the Institute of Education Sciences (IES) testing the efficacy of Academic Language and Literacy in Every Subject (ALLIES), an instructional capacity-building model that targets the academic language and literacy needs of English learners in grades 3–6. She has more than 50 publications, including articles in both research and practitioner journals as well as two books.

Dr. Robert Pritchard is co-founder of *EPF for Teaching* and Professor Emeritus of Education at Sacramento State University. He is a language and literacy specialist who has worked extensively with schools, school districts, and state departments of education on a wide range of professional-development projects. A classroom teacher and reading specialist for 13 years, Bob also worked internationally for nine years as an ESL teacher, teacher trainer, and curriculum specialist. He co-led a team in the development and testing of Essential Practice Frames that articulate high-leverage practices to meet the learning needs of K–12 students. He has authored numerous publications related to English learners, innovative uses of technology, and professional development for teachers, including *Common Core Standards in Diverse Classrooms: Essential Practices for Developing Academic Language and Disciplinary Literacy, Kids Come in All Languages: Reading Instruction for ESL Students,* and *Teaching Vocabulary with Hypermedia.*

Debi Pitta, vice president of professional learning for *EPF for Teaching*, was an elementary and secondary teacher as well as Assistant Superintendent of Curriculum and Instruction, where her primary responsibility was to provide professional development for teachers. Debi has been engaged with a

5-year project to develop, implement, and test a professional-learning model to build mentor and teacher capacity across disciplines to promote English learners' academic language and literacy development. She also supports the professional learning of teachers and administrators on topics ranging from implementation of Common Core State Standards to professional learning communities and differentiated instruction. Her publications include *Implementing New Technologies to Support Social Justice Pedagogy* and *Academic Language and Literacy in Every Setting (ALLIES+): Strengthening the Science Learning Ecosystem.*